1857 : VISIONS RESURRECTED
Shaping Ideas From Oblivion

1857 : VISIONS RESURRECTED

Shaping Ideas From Oblivion

Ranjit Sen

FRAME ETERNITY

Where Eternity is framed in knowledge

1857 : VISIONS RESURRECTED

Shaping Ideas From Oblivion

by

Ranjit Sen

First Published 2010

Published by :
Frame Eternity
78B, Shakespeare Sarani, Kolkata-700019

Exclusive Distribution
Maha Bodhi Book Agency
Publishers & Booksellers
4A, Bankim Chatterjee Street,
College Square, Kolkata - 700 073. India
Ph : 033-2241-9363, 9831077368, 9831529452
e-mail : mahabodhibookagency@hotmail.com
website : www.mahabodhibooks.com

Composed by : Joy Guru Printers
Printed by : Sagarika Press, Kolkata-9

ISBN : 978-93-80336-00-8

Price : Rs. 450

In memory of those whose blood made 1857-1859
the ruddy years of history

1857 FLAG-SONG

To us belongs our Hindustan
and to none else
Our sacred motherland
dearer than heaven
The world is aglow
with the light of her soul.
How old, how new
and unique of its kind
To us belongs our Hindustan
and to none else.

Ganga and Jamuna making
our lands fertile
And overhead the snow-clad
mountain
our sentry towering.
Beating against the coasts
below the trumpets of the seas.
And gold and diamonds from
our mines overflow.
Our pomp and splendour evoking the
envy of the world.

And then came the Firangi
and such magic spell he cast
Pillaging and plundering our
motherland
he ruled.
The martyrs call you.
O countrymen
do you hear ?
Smash up the chains of
slavery
and pour out fire,
Hindus and Muslims and
Sikhs–
all of us brothers.
Hail and Salute it.
Here is our flag of freedom !

Acknowledgement

No research work is a product of individual effort. This work is certainly not. All previous scholars who applied their minds in analyzing the revolt of 1857-58 have given me a lead in my research. I take my hat off and bow to them. The challenge with which the book was written was an outcome of a desire to find out a post-centenary golden jubilee perspective of the revolt. Those who wrote in the year of this jubilee have fanned my desire and to them I owe a world of debt. The staff of the Reading Rooms, National Library, Calcutta and the Maharashtra State Archives, Mumbai stood by me whenever I was in need of books, literature and records. Words cannot convey my gratitude to them. Ms Tanima Debnath, a research scholar under my supervision, was kind enough to prepare the index of this book. I offer my heartfelt thanks to her. Mr.. Jayadewa Jayawardana of Frame Eternity showed great affection to my work and took over the task of publishing it. The book is thus a tribute to his enterprise. The one who always is the first reader of my draft, who takes care of seeing it through the press and who inspires me by giving a critic's comment and a scholar's appreciation at the formative stage of the work, is my wife Dr. Snigdha Sen. Herself being a historian she shares with me the pains of prosaic moments of research and the ecstasies of moments of its fulfillment. I offer her what she deserves - a salute for comradeship. A crowd of mute mankind was always there with me when I wrote this book. They have sunk in oblivion over time leaving for me a memory of the service they rendered. They are permanent denizens in the world of gratitude which I carry in the innermost chamber of my heart.

Ranjit Sen

Preface

This book is a quest for an Indian standpoint in the historiography of the Indian revolt of 1857. It tries to come out of the frame of understanding about the greatest Indian uprising worked out by British historians for the last one hundred and fifty years. That history of the revolt which is taught and read in Indian schools and colleges, that one which is dicussed in seminars and symposia in India and abroad tell the stories of motivated history. In it the British escape from a near-certain collapse is presented with the glamour of an imperial achievement - a victory born out of disaster. A victory it was no doubt but it did not create the glory of a victor's exclusive feat. The British empire did triumph in the long run and the crisis of 1857-58 were ultimately over. But on its triumph it ceased to be the same as before and had to shed its triumphant rudeness in all matters of governance. The old empire of a mercantile company passed away and the Crown took over a huge Asian colony as its possession. It was not only a metamorphosis of an empire but also a replacement of a British mercantile stake in Asia by a British national involvement in global pattern of situating the west in the east. Some books give the impression that the failure of the revolt of 1857 was ultimately the failure of the Indo-Islamic culture in south Asia. Those who propound this theory forget that the fall of the Roman empire at the hands of the barbarians did not suggest the defeat of the Roman civilization in the west. If that civilization had left any message for history it was this that human spirit is the most pristine and the most profound element of human civilization and it is unbeatable because it creates and re-creates itself in various forms. Within a few centuries from the fall of the Rome empire two things happened in the west. First, Charlemagne's empire emerged in the continent. It was the first and perhaps the last major attempt at uniting and integrating Europe within one formation of an empire. The bonds of coalescence it created kept in tact the inner cohesion of the Christendom so that when Islam set out to conquer the world it was this inner strength of a Christian world that prevented Islam from penetrating into its interior.. The second event after the fall of the Roman empire was the growth of nation states in Europe. Roman law, Roman institutions and the memory of the glory and governance of Rome perpetuated a spirit that triumphed over the revolutions of time. The Roman empire was no more there but its memory and spirit lasted.

So it was in India. The Indo-Islamic empire of the Mughals passed away in 1858-59 but its culture left its legacy in a death-defying spirit to preserve its own entity under the most tortuous moments of the British rule in India.

How the elements of this entity regrouped, failed and ultimately triumphed have been discussed in the pages of this book. Thus this book in the final analysis stands out as the quest of Indian viewpoints in a historiography that builds its edifice on the unsound soil of lost Indianness. It tries to surmount the wall of a one-sided story of imperial victory and tries to peep into the other side of the wall to see whether the Indian aspects of the revolt can enjoy the light of a new dawn. It has no intention to revive old stories in new words but it certainly aims at purging misconceptions that had done great mischief to the reading of the events of 1857-59. New visions are rebuilt here, ofcourse not before old visions are resurrected.

The Day of Indian Independence Ranjit Sen
15 August, 2010
Department of Islamic History and Culture
University of Calcutta
Kolkata

Books by the same author

1. Understanding Indian History
2. Metamorphosis of the Bengal Polity 1700-1793 [Published by Rabindra Bharati University, Kolkata]
3. Economics of Revenue Maximization In Bengal, 1757-1793.
4. Social Banditry in Bengal : A Study in Primary Resistance, 1757-1793.
5. New Elite and New Collaboration.
6. The Twin in the Twist : Bose and Gandhi.
7. Calcutta in the Eighteenth Century, Vol.I.
8. Swadesh O Samakal (In Bengali) [Mother Land & the Comtemporary Age]
9. Abahaman Bharat (In Bengali) [Eternal India]
10. Mahabidroha O Bharati Udasinata [The Great Revolt and Indian Indifference] [Co-Author Dr. Snigdha Sen]
11. Bhabita Purush O Abhabifa Nari : Nari Prasner Sekal O Ekal (In Bengali) [Considered Men & Women Unconsidered : The Women's Questions : Past and Present]
12. The Stagnating City : Calcutta in the Eightenth Century [Barpujari Endowment Lecture delivered at the Institute of Historical Studies, Kolkata]
13. Swadesh O Savyata (Motherland & Civilization in Bengali)
14. Caste, Class and the Raj [Co-author Dr. Snigdha Sen]
15. Saptaturag [Seven Horses : in Bengali]
16. Bangladesher Rajasva Shashan : Atharo Satak [The Revenue Administration : The 18th Century] : (in Bengali)
17. Banglar Samajik Dakati : Ekti Prathamik Pratirodh 1757-1793 [The Bengali version of the book No. 4]
18. Mudir Dokan (ed.) [The Gorcer's Shop] : (in Bengali) It deals with the origin of some of the commodities in every day use, some of the Hindu ceremonies & practices gleaned from ancient sanskrit texts]

19. Banglar Shramashakti [The Labour Force of Bengal. (ed.) in Bengali]
20. History of the Chakmas (ed.) [in Bengali]
21. At The Crossroads of Change by Subhas Chandra Bose (ed.) [releasing soon]
22. Birth of a City : Calcutta [in press]
23. Vidyasagar Janani Bhagavati Devi (ed.) Bhagvati Devi the Mother of Iswar Chandra Vidyasagar] [in Bengali]
24. Shivnath Shastri : Englander Diary [edited Diary of my Visit to England] [in Bengali]
25. The Captive Lady (In press)
26. Lupta Satak [The lost Centuries, In Bengali] - [In the press.]
27. Rammohan Roy's Life (ed.) [in Bengali, also translated in Hindi] releasing soon
28. Documents on the Urbanization of Calcutta [editted & ready for the press]

Contents

1

1857: Redefining Boundaries and Cultures

Apparently the revolt of 1857 was a cross-cultural event transcending boundaries of class, ethnicity and regional rulership formations. Sturdy peasants of the interior fighting under the banner of princes and local barons was not a common phenomenon of history, here and elsewhere. A cross religious bonding was formed when the Hindus and the Muslims fought shoulder to shoulder against a foreign rule which they thought was out to defile the basic sanctities of their religion. Even there were attempts to efface the barriers of time. In a desperate bid the mutineers and the rebels sought to dislodge the British empire and restore the Mughal empire of the past. In all these attempts there was an effort to redefine boundaries—boundaries of religion, boundaries of culture and boundaries of time. This was significant in a double sense. First it was a spontaneous event and contained very little trace of pre-planned engineering spanning over time. It meant that the ferment was already there for such an event. The ground soil was prepared and the atmosphere was ripe for a general take off for crossing formidable barriers of life. Growing out of this there was a second significance. The whole thing was achieved through a mass effort. Such events are rare in history, as this, where the totality of a mankind in a given society is transformed into a warring community. Revolt, uprising, rebellion or any convenient word can be used to denote an effort to make things upside down – an effort to shatter the fetters of a settled order. But no word can be used to denote the effacement of certain basic facts of achievement that emerged out of the revolt of 1857. The revolt of 1857 did not allow the victors to impose their religion on the vanquished. It broke the isolation and the backwardness the Muslim community suffered in India under the British rule. It forced a very redoubtable and aggressive empire to go into the defensive and turn introvert in all matters of future administration in India. The process of history was given a new direction in India. The Indian National Congress was born in 1885 and the erudite leaders of the moderate Congress tore the mask of the British empire. Indian poverty was diagnosed as an effect of a hidden cause, namely an un-British rule in British India. All these meant that there was a massive attempt at redefining the give-and-take between the British empire and its subjects. Indian loyalty to the empire was redefined and a new culture of opposition now surfaced which first moved through a phase of agitation, then a phase of revolutionary terror and finally on to a new phase of non-cooperation and civil disobedience and then a national uprising forcing the British to quit India. All these came not in a day's preparation. The revolt of 1857 set the ball rolling. It certainly failed in its immediate mission to crush the British empire and restore that of the Mughals. But in the legacy it left it redefined boundaries of imperial aspirations, reset the sovereign yearnings of the subject people and gave them a new culture that was compatible with all their contemplative awareness of their own self and their new role in the changing world of modernity. In this sense the year 1857 was a landmark. It redefined boundaries and reset cultures of a complacent British rule in India. The achievement of the year of 1857 lies here.

The revolt of 1857 had forged a wonderful link between what Savarkar described as 'swadharma' and 'swaraj'— between one's own religion and the rule of one's own self. Out of the union of these two emerged the earliest rudiments of Indian nationalism.[1] Therefore, Indian nationalism must be considered as a direct outcome of the Indian revolt itself. This revolt left a legacy of courage, sacrifice and indomitable assertion. It was in the legacy of this that people stood up in later years to confront the Empire in their own terms. Dadabhai Naoroji, Romesh Chandra Dutt and men like them did the most remarkable thing that could be done in the context of the time. They sized up the economics of the Empire and wrote discourses on it.[2] Naoroji showed how un-British was the British rule in India for it had wrought poverty on the people by extracting from them the last dreg of social surplus. Romesh Dutt showed how Indian wealth was drained out to sustain the apparatus of the Empire, here and in Britain and how the subject people in India were squeezed tight against the margin of subsistence. The boldness of this assertion could not be a product of a defeat. It was, on the contrary, the product of a milieu that was created by the ferment of the uprising

[1] " The events of 1857 also therefore stand as an important landmark in the evolution of Indian nationhood. In 1857 it was primarily religion which defined the identities of the two peoples–the Hindus and theMuslims–and it was their religious fervour and passion which provided motivation for their actions. Such religiously informed sense of community had no place in the later day modern secular concept of nation nurtured by Nehru or Congress. However, Indian nationalism was never a monolithic structure and it is interesting to note how various strands of nationalism across the political spectrum, each looking for myths and heroes, tried to appropriate the history of 1857."– Sekhar Bandyopadhyay, "Eighteen-Fifty-Seven and Its Many Historians" in *1857 Essays From Economic and Political Weekly,* in association with Orient Longman and Sameeksha Trust, Hyderabad, 2008, p.16.

[2] In 1897 Romesh Chandra Dutt's book *England and India : A Record of Progress During a Hundred Years 1785-1885* was published from England. In the same year he wrote an essay on famines in India in the prestigious journal *The Fortnightly Review.* It is said that this essay was the first major fruit of his thinking about the economics of the Empire. His *A Record of Progress* was in no way an economic history of the British rule in India. But many a thing which was written there eventually came to be accommodated in the two volumes of his later work *The Economic History of India.* In 1900 Romesh Chandra wrote his *Open Letters to Lord Curzon.* In 1875 he wrote his book *The Peasantry of Bengal.*

of 1857. To make an assertion such as this in an age when the Empire was resting in Victorian complacence showed in what spirit the Indians had learnt to address themselves even when they were in a state of misery and woe. This was the real achievement of the revolt of 1857. To make an anatomy of an imperial economics in the way Naoroji and Dutt did was a rare feat not paralleled by any subject people under any imperialism in the world. When the discourse of poverty was being worked out the all-India political platform was constructed under the title Indian National Congress. A new India was emerging out of the memories of 1857.

What happened in the aftermath of the revolt must be taken into consideration in order to assess the significance of the events of 1857-59. The history of the uprising that was appropriated by the empire was broadly a one-sided presentation of the great events. To the imperial historians the quintessence of the story of Indian uprising was defeat in the long run and beyond defeat it was a story of suppression of a formidable rising against the Empire. The early stereotype of the imperial historiography of the revolt was a two-fold approach to the events of the uprising — that it was a mutiny born of a conspiracy and that it was a mutiny at one stage and a mass rising at the other only when it was joined by unruly mobs at places where the popular elements of governance temporarily withdrew from operation. This view, an upright imperial understanding during the revolt and in its immediate aftermath, was later bedecked by a well-knit suppression theory that was required to boost the morale of the Empire. A recent observation on the point runs thus:

"However, the more dominant imperial stereotype... was that it was primarily a mutiny of the sepoys, later joined by the unruly mob, taking advantage of the general breakdown of law and order. However, around the same time there were people like Benjamin Disraeli or Karl Marx who could see the element of 'national revolt' in what was being commonly described as the 'Military Mutiny."[3] Several years later in 1864 John Kaye wrote the official history of 1857, *A History of the Sepoy*

[3]For details see Snigdha Sen, *The Historiography of The Indian Revolt of 1857* Punthi-Pustak, Calcutta, 1992, pp 59, 90-91, 159, 179, 180-201, 204, 209, 218, 248

War in India 1857-58, and James Fitzjames Stephen, the conservative utilitarian ideologue of the empire, could immediately use it in defence of the empire. In what happened in India in that fateful year was for him evidence enough to show that no one in that country, 'had in him any power of improvement or any wish for it'. Hence they needed the enlightening touch of the Raj. In the writings of Charles Ball, John Kaye and George Trevelyan the history of 1857 became the history of its suppression, a history of the valour and courage of the English race and the glory of the empire. Recently, Tony Balantyne has shown that even in far-off New Zealand the indigenous Maori population were being told the stories of how the mutiny was suppressed in India, with a not-so-covert message about the futility of resistance to the empire and its possible consequence."[4]

This way the revolt of 1857 defined anew the boundaries of relations between the Empire and its subjects. The apparent victory of the Empire was used as a tool to keep other subject people elsewhere under surveillance. The arrogance that was displayed by the Christian Evangelical missionaries, army officers and bureaucracy before the revolt of 1857 created insurmountable barriers of distrust between the Indians on the one hand and their masters on the other. By the middle of the nineteenth century practically the whole of the Indian subcontinent was under the rule of the British. From absolute dominance was born the paramountcy of power, a concept that bred arrogance.[5] This arrogance was now beaten to the dust by those who rose in arms against the Empire. The Empire now became introvert. In all give and take between the Empire and its people now a new barrier emerged. On

[4] Sekhar Bandyopadhyay, *op.cit.,* p.2.

[5] Under the influence of power the British psyche underwent a change. Everything Indian now became a matter of contempt to the British bureaucracy and men of authority. The mentality of sobriety and accommodation which had been the characteristic mark of administration under many a governor-general in the past was now thrown to the wind. Absolute power now gave birth to its most degenerate form—arrogance. As the British were "absolute masters everywhere", wrote one of them, "restraint is cast away—and [they display] a superfluous arrogance and contempt of the people"—quoted in Christopher Hibbert, *The Great Mutiny, India 1857,* Allen Lane Penguin Books, London, 1978, p.29.

the British side it was suspicion. It was hatred for the British on the Indian side. Previously it was the opposite. On the Indian side there had always been a suspicion that the British Empire was out to undermine Indian institutions and life. Hatred for the Indians were there on the British side. Situations now reversed. An overt racialism which was the hallmark of British imperialism in the pre-1857 days now sought to hide itself behind a very apparent show of benevolence exhibited in the Queen's Proclamation of 1858. The British attitude to the Indians who lived in England now changed. Diaries and memories of Englishmen which started pouring in England right from the time of the revolt maintained its flow upto the twentieth century. Most of this literature contained horror stories that filled the minds of the avid readers there. The philanthropy and paternalism which had characterized the British governance for the past half a century or more now vanished altogether. What is more the British domesticity in India suffered the stress of an unknown fear. The British women after the revolt woke up to the stark reality of lost complacence and the comfort which they had enjoyed in the heydays of the Empire in dealing with their household staff was gone altogether.[6] Relations now were defined within the complexities of a changed situation.

After the revolt of 1857 two different identities faced each other –the British imperial-national identity and the identity of the Indian nation. This had substituted the old master and subject identity so meticulously worked out during the long stretch of British rule in India, from the time of Lord Cornwallis to that of Lord Dalhousie. The imperial-national identity of the British emerged at the time of the revolt itself. The huge massacre of mankind and the destruction of property perpetrated by the British in the process of the suppression of the revolt were consciously unleashed to retrieve the lost honour of the British nation. The British imperial national identity in India was thus initiated with a mark of blood and through acts of violence. The British violence was the 'backlash' of the indiscriminate killing of the British men and women in which children

[6]For a further exposition of the point see Jane Robinson, *Angels of Albion,* pp. 253-54.

were not spared.[7] The massacres which the sepoys committed in a fit of rage and vendetta were unrestrained and uncalculated acts that burst out in agonized response of souls so tyrannized over the last one century. Brigadier General James Neil's atrocities during his march from Allahabad to Kanpur were often claimed to have been the backlash of Nana Sahib's treachery. This point, so vigorously denied by recent researchers, only shows how the British valour, when required, could be an offensive armour in defense of the honour of the nation. The prowess of the Empire thus exercised in defense of the country's honour assumed the mark of a national identity in an imperial setting. An imperial violence since the time of the revolt itself was construed as an act of retribution–a retaliatory act – spurred by a sense of humiliation and injustice.[8] It was in these ideas that the imperial-national identity of Britain was working out itself in India.

National identities cluster around symbols of national respect. British women since the time of the revolt became symbols of British national respect. Any act of outrage on their honour was considered to be an atrocity on the honour of the nation itself. The ignominy supposed to have been inflicted upon British women during the revolt was considered to be a national 'dishonour' by all, the British generals, bureaucrats, missionaries, press representatives, in a word the British community as a whole. This eventually became a rallying point for the imperial-national identity of the British nation. 'Dishonour' was a part of injustice and injustice done to the British was the logic that justified indiscriminate killing as a form of retribution. This has become so settled a point in the historiography of the revolt that in the post centenary golden jubilee of the revolt a historian observes with confidence that 'dishonour' to British women was one act of transgression that added to the sense

[7] The sepoys had perpetrated in three major massacres, the *Satichura Ghat* and the *Bibighar* massacres and the massacre in Delhi which took place when the rebel sepoys assembled there to invoke the blessings of the Mughal ruler.

[8] This sentiment is expressed in Saul David's *The Indian Mutiny 1857*, Viking, London, 2002; Andrew Ward, *Our Bones are Scattered: The Cawnpore Massacre and the Indian Mutiny of 1857*, Henry Holt and Co., New York, 1996; Michael Edwards, *Red Year: The Indian Rebellion of 1857*, Hamish Hamilton, London, 1973.

of injustice suffered by the British.[9] "What would India be without England? And what would the British Empire be without Englishwomen?"[10] This was the question that haunted the British mind all through the years, from the days of the revolt to the modern times. The British femininity became human symbols of the purity of a nation and the British mind harping irresistibly on the disaster that befell the English womenfolk in north India during the fateful year of 1857 became a chiselled instrument for salvaging the outraged honour of the nation. Only such a mind could furrow the soil in which seeds of retribution could be sown. In any case the whole question of a national 'dishonour' born out of the sufferings of British women in India has been very powerfully integrated into the historiography of the revolt. Even in the writings of Indian historians its resonance is heard.

"The memsahibs in India represented national purity and the alleged 'dishonour' of women caused a national rage, both in India and in London. At Meerut, Delhi and Awadh, writes John Premble, 'the blood of European women and children had been shed; and with its shedding warfare was suddenly loosed from its customary restraints.' [11] Although later inquiries revealed that there was no rape, what was important however was the perceived sense of injustice that easily excited emotions. 'The outbreak would not have been half so humiliating to the British', wrote Jane Robinson, 'had the women not been there...'[12] The centrality of women in the working of the imperial-national identity of the British nation was not a post-upsurge phenomenon. A national identity of the British now clearly manifested itself through vengeance. The pages of the famous journal *Calcutta Review* for the years 1858-1860 are replete

[9] "To the British sense of injustice and vengeance one may add another act of transgression, i.e. the alleged 'dishonour' to British womanhood."— Bandyopadhyay, *op.cit*, p.9.

[10] Maud Diver, *The Englishwomen in India*, London, 1909, p.7, quoted in Jane Robinson, *Angels of Albion: Women of the Indian Mutiny*, Viking, London, 1996, p.248.

[11] For the Indian understanding of the point *see* S. B. Chaudhuri *Civil Rebellion In The Indian Mutinies 1857-1859*, The World Press Pvt. Ltd., Calcutta, 1957, pp.258-261.

[12] Bandyopadhyay, *op.cit.*, p.10.

with pledges for 'vengeance for vengeance' was the means through which the national mind of the British could express itself. Here is an example of the Anglo-Saxon swaggering so common in the said Journal at that time :

"England should beware of showing too much magnanimity in a country where compliance is understood to mean fear and with a people devoid of patriotism and for whom we believe *the pressure of the heel upon the neck* or in other words, a strict yet just despotism was the normal government."[13] (Italics ours)

This expression of the British public sentiment must not be thought of only as indicative of national vengeance. In it was sheltered the 'charged mood'[14] of a nation that sought to reset the boundaries of its civilizing missions so eagerly pursued by the colonial masters of early generations. An event that shook up the British Empire in India from its foundation had also given the Empire an incentive for an internal search. This search resulted in the shutting down of the Company's rule in India and the takeover of the Empire directly by the British Crown. This eradication of the rule of a body of merchants clearly meant that the British national entity had so long been wrongly represented in India and now the nation as such wanted to assert itself through the majesty of its most august institution, the Crown. This cancellation of representation through proxy was found to be a national error and in mending the error the British imperial-national entity was asserted. One form of this assertion was mild and benevolent as was revealed in the

[13] *Calcutta Review,* 1860, vol. 34, pp. 196-197.

[14] "All these [the vituperations that were published in journals of the time] gave a sharp edge to the charged mood of the people. To them the accusation of cruelty to the natives would not arise for the treachery of capitulation and the brutality of the massacres called forth sternest retribution, but to call such slaughter 'as fearful revenge' would be mere maudlin sentimentality. So black life was never so cheap as in 1857 in India and writers freely quoted from Martin Tupper, the English poet of the 'Rebellion', 'whose popularity was a most astounding fact advocating rigorous repression' " .— S. B. Chaudhuri, *English Historical Writings On The Indian Mutiny 1857-1859,* The World Press Pvt. Ltd., 1979, p. 259. Chaudhuri must be read along with the following : *Calcutta Review,* 1858, December, p.550, 1858, vol.31, pp. 330-331, 73, 363.

Queen's Proclamation of 1858. It was the first major act of assertion of the British nation now vigorously out to retrieve and consolidate its imperiled imperial stakes. The other form of assertion was ruthless vendetta propelled by the unquenchable thirst for native blood. This latter aspect found an outlet in the verses of Martin Tupper who made the blood-sucker's barbarism the murmur of his soul. Here is one such verse in which the aggrieved mind of an agonized nationalism sought to manifest itself :

> "And England, now avenge their wrongs
> by Vengeance deep and dire,
> Cut this canker with sword, and burn it out with fire;
> Destroy those traitor legions, hang every Pariah hound,
> And hunt them down to death, in all hills and cities round."[15]

While the most popular British poet of the time prescribed death for the Indians, Her Majesty's government in England offered fillers of regeneration to the subjects of the Empire. It was between these two opposite spirits of vengeance and clemency that England shaped its entity in the immediate aftermath of the revolt. Her imperial-national entity was thus a product of two opposites, a civilized instinct for restraint and a barbaric urge for excess. At the base of restraint there was a fear that a habitually submissive Orient might burst into violent distemper if the values it cherised were made to capsize under the caprice of the Empire. The excess of evangelical Christianity and the megalomania of imperial British bureaucrats and army officers mingled into an arrogance that had destroyed the genial flow of a broad utilitarian and humanitarian British culture. To this the Orient had displayed its anger and it was this anger that had tamed imperial arrogance into the sobriety of a new culture of accommodation and adjustment. The rulership mania of the English that had vitiated the chemistry of administration in the past now dissolved into an educated mentality for governance. Justice and ethics were now recognized as the nuances of the new rule. This was where the revolt of 1857 had defined the boundaries of the old imperial culture of the English in India. The triumph of the revolt lies here.

[15] *Calcutta Review*, 1858, vol.31, pp.73, 410-411.

2

The Post-Centenary Golden Jubilee Retrospection

In course of the one hundred and fifty years of the Indian revolt of 1857 we have hardly been able to build up an Indian stand-point. The two books written by two contemporary Indians, Kishori Chand Mitra [his book *The Mutinies, the Government and the People*] and Sambhoo Chandra Mukherjee [his book *The Mutinies and the People, or A Statement of Native Fidelity Exhibited during the Outbreak of 1857-58*] were published under disguised authorship. Their main effort was to exonerate the guilts of the Hindus. Syed Ahmed Khan working under allied intentions wanted to prove that the revolt was the handiwork of base Muslims who lived in the rim of the society. It took nearly fifty years for the Indians to come out of this psychological inhibitions and propound a proper theory of the Indian revolt. Savarkar did it only in the beginning of the twentieth century after which nearly another fifty years elapsed and there was no conscious Indian effort to size up the revolt, in Indian terms. The next man to do it was Sashibhusan Chaudhuri who took great pain to prove through exhaustive research that the first century of the British rule in India was one of incessant civil disturbances which eventually led to the civil uprisings during the revolt of 1857. He was accompanied by P. C. Joshi who in his edited book *Rebellion 1857 : A Symposium (1957, 1986)* showed that a proverbially un-British rule in British India had led to a tremendous economic squeeze which created the base of the revolt in the country. This was also the findings from which Promod Sengupta wrote his account in Bengali (*Bharatiya Mahabidroha* in 2 vols.) his work being more massive than that of P. C. Joshi.

Broadly speaking, this exhausts the stock of Indian writers who could work out Indian standpoints in a very unorganized and rudimentary fashion. The present chapter discusses as to what the subsequent historians wrote about the revolt and what the post centenary golden jubilee Indian historians in our contemporary times are thinking about the character of the revolt itself. Could they build up an Indian perspective, or they fall in the line with British colonial historians who had maligned the revolt with purposes consistent with the logic of the empire. This chapter will be a 150th year's recall of Indian memory of the first great Indian revolt for independence and a tribute to an effort that was rarely shown in Indian history in terms of unity, coalescence and action, self-motivated and self-driven. The chapter will also discuss as to whether there is any element of iconoclasm in Indian History which seeks to malign the Indian revolt the way it was done by British historians.

The revolt of 1857 has been viewed from two contradictory standpoints. To the British historians it was a crisis of the empire. To the Indians it was a war of independence. The first batch of British historians who were contemporary to the revolt had one task to perform. They were to relieve the empire of its psychological shock. The first batch of Indians who lived at the time of the revolt similarly had one task to which they set themselves. They offered apologies to their masters for the Indian involvement in the upsurge. This subservience of Indian standpoint continued thereafter so much so that till date we are unable to recognize any standpoint as firmly Indian. Savarkar [his book *The Indian War of Independence 1857* (1907)] was the first Indian to rescue the Indian historiography from his misery. His book was polemical and as such was not history. All that he did was this. He accepted 1857 as a moment in Indian history, instilled into it a very powerful nationalist sentiment and kept it as a store of inspiration in the memory of the nation. This was a unique achievement for it converted a nation's memory into a weapon for a psychological warfare against the English. This was done in the backdrop of a resurgence of a nationalism in India. This nationalism expressed itself in three forms. A political platform namely the Indian National Congress was created on which nationalism could rally itself. A politics of agitation was evolved through which the Indian public opinion could manifest in an organized form. And finally a new economics was discovered which revealed the tyranny of British exploitation in a most un-British form leading to the poverty of the masses. the economics of mass poverty was thus unearthed by Dadabhai Naoroji whereas Romesh Chandra Dutt unmasked British rule that allowed drain of Indian resources to hide itself under the show of a shallow justice. All these were the achievements of the moderate phase of the Indian National Congress. During this phase of Indian assertion the revolt of 1857 did not find a very major reception in the Indian mind. India was massively engaged in evolving a political organization, a system of people's politics and finally a new political economy of the country that was seething under the squeeze of the British rule. This was not the time to discuss an event that ended in defeat. Hence radical writings did not come out from Indian pen during this phase of the Indian national movement.

Yet the aftermath of the revolt of 1857 was the period when in the retrospective awareness of its own self the Indian mind could slowly return to the legacy of the revolt. Rabindranath Tagore wrote a moving essay on the leaders of the revolt in 1877 when he was only sixteen years of age. Titled *Jhansir Rani* [The Queen of Jhansi] this essay was basically an exercise in building the image of Indian leadership. It said : "Tantia Topi and Kumar Singh are not merely two petty rebels. If history is to be written their names should be placed by the side of some great heroes of the world. I cannot but be in praise of that octogenarian Kumar Singh who riding on a horse with sacking eyebrows supported with strings, wielded swords in two hands and put to rout the Highlander army and that Tantia Topi, who could send tremors into the rule of foreigners in India with only a few bodies of scattered soldiers who had no arms, no food and no money with them".[1] Tagore's source was Russell's *My Diary in the year 1858-59* which inspite of being a typical British narrative failed to captivate the juvenile Indian mind that was coming to shape in the aftermath of the

[1]Rabindranath Tagore, "Jhansir Rani" in *Rabindra Rachanavali*, Janma Satabarshiki Sanskaran, 1368 Bengali year, (1961), p.464.

revolt of 1857. One year after Tagore wrote his essay Rajani Kanta Gupta published his book *Sipahi Juddher Itihas* [The History of the Sepoy War] a five volume book that patterned itself on Kaye's *History of The Sepoy War.* He wrote this work to show that the direction of the sepoy war was basically to transcend the ephemeral shortcomings of a military war. It emerged out of an inspired nationalism and was directed towards fulfilling its mission. He wrote: "If a historian thinks of its causes, extent and duration then it will be drawn on him that the great revolution was not confined to the sepoys only".[2]

Inherent in these words is a new approach to history which Snigdha Sen calls *History with Mission.* [3] This mission, Sen says, was not an output of a stirred aftermath. It grew as a phenomenon contemporaneous to the revolt itself. Sen writes: "The contours of the historiography of the revolt of 1857 were drawn not in the aftermath of the revolt but during the revolt itself. In the aftermath competent hands of British historians had offered deeper shades into them. But concurrent with this the Indian mind did not remain idle. It was musing over gigantic events which on the one hand shook the pillars of British complacence in India and on the other offered the Indians an opportunity to reset the pinnacles of its fallen glory. During the first five decades of the revolt two Indian minds returned to these events and their avowed mission was to restore the Indian image that was otherwise fractured under the colossal thrust of the British pen. They were Rajani Kanta Gupta and Vinayak Damodar Savarkar. They laid the first foundation of Indian bridgeheads in the territories held by British historiographers."[4]

It was this mission which Tagore initiated in history writing as early as 1877. Borrowing from Russell certain facts of history he mingled his own emotions to create what may be called the patriotic historiography of the revolt of 1857. He presented in his essay Indian

[2] Rajani Kanta Gupta, *Sipahi Juddher Itihas,* vol. v, p. 100. For details on Rajani Kanta Gupta *see* Snigdha Sen *The Historiography of the Indian Revolt of 1857,* Punthi-Pustak, Calcutta, 1992.

[3] Sen, *op.cit.,* p. 133.

[4] *Ibid*

leaders, Tantia Topi and others, whose flaming spirit, he believed, manifested in their utterances. Thus Tantia Topi said and Tagore reports : 'I don't expect from the British Government anything but death. Let this be my only prayer : my death sentence be executed soon and may not my innocent family, prisoners now, suffer because of me". [5] In his gallery of heroes Tagore placed three more personalities, Rana Beni Madho, the Rajput hero of Sankarpur, Nripat Singh of Royar and the Rani of Jhansi. As a vassal of the Nawab of Awadh, Beni Madho had a large influence over the territory he held under his command. Yet he cast his lot in support of his masters. The British Government for strategic reasons wanted to condon him and return him his property only if he submitted to the government. Beni Madho declined, mingled his fate with the lot of his masters and escaped to Nepal to protect the fugitives of his master's family. There he died as a penniless man who had no remorse for his lost regalia. Tagore comments: "Who other than a Rajput hero can suffer such a sacrifice in order to maintain his own oath [of fealty] ?" By the side of Rana glitters another personality, Nripat Singh, the lame feudal lord, who identified himself with the cause of the rebels. His spirit is revealed in his own speech which Tagore reports thus : "God has taken one of my limbs. The remaining parts of my body I shall sacrifice for my motherland". This was a kind of patriotism that struck the Indians long before western type nationalism formalized itself in India. One of the greatest symbols of this patriotism was the Rani of Jhansi and Tagore's eloquence was finally marked in the poignance of praise for her. He writes : "Yet we salute with reverence the greatest of all heroes Lakshmibai, the Rani of Jhansi".[6]

This appreciation of the leaders of the revolt was not an outcome of a juvenile amazement. Rajani Kanta Gupta often displays similar appreciation of the sepoy for their warrior-like characteristics and the melody of his praise somewhere resembles and sometimes mingles with the tune of Tagore's eulogy. He writes : "These men did not shrink from sacrificing themselves for freedom. In many a place in the present history their bravery and courage have been exhibited. In the

[5] Tagore, *op. cit.,* p. 465.

[6] Tagore, *Ibid.*

account of these sepoys one may see how robust men, when inspired by nationalism and freedom, can display their own valour. Many of their brave achievements have illuminated a good number of pages of the present history. The feat of many has, however, also not found place in the accounts. Foreign historians on many occasions have proved themselves averse to writing the flaming achievements of their opponents who are foreigners to them. If it were Europe the glory of these heroes would have been sung ....But in this unfortunate country even their names do not appear in history."[7]

[7]Rajani Kanta Gupta, *Sipahi Juddher Itihas*, vol.3, p. 33.

3

1857 : The Missing Indian Standpoint

The historiography of the revolt of 1857 has no specific and consistent Indian standpoint. The contemporary historians, a Sambhoo Chandra Mukherjee, a Kishori Chand Mitra and a Syed Ahmed Khan, wrote to hide the skin of their own kinsmen. To them the revolt was the handiwork of bogus Indians geared to base intentions. In the aftermath of the revolt Rajani Kanta Gupta copied in Bengali Kaye's masterpiece *The History of the Sepoy War* where he allowed a mellow nationalism touch the rim of his narratives. Thus in the entire history of the narrative accounts of the revolt Rajani Kanta was the first Indian to stop the quick march for capitulation of the Indian standpoint. He was also the first to take a right about turn towards Indianness. But then where was the Indian standpoint? Could he create it or discover any of its kind ? No, because the time was not ripe yet to do that. In the wake of Rajani Kanta came V. D. Savarkar who let loose the torrential passion of nationalism to sweep away the pusillanimity of Indian chroniclers. It was not history that he wrote. He discovered a moment for Indians in history and then recreated history itself in his own way where that moment could be stored as an inspiration for ever. In the centenary year a bunch of vacillations and contradictions appeared in the Indian historiography of the revolt. The Marxist historians under the strong leadership of P. C. Joshi analyzed the economics of the revolt. In doing this they superseded the earlier thesis of the Marxist pioneer M. N. Roy who considered the revolt as a feudal outburst at the threshold of a change in India. This provided cue to Nehru's interpretation of the revolt as a spasm of the old order. To consider the revolt as an upsurge of ancient regime in the Royist and Nehruvian line was to denigrate a movement that had preserved the Indian genius for continuity and steadfastness in all processes of change. The officially commissioned centenary history of the revolt, S. N. Sen's *1857*, has carried Indian standpoint nowhere. The revolt, he says, had its origin in the sepoy discontent and it derived strength from the widespread disaffection of the civil population. This was not the thing which he or the Indian historians had declared first or which they had spoken exclusively for themselves. The British administrator and the English historians had said this long before this had dawned in the Indian mind. Other centenary historians, R. C. Majumdar and H.P. Chattopadhyay had formed a club with Sen in enunciating a viewpoint which was not Indian in the true sense of the term. Majumdar's book was titled *The Sepoy Mutiny and The Revolt of 1857* and the search he unleashed there systematically wiped out any Indian pretension to glory that could have lurked for them behind the events of 1857. He wrote: "On the whole, it is difficult to avoid the conclusion that the so-called First National War of Independence of 1857 is neither the First, nor National, nor a War of Independence". Close in the heels of Majumdar we have H.P. Chattopadhyay who slapped on his book a short, curt and a straight title *The Sepoy Mutiny, 1857* thus avoiding two very poignant and suggestive words *'the Revolt'* which even Majumdar could not discard. Chattopadhyay upheld Majumdar's conclusion saying that "...the participants in the Mutiny had no such common political aim in view as India's emancipation from British authority." Why was then, the question will legitimately arise, Bahadur Shah II proclaimed as the Emperor of India by the sepoys ? Does not such a proclamation point to the fact that the revolt of 1857 was a struggle for Indian independence, the first of its kind in terms of the depth of people's participation and the area of the expansion of conflagration ? The centenary historians did fail to discover a proper Indian standpoint from which the events of 1857 could be looked at. Only S. B. Chaudhuri was one historian somewhat away from the rest who was trying to project an Indian mind into the study of the revolt of 1857. In the centenary perspective he looked back into the events of 1857 and discovered almost an endless series of civil rebellions marching inexorably towards the finale of the historical process created by the rule and the misrule of the English East India Company. But then where was the story of Indian triumph in the midst of catastrophes and disasters ? A handful of British army did not suppress the revolt. The rule of the East India Company, the might of the English nation and the valour of the British generals -- all were at the mercy of the Indians, the multitude of both the princely and the lowly Indians, the soldiers and civilians, the supporters and collaborators, the rugged and the rustic, the townsmen and the countrymen, both the rich and the one rolling in the dust without whose support success would have been a distant dream for the English in 1857. The story of the support the Indians offered to the British rule in India in the moments of its crisis must be told and retold in equal jest and vigour along with the story of the Indian defeat and Indian failures in all their movements of 1857. In a recent work Rudrangsu Mukherjee questions whether Mangal Pandey was 'a martyr', or 'an accidental hero' and in the other Tapti Roy questions whether the British were responsible for creating a larger than life image of the illustrious Rani of Jhansi, Lakshmi Bai. All these go to build up the post-centenary golden jubilee understanding of the revolt of 1857. The centenary appreciation of the revolt smashed efforts to look into the event as a war of independence. Now a post-centenary golden jubilee appreciation is made in which Indian admiration for popular heroes is sought to be scuttled. A very rude iconoclasm borrowed from the West now makes its inroad into the loose, unsystematic and lax structure of Indian historiography about the revolt of 1857.

The major points of Indian achievements in course of the two years of 1857-58 have remained largely unmarked in the entire historiography of the revolt. The victor's religion could not be imposed on the vanquished by force. This point was very powerfully settled through the revolt of 1857. For one century the Christian missionaries, the British administrators, the army generals and English reformers had enjoyed a very tacit patronage of the state in all their moves to gain Christian converts in this country. The most unique of the world's plural society the Indians kept their windows open and allowed the wind of change to come in. Yet they refused to be blown of their feet. The British policy to convert Indians to Englishmen, writes Burton Stein, a historian of our time, so ceremoniously inaugurated during the Bentinck era, was dashed to the ground. Indian accepted modernization but rejected the one that did not incorporate Indian values, Indian culture and Indian ethos of life. While being modernized Indians refused to be westernized. These were the moral triumphs of the Indians at moments when their material strength was waning out. The Indian Musalmans, a very robust part of the Indian mankind, refused to be treated with neglect and pushed into the gloom of oblivion. After the revolt they were restored to status and rehabilitated in honour which they deserved. These were Indian triumphs. The mercenary rule of a body of merchants, the East India Company, was swept into the limbo of history and the British Crown had to replace its franchisee and take over the direct administration of India. In the Queen's Proclamation a definite pledge was given that henceforth colour, creed, religion and race would be no bar to the fulfillment of Indian ambitions. These were principles of benevolent administration and they were extracted from a reluctant rule of foreigners. By no means they were as meagre achievements on the part of the Indians but they have been construed as acts of British benevolence that were showered on wayward subjects as measures of shepherding them into the right fold. How much blood the Indians had to shed before they could force the British to keep away from principles of racialism and hatred as functioning creeds of the British rule ? How much blood did the Indians shed for restoring the Empire of Great Britain to its masters ? Was the restoration of the empire entirely a British achievement ? No army from outside, it should be noted, not even from England, was required by the English to gain back their lost possession in India. It was mostly Indian blood, Indian money, Indian labour, Indian strength and above all Indian goodwill on which the British had to depend till the last. There is no reason to suppose that the British success in 1857-58 was entirely an achievement of the empire itself. Think of those crucial days from the Meerat rising on 10 May 1857 to the fall of Delhi on 20 September, 1857 when the British Government, the British administrators, the British army and the British generals, in a word, all representatives of the British nation in India remained dependent on the Indians, those Indians, the affluent and poor, better or battered, perpetually oppressed but traditionally loyal without whose cooperation and help it would have been difficult for the English to prevent the renewal of the Mughal empire in India. If the British had lost their empire it was mainly due to their malevolence that hurt the Indians. If they could regain it, it was due to their benevolence which touched the Indians and secured their collaboration. This is the message the revolt of 1857 leaves for posterity. Rulers' malevolence faces retribution. Their benevolence is rewarded by history. Hegel once said that history drags the fool and leads the wise. Dregs of Englishmen who tortured Indians for one century since the days of the Plassey were adjudged fools by history in 1857. They were dragged and were made to suffer penance. But then history ceased to be merciless because the British also had their own virtues on which they had based their existence in India. In the long run they were, as Marx said, the unconscious tool of history for the regeneration of India. In the crucial year of 1857-58 a regenerated India stood by the British. A hundred years of benevolence of the British rule paid its dividend.

The story of the revolt has two sides. So far as it was directed against the British rule it was meaningful for in some respects it was an act of tyrannicide. But so far as its professed aim was the restoration of the Mughal empire it was an anachronism for history does not allow a march to the past. History is forward-moving in a course that is zigzag or non-linear but eternally progressive. Contradictions do appear and do resolve in its course but contradictions do not block the path of progress. The revolt of 1857 was bound to fail from the moment it sought to bring a dead empire back. From the time of Aurangzeb, writes Sir Jadunath Sarkar, the Mughal empire was caught in a crisis. It sinned against the people and was chased by a pitiless Nemesis that drove it to destruction. To bring such an empire back was moving against the current of history. To champion its cause meant that the ulterior aim of the revolt slipped out of the time frame of history. Every progressive event in history has to be consistent with time. In the case of the Indian revolt the time adjustment was a compound of two, one positive and the other negative. The positive aspect was that it happened just when it was required to happen. The whole of north India was vacant of white army. The sepoys had the chance to operate in a military vacuum. The Bengal army at that time numbered 1,51,000 men. Of these men 23,000 were Europeans. A bulk of these Europeans, about 13,000 were outside India fighting beyond the Sutlej, guarding Indian territories there. Many of them were sent to fight either at the Crimean or the Persian Wars and were yet to return to their own stations. A colossal vacuum was created unknowingly. The dynamics of empire needs expansion and chasing the mirage of expansion the British left their own territory defenceless. The Indian army and the Indian leadership failed to take advantage of this. They turned their face back. Their rallying point was sought in an old and decadent ruler, Bahadur Shah. This was certainly a very powerful bid for independence but that independence veered around an infirm reed to regroup its strength. Bahadur Shah was in Delhi and Delhi was not far from Punjab. The Sikhs of Punjab had nothing to gain from the restoration of the Mughal empire. The tyranny of Aurangzeb and some of his successors was not lost in their memory. They were antagonized and thus the most warrior mankind of India was estranged from the cause of the revolt. It was from this vast multitude of alienated but rugged Indians that the British drew their necessary strength. The rebels were not at home with the trends of time and they tried to put the clock back. From then on the dynamics of the revolt became backward looking. The logic of the situation did not favour a backward looking movement and the movement in its essentials got negatived in the process by the requirements of time. The revolt, so powerful and spontaneous in its origin, thus became inconsistent with its own time frame. George Campbell in later years rejoiced at the fact that the English annexed Punjab. He said that it was Punjab which saved the British empire and we may add that in saving the British empire in 1857 Punjab acted as an adjunct to the unconscious tool of history for Indian regeneration.

The revolt had a powerful moral undertone that shaped its belligerency. The Indians rose in defence of their faith that was trampled, their rights and privileges that were disregarded and their honour that was mowed by racialism. Their courage, their actions and passions and all their sacrifices were directed to one end, namely the liberation of the country, their *watan* from the *faringis*, the aliens. Yet their ideology was wrongly understood and their place has not been properly marked in history writings. That is why even today we question whether Mangal Pandey was a product of circumstances or of a collective will to avenge historical injustices ? Rudrangsu Mukherjee while raising this question writes : "Indeed, in one crucial way, Mangal Pandey's action was somewhat contrary to the spirit of insurgency. A rebellion's real strength lies in the collective. A rebellion represents a collective will to overthrow an oppressive order. Mangal Pandey's action was that of an individual. His defiance may have been grounded in a collective sense of fear, suspicion and anger but its manifestation was individualistic" *(Mangal Pandey : Brave Martyr or Accidental Hero,* pp. 52-53*).* Mangal Pandey's revolt took place at critical juncture of time. The Baharampur revolt happened a few weeks ago and the Meerut uprising occurred a few weeks later. All these were collective uprisings. Many more were there such as the rising at Barrackpore in 1824 or at Vellore in 1806. The sepoy discontent was general and the spirit of uprising was universal. Individuals were as much a part of the ferment as a collective body of mankind is. Do not the innumerable civil rebellions S. B. Chaudhuri speaks of *(Civil Rebellions in the Indian Mutiny)* or the Sepoy Mutiny at Barrackpore in 1824 Premangsu Kumar Bandyopadhyay writes about *(Tulsi Leaves and the Ganges Water : The slogan of the First Sepoy Mutiny at Barrackpore 1824)* make it clear that squeezed tight against the margin of subsistence the rank and file of the Indians, the sepoys and the civilians alike, were seething in discontent ? The British administrators and the generals knew that an outburst was imminent. Every social outburst is a product of tensions that brew up over time. They manifest at destined moments taking individuals or groups as required tools of history. Individuals then become parts of a collective entity acting under the direction of an impersonal force which is the destiny of a nation. This destiny is called in Hegelian parlance *'the cunning of reason',* the sovereign spirit of a time, that sets human passions to actions and propels mankind toward the fulfillment of its tryst with destiny. To ignore this is to ignore the real perspective of history, here and elsewhere. For many years our history writings remained as appendages to the intellectual outputs of British historians and even today examples are not rare as to how in history writings in India a British mind reflects itself through a disguised Indian mouthpiece. Many years ago Percival Spear wrote : "The passions of the mutineers were centred on their grievances, not on larger ideals. They knew what they disliked, but not what they would wish to set up in its stead. So they gained little advantage from successes and nothing but despair from their defeats. Their resistance was made desperate by the knowledge that they had burnt their boats, that they had committed the unforgivable military sin. However courageous their resistance it was therefore despairing rather than purposeful. They fought to the end, because the chance of death from surrender was equal to that from continued battle." (Percival Spear (ed.) *The Oxford History of India,* 3rd edition, pp 671). Spear denigrates the collective action of the sepoys as Rudrangshu Mukherjee denigrates the action of Mangal Pandey. An accidental hero has no purpose of action just the way the sepoys in spite of their courageous resistance had no purpose for an indeterminate cause. Spear writes the conspicuous history of the English in which their opponents fade into insignificance. Mukherjee maintains the subordinate partnership with Spear blurring an opponent of the British and thus demonstrating in the process the persistence of the colonized spirit of history writing in India. This is where the Indian historiography of the revolt of 1857 stands today. We go shopping to the West for intellectual wares and in all our admirations we act as brain-washed Indian agents who function as necessary remote controls of foreign historians. With such human instruments readily available they easily blast of the perspective of our own history. The result of this is catastrophic. At the end we come to feel how poor we are and our native admiration for a native hero is gradually dimmed. We lose our heritage. We remain shut in the obscure corridor of British conspicuous history.

Thus the main thrust of this essay is clear. The episode of the revolt of 1857 has to be looked at from the perspective of India, a flaming India or a quiet India, India of unity or India of diversity, but India that stays perpetually at the core of the Orient, always plural, but eternally corporate. Time has come when we spoke in clear Indian terms the story of this India where in 1857 tyranny and tyrannicide matched each other to form the moving balance of two antithetical forces of history. Such balances had always been the routine features of Indian history and it was not new for British India. What was new in British Indian history was the stark arrogance of the British rulers and the bitter racialism of the English people which was sought to be curved by the Indian uprising of 1857. Such arrogance the Mughals had never displayed, not to speak of the other rulers of the past. Percival Spear who had always been very dexterous in amplifying British glory by marginalizing Indian achievements had to admit that at the root of the Indian revolt lay the incorrigible haughtiness of some unaccommodative members of the British ruling elite. He writes : "To the fact of conquest many of them added an aggressive and superior air which could not fail to be both offensive and alarming. Their type of talk is illustrated by one of Sir Charles Napier's typical outbursts : 'Were I Emperor of India for twelve years she should be traversed by railways and have her rivers bridged.....No Indian Prince should exist. The Nizam should be no more heard of...Nepal would be ours........" [Spear, *Ibid.*, p.664]. This is the true spirit of aggrandizement which imperialism begets and on the eve of the Indian revolt this spirit was the reigning sovereign in English mind. The defeat of the revolt escalated it. Kaye, the greatest English historian of the revolt carried English egotism to its Olympian height. He wrote : "The story of the Indian Rebellion of 1857 is, perhaps, most signal illustration of our great national character ever yet recorded in the annals of our country. It was the vehement self-assertion of the Englishman that produced this conflagration; it was the same vehement self-assertion that enabled him, by God's blessings, to trample it out. *It was a noble egotism, mighty, alike in doing and in suffering*....If I have any predominant theory it is that : 'Because we were too English the great crisis arose; but it was only because we were English that when it arose it did not utterly overwhelm us". (italics ours); Sir John William Kaye, *History of the Sepoy War in India,* vol.I, Preface; vol.II, p.xii). Thus the British temperament remains to be persistently egotist. No revolt could check it; its depth and bearing were unfathomable. The robust egotism of Kaye turned more sophisticated and cute with the passing of time. Kaye wrote in the first flush of triumph when the empire was regained. Napier-like arrogance did not wither away altogether. Then came the inevitable moment. The empire was lost. The British historians then traversed the memory lane and the rude voice of British arrogance of the nineteenth century became metamorphosed into a subtle tune of contemplative pride. The reminisced fragrance of this can be found in the late twentieth century history writings of the British. Here is one such reminiscences from Spear : "It must always remain an object of wonder that forces so small should defeat opponents so numerous animated by such desperate courage in so short a time. But in fact the forces arrayed on each side were not so unevenly balanced as appeared at first sight. While at first the balance of material factors weighed heavily on the side of the rebels, the balance of moral factors weighed heavily on the side of the British. They only needed time to convert their moral assets into material terms, and thus their determination and confidence in themselves, no less than their courage, enabled them to do." [Spear, *Ibid.*]

Thus pride surfaces when memory unfolds. This is where the British historiography of the Indian revolt triumphs. Such triumphs are the lasting phenomena of British history writings on India.

Could we, the Indians, ever catch up this pride of the British historians ? This question remains unanswered. It can be answered only if we stop hiding our heritage behind a sham digital nomenclature '*1857*' or a profoundly inexpiable expression 'the sepoy mutiny' which is reminiscent of what the British historian calls an '*unforgivable military sin*'. Our respect for our heritage must be reassured. Our road to it will be lost if in the post-centenary golden jubilee of the revolt we go into any exercise of iconoclasm. In the age of globalization the trap is set for us. Shall we step blindfold into it ?

This question becomes meaningful in view of two things. First, ever since the centenary historians wrote their books no authentic history from an all-India perspective has been written. Archive-based research which is essentially very painstaking research found no favour with historians for the last fifty years. We have a good number of micro-studies in the field, studies relating to Oudh, Bundelkhand, Malwa (K.L.Srivastava, *The Revolt of 1857 in Central India–Malwa*) etc. but superseding the viewpoints of regional studies no attempt was made to discover an all-India story of the revolt. One reason for this is the fact that the regional or the state archives situated in Mumbai, Chennai and Kolkata had not been properly visited by scholars so that an all-India perspective of the revolt did not grow. Our conception of the revolt remains largely confined in the inconspicuous cell of a narrow perspective. It was the perspective taught by British historians that the revolt was essentially an event of the Bengal Presidency and an upcountry affair. What tremor the revolt sent in the Presidencies of Bombay and Madras we do not know. In a recent excavation of records in the Mumbai archive the present author discovered how the small revolts in the Bombay Presidency, the uprisings of Poona, Satara, Nagpur, Naurgond, Ahmedabad, Mount Abu, etc. caused tremendous concern to the British administration there. A series of measures were adopted by the Government to prevent the ferment from spreading far and wide. This included disarming of the people, complete news blackout in the entire Presidency from the Sindh to Karnatak, cordoning the military lines by thick police posting so that no communication between the civil population and the army personnels could take place, importing British and European soldiers from outside, imposing martial law at places, enacting new laws for apprehending suspect people and conducting a search in their houses, inflicting of corporal punishments on those caught on specific charges, valid or concocted, inciting the Bheels and the tribal people through prize money and bribes to surround the rebels who moved into villages and so on. These emergency measures were deep, wide and far-reaching and created new tensions among the people of some areas like the south Maratha countries. They show that the uprisings in the Bombay Presidency although not powerful enough to be ranked with the revolts in North Western Province, Oudh and Bundelkhand, do in certain degrees merit appropriate posting in the general map of revolt. The British study of the revolt so far has been an exclusionist approach, their natural tendency was to exclude certain areas of the country from the map of the general uprising in 1857. Our approach, the one we call an Indian approach, will be an integrationist approach whereby we study facts ignored so long because of colonial motivations, appropriate the information provided by them and round up the story in the perspective of a territorially sprawling but nationally integrated phenomenon. In this story of integration the revolt at Vellore in 1806 or that of Barrackpore in 1824 do not stand as isolated events separated by time and distanced by their geographical locations but integrated in our annals of a resistance which was coextensive with the British rule itself.

There is a second reason which makes an all-India perspective illusive to us. This emanates broadly from the results of the defeat of the revolts of 1857. The English in the immediate aftermath of the revolt did two things. First, they imposed on the Indians a mentality of defeat. This was done by constantly harping on the glamour of British military success in the revolt. The second thing was deeper than this. In the immediate aftermath of the revolt the British introduced in their academic curriculum the study of English and European history and the poetry of Tennyson and Wordsworth. In the Tennysonian rhythm the Indians found the space of the British movement. In the worship of nature in the Wordsworthian manner the Indians learnt to return to their ancestral peace of a country life. The Indians forgot that the supreme question that concerned them in 1857 was whether to accommodate change or not, whether to remain in the contemplative mood of inner satiation or to keep itself moving in tune with time. In western India, in the Bombay Presidency the Indians largely did not participate in the revolt because there the Gujaratis, Parsis, the coastal Muslims and the sprawling community of Christians were engaged in trade and the new livelihoods that were opened before them by the British empire. The Marathi people were yet to recover from the shock of their own collapse signified by the fall of the Peshwa in 1818. In the north the Muslims identity, whatever of it remained there, still clustered around Luknow and Delhi, the two eastern outposts of the western and central Asian cultures that lost their streams in the philanthropic wilderness of the Indian pluralism. This culture of the Mughals in India was too sublime to fight against the incoming new culture which unleashed in this country the might of three superior forces of history, namely science, technology and reason. The tranquility of oriental culture manifested in the emotions of Ghalib and the romanticism of Bahadur Shah Zafar was essentially the old order tranquility that could not survive the stress of time. The political culture of the age was one of competitive hegemony centripetal in its spirit and ruthless in its form. The Mughal empire from the beginning was too accommodative, too partnership-oriented and too contemplative as a distant Majesty to compete with the master performers of this hegemonistic racial centralism. As a result when Bahadur Shah Zafar and Ghalib died respectively in 1862 and 1869 in the wake of the collapse of the two Muslim centers of culture, Delhi and Lucknow, the world of the Muslims turned into a vacuum, an irretrievable abyss from which there was no prospect of return. In this situation life had to come to terms with the new order. What this new order was has been brilliantly explained by Maulvi Muhammad Baqar's son, the poet and critic, Azad. "The important thing is that", writes Azad, "the glory of the winners' ascendant fortune gives everything of theirs – even their dress, their gait, their conversation – a radiance that makes them desirable. And people do not merely adopt them, but they are proud to adopt them".[1] It was in this situation that Syed Ahmed Khan defined and organized his overtures with the West. The Hindus, the majority community in India, did not have much to lose in material terms from the defeat of the revolt. In Delhi the Hindu *khatri* class, merchants and moneylenders stepped into the vacuum created by the fall of the Muslims. Dalrymple writes: "Most of the confiscated Muslim properties put up for auction by the British were bought en masse by the Hindu *khatri* (clerical caste) and Jain bankers of the city, such as Chhunna Mal and Ramji Das. These were the only Delhiwallahs who still had access to liquid cash, their main centre of Nil Ka Katra having bought immunity from the depredations of the prize agents on the payment of a large sum soon after the fall of the city. Hindu traders and bankers even bought up two of the city's most famous mosques: Chhunna Mal bought the Fatehpuri Masjid, while a Hindu banker bought the beautiful Zinat-ul-Masjid, one of the main jihadi centres throughout the uprising". "All this exacerbated the sudden shift of power from the Muslim elite, who had dominated the city before the uprising, to the Hindu bankers, who were its most wealthy citizens afterwards". Thus a peculiar age of fulfillment was ushering itself in some parts of the country and among some sections of the Hindu community in India. Standing on the debris of the great city of Delhi in 1858 Edward Campbell wrote : "The capital is in the hands of one or two men like Chhunna Mal and Mahesh Das".[2] The Hindu money-makers were truly regrouping themselves in Delhi and was building up the money stability in the devastated economy of the country. In Bengal the Hindus were going the other way round. They were building up their language identity, so crucial in the formation of their own race. Anchoring on Sanskrit as the most ancient base of Indian culture

[1]Cited in William Dalrymple, *The Last Mughal, The Fall of A Dynasty*, 1857, p. 478.
[2]William Dalrymple, *Op. Cit.*, pp. 461-62.

the Hindu Bengalis steadily crossed over from the turmoil of the Young Bengal age to the new construction in the age of the Universities. The agenda of a radical break with the past upheld so tumultuously by the members of the Young Bengal was cautiously rejected in Bengal in the years immediately preceding the revolt and change there was ultimately accepted as a force only in the vicinity of tradition. Thus the frame of tradition was retained and within it the agenda of modernization was embarked upon. It was in this situation that Iswar Chandra Vidyasagar, writes Amales Tripathi, defined his role as a *traditional modernizer*, making himself the first human symbol of the cultural synthesis of the new age.

In Bengal thus a peculiar thing was going on -- tradition was being mingled with modernity giving rise to the context in which the Hindu intelligentsia could make a meaningful use of their renaissance talents. This was the time when Bengali language was being provided with its own limbs. It was becoming self-reliant. Its structure was being created by Iswar Chandra Vidyasagar in his prose and its elegance was being supplied by Madhusudan Dutt in his poetry. Western forms were fitted in Eastern images. There was the rhythm of a new life, the ecstasy of a new creation everywhere. In this age of creation Bengal was in no mood to accommodate any agenda of subversion that was being followed elsewhere in the country. Weak in their limbs the people of Eastern India made little contribution toward making the military manpower of British India. Bengal perennially devoid of rugged humanity supplied no single sepoy in the so called Bengal army and as such never had experienced the return of disbanded soldiers burning with the passion of revenge against the English. The upcountry motivation for revolt was sadly absent in Bengal.

From all these there has grown a tradition of indifference to the Indian perspective of the revolt of 1857. This indifference has obscured our visions to Indian triumphs. The revolt in no sense was an unhappy incident. In no way it ended with its suppression. Opposition certainly was driven underground and did not express itself in overt rebellion any more. In a few years' time a new kind of opposition surfaced. It was an opposition both to the politics and economics of the empire. The economic failure of the British empire was analyzed threadbare;

the masks of British justice and the British pretension to paternalism was torn asunder and the British exploitation of India was exposed and quantified in minute perfection. All these were done with extreme keenness that was suggestive of a warrior's determination to avange its own defeat. This innovative Indian mind and the contemplative Indian genious sprang up only when the fire of direct warfare was over so that Calcutta, Bombay and Madras could swing into a different warfare to complete the task left unfinished at Kanpur, Meerut and Delhi. In three decades' time the image of invincibility the British gained in 1857-58 became memories ineffectual in new battles of ideas which the Indians raged against the British empire. The grandeur of the British rule and the Majesty of the Queen's Proclamation of 1858 were eventually replaced by a picture of an economic catastrophe of an unparalleled magnitude. Nowhere in the world have the subject people studied and scanned the economics of empire so thoroughly as did the Indians under the British rule. Nowhere in the world under no system of imperialism the imperial economics had been appropriated by the subject people and converted into instruments against their masters as it was done by the subjects of the British empire in India. This was done in the immediate aftermath of the revolt of 1857. This was India's triumph.

Being in this new warfare the British became conservative and shaky. Resources now at its command seemed inestimable but it faced an India which was not as divided as it was any time in the first half of the nineteenth century. Thompson and Garratt writes : "The British, unlike any previous invaders, became more aloof the longer they stayed, more foreign, more efficient. They could neither be assimilated nor expelled, and thus naturally, if not logically, the idea of an Indo-European civilisation grew more remote and less desirable."[3] What does this '*Indo-European Civilisation*' really mean ? It means the civilization envisaged by Bentinck and Macaulay whereby brown men would resemble white men in tastes and culture so that a massive outpost of a Christian civilisation could be planted in the Asian soil. India refused

[3] *The Rise and Fulfilment of British Rule in India*, Central Book Depot, Allahabad, 1962, p. 462.

to tread the Western way. She was ready to change and she did change but not any more on terms of the metropolitan power of Britain. After the revolt of 1857 domination continued as before in all Indian institutions, political economic cultural, but there was no attempt to substitute indigenous institutions with British or European ones. The nature of British domination also slackened. This was a very queer situation for the English. After the revolt the British rule in India became more compact and its administrative apparatus became more solid than ever before. But it became alien, distant and totally London dominated so that it lost its Indian character. Commenting on this Burton Stein said : "Until 1858, the Company had taken part of its ruling title from the Mughal emperor ... (and, albeit less and less convincingly, had presented itself as an Indian state.) Now the foreign character of British rule became incontestable and a focus for political response and organization."[4] This was an Indian gain in the aftermath of the revolt. In 1857 it was difficult to identify the British empire as an enemy of the Indians. Hence the target of attack could not be properly defined. Now the paradigm could be set in very clear terms – *'they and we', 'England and Hindoostan', 'the British and the Indians'*. No Indian could forget the British cruelty that swept the whole of north India after the revolt and this dichotomy between the rulers and the ruled was now written with the blood of the Indians. Henceforth the Indians did not fail to identify their target of attack. It was no longer the *Raj* for the *Raj* was sloth, inchoate and hence discredited and finally superseded. The target was now directly the British empire, the British government and the British power – all un-Indian and hence all foreign and impinging. The Indians did not take much time after the revolt to realize that the fight between them and their oppressors was imminent. They now had their all-India public platform–the Indian National Congress. Their armoury was now their intellect, their public newspapers, a vast stratum of their lawyers and professionals, up-coming civil servants and politicians equipped with techniques of agitation. All of these grew in a generation that matured in the time span of half a century since the revolt. That was the time when very

[4]Burton Stein, *A History of India*, Oxford University Press, 1998, p. 239.

important developments took place. The political platform was erected - *the Indian National Congress*; the ideology of warfare was worked out – *agitation*; the political slogan was made available – *Bande Mataram*; preachers of agitation appeared – *roaming politicians* from Bombay and Calcutta and other parts of the country. It was realized that the outburst of an unprepared moment - 1857 - was a disaster and it was not to be repeated. Twenty years later, in 1877, Tagore wrote his famous article *Jhansir Rani* (The Rani of Jhansi) where he extolled the sacrifices of Indian leaders, their fealty and commitment to the cause of their country. This article was a signifier of a change in time. Tagore was only seventeen years of age when he wrote this article. It manifested the mind of a generation that was born after 1857. The gallery was now raised for the fallen heroes of 1857. The spirit of the revolt did not die. It was now being revived. At the crest of this revival came Savarkar. What was a mutiny and a revolt at one point of time now became the *First War of Indian Independence.* A new confidence was ascribed to the year 1857 and the series of episodes it unleashed. India was now experiencing its moment of triumph. Purged of its ignominy the revolt of 1857 now returned as an event of sacrifice and hence a source of inspiration. What was resurrected in the process we do not know – the events of defeat or the mind that was defeated in 1857. In the reflective awarness of its own failures and achievements the Indian mind was now re-set to its purpose. This mind re-set in its appropriate perspective is the sovereign of history.

4

The Indian Muslims and The Perspectives of The Revolt of 1857

The revolt of 1857 affected the Indian Muslims in four ways. In the first place it was suspected that the revolt was an outcome of a Muslim conspiracy. There was no basis of this suspicion yet it was inflicted upon them and they suffered the wrath of the Imperial Government. Secondly, the Muslims lost the stability of their life after the fall of Awadh and the collapse of the revolt in 1857. The centres of their culture, Delhi and Lucknow, were destroyed and their centuries-old rallying points were crushed beyond recovery. Thus Muslim life became miserable. For nearly one hundred and fifty years since the death of Aurangzeb their life was degenerating into chaos and anarchy. Now the very core of their existence was shattered and there was no sign of recovery. Since this time onward the Muslim resistance to the British, if there were any, was sporadic, casual and unsystematic and was carried mostly on individual score or as a group effort. Community resistance to the British henceforth became a matter of the past. The third way the revolt affected the Indian Muslims was totally antithetical to the two other ways in which it touched them. The Muslims staged a turn around. Centering on Aligarh the Muslims of north India experienced a regeneration. The British government took a pro-Muslim stand after the revolt and provided them with adequate state support so that they could regroup themselves as a force integrated to the British Empire. Inspirations also flowered in their own mind from their own indigenous feeling that they had to come to terms with the

West in order to effect their own transition to the modern world. The Calcutta-based Indian renaissance did not very much take the Muslims in its fold. This gave the Muslims a feeling of being left-out. This hurt the Muslim mind. It was not that the leaders of the renaissance were unwilling to take the Muslims as their partners. But the forces of circumstances kept them apart and the Muslims were dropped out from all agenda of the renaissance movement. This Calcutta-based Indian renaissance absorbed the stimuli of the West and sought to mingle them with the very powerful incentives which it derived from the classical Hindu culture of the past. Therefore the Muslims found themselves difficult to adjust with this very modern south Asian renaissance, however vivacious and dynamic it was. It had powerful Hindu ethos in it which could not be negotiated into a compromise by the Muslims. The Muslim community that had fallen from its status as a ruling people in India was still steeped in the stereotype of its primeval existence and failed to come to terms either with the education of the West or the renaissance of the East. Thus in the middle of the nineteenth century the Muslims in India were a desolate community, absorbed in the contemplative awareness of its own isolation unable either to come to terms with the change around or to take life in the confidence of a partnership with the rulers.

The revolt of 1857 burst forth in this situation. The Hindus and the Muslims sank their differences, struck a new bond of unity and ushered in a form of resistance not known in history before. The fourth aspect of the revolt touched the Muslims here. They experienced a communal compatrictship in war and resistance the underlying solidarity of which was their flaming passion to save their own religion from foreign aggression. This aim born essentially of a native psyche was powerfully tradition-driven and directed towards self-preservation. That way it was introvert. It became extrovert only when in a megalomaniac frenzy it sought to destroy the structure of the British empire in India. The sensibilities that connected the introvert motivations with the extrovert actions were in their entirety archaic, revivalist, and certainly not in tune with the spirit of the age. The rebels wanted to revive the Mughal rule in India, a decadent and moribund institution as a substitute of a modern state, the British empire. In doing that the Hindus and the Muslims left out another very powerful element of the Indian population from the orbit of their unity, the Sikhs of the Punjab, whose persecution by the Mughals left them in a perpetual state of resistance to them. This failure to integrate the Sikhs in the movement against the English was a colossal mistake on the parts of the Indian rebels and their leaders and eventually left a massive crack in the resistance efforts of the people fighting for almost a millennial change in the country. Thus the Hindu-Muslim unity at one given moment of Indian history operated as a detriment to another Indian community that was determined to stop their nightmare days from returning in their life again. We speak of the Hindu-Muslim unity in the revolt of 1857 as an illustrious event of Indian history which it truly was but in doing that we forget to note how this unity worked in favour of an obscurantist force that turned its face to the decadent institutions of Indo-Islamic culture. The solidarity of the Muslims and the Hindus which had once supplied the dynamics of a powerful empire in south Asia now dissipated itself in a moment's effort to undertake a journey to the past. The moment was inopportune, the exercise was fatuous and the unpreparedness of the whole scheme condemned the revolt into a failure. Thus the lesson of unity fell asunder. From the failure of resistance the Hindus regrouped in three lines. First, they withdrew their collaboration with the British, organized their resistance through the Western technique of agitation and grew the spirit of an argumentative Indian to look into the concealed economics of the conspicuous British empire. This was the economics of poverty which Dadabhai Naoroji, Romesh Chandra Dutt and Madhav Govind Ranade laid bare before the world. As soon as the Hindu collaboration sank the Muslims under the leadership of Syed Ahmed Khan stepped in and the partnership pattern within the British Empire metamorphosed in the twinkling of an eye. The revolt of 1857 had thus two aspects involved in it. It was an immediate unifier between the Hindus and the Muslims but a colossal divider in its long run aftermath effects.

It is truly unfortunate that the greatest effort at the Hindu-Muslim unity in Indian history had tried to balance between two opposites, a progressive and an anachronistic aim at the same time namely the expulsion of the British and the restoration of the Mughal empire. In upholding the latter it had addressed itself to an obscurantist and hence a wrong end and dissipated its spirit in a mission that was absolutely out of tune with the general spirit of the age. The age did not favour the revival of a dead empire for modernity was knocking at the threshold of the country. The age of the Railways and the Telegraphs had already set in. New education was in the horizon. The age of Universities had already dawned. The age of Agency houses was gone and the new Banking system was in the offing. In Calcutta the Union Bank had collapsed in 1848 and the Indian capitalists were thrust into the dust. The Business communities were in no mood to face a turmoil in place of the peace of the British rule. The experiments with the Indian land-settlements which began in Bengal sometimes in the middle of the eighteenth century had just come to an end and the Indian mind had not grown its motivations along a right line of action. The Indian state system of the olden times had crumbled and with the surrender of the Peshwa in 1818 the last Indian resistance was beaten to the dust. By that year the Hindu College had come into being in Calcutta and before the Hindus stretched their arms for unity with the Muslims in 1857 the latter community was already three decades backward than their Hindu brethren. The result was that when the Muslims clasped the hands of the Hindus it was not the educated, progressive Hindus whose hands they could hold. The Hindu elements of the *ancien regime,* those whom the revolutions of time had thrown into the limbo, now joined hands with a substantially backward community in India, the old-world Muslims who had turned their face from modernity and progress. The communal unity had a force. It was a social dynamite that could erode the British empire which it really did at times and at places. But that erosion was not universal and the expulsion of the British had never been a sustainable event. The result was that for nearly fifty years the question of the Hindu-Muslim unity did not arise again. It was whipped into action fifty years later when Savarkar wrote his book and designated the uprising not only as a revolt but also as the first war of Indian independence. The scene of Mangal Pandey's revolt which he had drawn in his book and the words of appeal for a general uprising which he put on the lips of this rebel-hero were tinged with an astounding sense of patriotism that could enmesh the Hindus and the Muslims in a corporate mission for liberation. That was unique. Because it wakes up a memory of Hindu-Muslim unity and tried to utilize it as a force of history. Thus while describing a moment of Hindu-Muslim unity in Indian history he revives the romance of history in his own way and like a perfect story-teller, and certainly not as a historian, he creates and recreates a moment for the Indians which could be stored as a source of future inspiration for the people of his country. It is thus a paradox of history that one who later turned out to be one of the greatest exponents of aggressive Hinduism in the country began his carrier as a revolutionary to whom the communal distinction between the Hindus and the Muslims were totally blurred. The greatest importance of the revolt of 1857 was thus for once broke the frontiers of separation between the two communities and ushered in the majestic force of unity in a country that was marked by diversity and among a people that was afflicted with the culture of pluralism.

What did the Hindus and the Muslims eventually gain from their unity in 1857 ? Apparently not much in short term view but something great and tangible, majestic and unique, on a long term perspective of Indian history. Collectively they forced an extrovert empire and its megalomaniac rulers to become introvert. They swept away the rule of a body of merchants, the English East India Company, and forced the British Crown to takeover India on a declared mission of benevolent administration. The ignominy that was inflicted on the Indian Muslims over one century of British rule was effaced from their existence and the robust mankind among the Indians, the Muslims, were restored to their honour. The principles of benevolent administration and institutions of welfare were promised to people irrespective of caste, creed, sect and religion. "The British colonial administration embarked on a program of reform, trying to integrate Indian higher castes and rulers into the government and abolishing attempts at Westernization. The Viceroy stopped land grabs, decreed religious tolerance and admitted Indians into civil service, albeit mainly as subordinates."[1]

It was only in the context of this that the regeneration of the Muslim community in India could set its sail in the aftermath of the revolt of 1857. Nothing could be achieved and gained for the Hindus and the Muslims in India if this communal unity had not been a force in social and political mobilizations in India in the middle of the nineteenth century. This unity was both spontaneous and engineered. It

[1] "Indian Rebellion of 1857", *Wikipedia, The Free Encyclopedia,* p. 21.

produced three things : the courage of an uprising, the spirit of revolt and the force of mobilization that had made the Indian uprising so powerful. It was this unity which made the uprising a national event. Three aspects of this unity bore a national character : firstly, in all sense it was patriotic ; it served no regional purpose and did not try to revive any regional kingdom. Secondly, it was designed to be effective as an instrument to free the nation comprising all people irrespective of caste, creed, religion and sect. Finally, absorbed by a nostalgia that was specifically national it sought to restore a national empire, the Mughal empire. Thus at the crest of success where tensions were high the interest of the nation was not forgotten. A national logic was powerfully driven to a national end.

It should be noted that the central theme of the revolt was not one but an amalgam of four : the unity between the Hindus and the Muslims, the extinction of the rule of the East India Company, the baffled attempt to restore the Mughal empire in India and finally the collapse of the time-old Indo-Islamic culture in this country as a sequel to the passing away of the Mughal empire itself. These four aspects provide the real Indian standpoint from which the revolt of 1857 must be looked at. The revolt in any case was never a sepoy war as has been contemplated by Kaye and other historians because the sepoys had never had a prepared mentality for war nor an organized preparation for it. Nor even did they have an articulated and integrated direction to which the war could be driven. Their direction, if any, was split. On the one hand they aimed at the liquidation of the British empire and on the other they endeavoured to bring the Mughal empire back. The liquidation of a modern state and the restoration of a medieval one could not match each other as parts of the same aim, the one complete and indivisible goal to reach. The attention of the rebel sepoys was bifurcated because they had no premeditated alternative to the British rule in India. The rising was spontaneous and the heat of militancy which the sepoys carried with them was the result of a pent-up grief that found outlet through double passions, a hatred for the foreigners and a spirit of self-assertion. None of these passions had immediate gratification. The rule of the foreigners ceased immediately. The self-assertion of the Indians melted in their failure to bring their own Indian empire back. But out of the ashes of failure emerged the sphinx. For the Hindus the age of the renaissance now gave to a new age of politics. For the Muslims a new age of modernization dawned in the country, thanks to the efforts of Sir Syed Ahmed Khan.

It is here that the revolt story for the Indian Muslims unfolds itself in two aspects. One is a broad morbidity born of a collapse of the Indo-Islamic heritage in India. The other was an optimism born of a spirit of regeneration caused by the touch of a cultural West wind. Between 1857 and 1947 when Pakistan was born the spirit of the Muslims in India underwent a metamorphosis. The Hindus took a span of half a century, from Rammohun's time to the birth of the Indian National Congress in 1885, to build up their political forum. The Muslims in India took as little time as the Hindus—about fifty years from the time of the revolt to the birth of the Muslim League in 1906— to organize their own forum for self expression. Yet they did it when they were half a century behind the Hindus in their march to modernization when they began their journey from Aligarh in the sixties of the nineteenth century. The robustness of the Indian Muslims lies here. The political degeneration which the Muslim community had been suffering since the time of Aurangzeb reached its nadir in 1857. After this date their living was in total despair. They could neither rally their old centres of culture, nor could they revive their old institutions of power. Academically backward, culturally sunk and financially wrecked they could not maintain their compatriotship with the Hindus who in the aftermath of revolt took to the path of political agitation. Thus the aftermath of the revolt of 1857 saw the two communities of the Hindus and the Muslims move in two different lines — one on the road to agitation and the other prevailed upon by regeneration. The Hindu partnership with the state broke down. The Muslim partnership with it was re-structured.

This is a very important point to note. The Hindu-Muslim communal bond and amity were worked out at a time when under the stress of a feudal outburst a joint action became a desperate necessity. But in the peace-time agenda for survival their methods of self-search and sustenance differed. They were flung on the opposite routes for their own quest. Why ? Were their bonds frail ? Were these bonds only products of a crisis ? The answer would be broadly 'no'. In the aftermath of the revolt the Muslims were in the process of a community formation which task the Hindus had completed fifty years ago. They were having the first truce with modernity. The Hindus on the other hand had absorbed from the West the rays of nationalism and they were in their own process of nationality formation. Thus in the making of the two communities the processes of history differed. The Muslims accepted modernity subject to their allegiance to the sovereignty of Allah. The Hindus were shifting their allegiance from the prospect of the divinity to the mundane. Under the leadership of Bankim Chandra motherland was identified with the mother and a mundane image was created to serve as an icon for nationality. This is where the Muslim and the Indian minds differed. At this critical juncture of national psychology the character of the imperial masters changed. The Company-Raj was transformed into the Crown-Raj. The Proclamation of Queen Victoria underlined this change. A new Majesty was ushered in the entire process of transformation. The Queen's promise of a benevolent rule and non-interference in religion offered a double boon to the Indians. Every community in India was assured of the safety of its own religion. Individuals of every community were assured of the reward of their own talents. Private aspirations were fanned and public security was ensured. It was certainly a new beginning—an extension of the Whig benevolence to India in the package of a Victorian peace. For the last one century the Muslims in India had no avenues in public life to satisfy their ambitions. New opportunities were now declared to be open for them. A colonial state suddenly unrolled its scroll of welfare. The Muslims were a defeated community, reeling in misery, mourning the loss of their empire and their own cultural centres. Now a mighty state suddenly stooped to them, stretched its hands of support and cooperation to them and took them in confidence. Those who were suspects in the masters suddenly found their status redeemed. They were now in the substitute role of the Hindus as the partners and collaborators of the imperial victors. This was indeed a new situation and a new age in which a defeated and degenerate community found opportunities of its own resurrection. The Muslims now went into a process of self-purge – a process which the Hindus had experienced throughout the course of the last one century. Thus from the defeat of 1857-58 the Indian Muslims emerged into a new dawn. Prospects of modernity, partnership with the state and a regeneration of a moribund life – these were the hopes of a new dawn. The Muslims were in it.

It was not that security was not there for the Muslims in the past. It was there. What was lacking, they thought, was assurance. Now assurances became declared parts of a colonial state. For the Muslims now had come the moment of opportunities. Since the sixteenth century global Islam had been locked up in stagnation. Their hey-days were gone. The ascendancy of the West through geographical discoveries, the Renaissance, the Reformation, the conquest of new lands, mastery on the seas, the French Revolution, the industrial revolution, the military revolution and so on had overshadowed the Islamic glories of the past. This was the time when the Ottoman Empire was tottering. The messages of the French Revolution were corroding the fabric of the empire which had already been lacking its cohesive force at its core. The Ottoman Sultan was considered the *sick man* of Europe so much so that the liberal Prime Minister of England, Gladstone was speaking of driving the Muslims bag and baggage from Europe. It was in this situation that the Indian Muslims after the revolt of 1857-58 turned to the West. This was a peculiar juncture of moments in history for the Indian Muslims. They saw their empire to sink. They at the same time saw their regeneration to sprout. The years of 1857-58 were thus one of the greatest watersheds in the history of the Indian Muslims. They battled to bring back their lost empire. They failed because they slipped out of the time frame of history the inexorable force of which was moving towards modernism. An espousal of an archaic cause—the substitution of a modern empire by a medieval one—was bound to fail. The revolt of 1857 failed because of this—because its direction was to the past. The forward-looking Indians did not consider this to be a blessed situation to embrace and they turned their faces away from the event. The result of all these was that a new paradigm in Indian history was created. The old-world Indians—the Hindus and the Muslims—united. They did it primarily for their religion and secondarily for their *watan*—their own land. In a world where reason, science and technology was being ushered in as the ethos of global transformation religion seemed to be very primeval motivation for action. A modern state bent on switching over to modern armaments and modern logistics could not tolerate resistance to it. It rallied every force around it—its police, its law courts, its army, its modern transport and its modern communication and transmission system, its paramountcy for mobilizing support and its political and military will—all it had in its arsenal to crush this resistance. Hence the revolt failed. The Hindus and the Muslims experienced the might of a modern colonial state and the progressive elements among them henceforth turned away from the path of resistance. The dichotomy of the story of resistance lies here. The most effective internal motivation of the revolt was religious patriotism. This became irrelevant after 1858 when the colonial state declared its secularism in the form of the Queen's Proclamation. True, this secularism was an imperative of an imperial rule. But the catastrophe of 1857-58 this secularism brought in its train a new hope and the new generation of Indians flourished in it. In many places the revolt had racial dimensions. The rebels in good many places in north India, as in Bareilli, were actuated by anti-Bengali sentiments for the Bengalis were considered to be the agents of the English. This was a very catastrophic sub-nationalism that ran counter to the broad nationalistic genre of the revolt itself. National aspiration of the rebels accommodated a worst kind of sub-nationalism out of which an internal contradiction arose which was never resolved. This had sapped the vitality of the uprising. In later years even the greatest Muslim spokesman of the time Sir Syed Ahmed Khan could not make himself free from this sentiment. He feared that the end of the English rule would mean the rule of the Bengali Babus. This revulsion for the Bengalis shaped the minds of the first Aligarh generation and did not wither away even at the time of the formation of the Muslim League in 1906. This functionally operative sub-nationalism considered the Bengali dominance as a kind of sub-imperialism which it wanted to destroy. Therefore, at many places the rebels had directed their attacks against two targets—the *firingis* and the Bengalis. Thus the apparent communal unity had a racial crack in it. In most cases the dynamics of revolt satisfies double passions—a hatred against foreigners and a hatred against class-enemies, *zamindars, sahukars and mahajans.* It was these double passions which made the revolt spontaneous, impulsive and random underlying the absence of a programme at its inner core.

All the massacres perpetrated by the rebels were basically impulsive, isolated and sporadic.

Emerging out of these experiences the Hindu and the Muslim mind did not find any common ground where they could meet. The Muslim mind became introvert musing over the morbidity of collapse. An all-round pessimism grabbed their spirit. From this pessimism Sir Syed Ahmed Khan released them. The Queen's Proclamation followed by the British support of the Aligarh College offered to them the promise of an oasis in a desert. This promise never turned into a mirage. This is why the Indian Muslims could effect their transition from the pessimism of Mirza Ghalib to the optimism of Iqbal. The revolt of 1857-58 and their failure acted as a catalyst to the Muslims of India. It rescued them from the prison of despair and frustration and set them free in a space from which in a span of time less than a century they could create their own state—Pakistan. From 1857 to 1947—the period of nine decades—were utilized by them to create a community and its potential platform. The British gave the Hindus three things, education, command and participation with which they could organize their own formations—their society that shed archaic institutions, their culture that assimilated the West and their aspirations that federated diversity into an unity. To the Muslims it gave their education, their cohesive entity and their confidence with which they shaped their own institutions—their party, their ideology and their own state. The Hindu-Muslim unity in course of time thus drifted into a dichotomy which their destiny ordained and their history failed to reverse.

Were the Hindus and the Muslims themselves really responsible for their own fall out ? The answer would be broadly 'no'. The aftermath of the revolt of 1857 was the period when the British Empire became introvert. The imperial heydays of a mercantile Company were over. Now began the phase of a new imperialism, namely that of the imperialism of the British nation. Sarvepalli Gopal observes: "The years after the suppression of the revolt in 1858 marked the heyday of the *raj* in India. The British regarded themselves as a superior race ruling by right of conquest, and they saw no reason why they should not remain in India indefinitely. There was little hesitancy about accepting this position".[2] Gladstone in one of his letters[3] used the expression : "When we go, if we are ever to go...." etc. It suggested that the British mind was contemplating a lasting stay in India. In their new urge to regroup themselves in India the rulers needed new partnership for a new kind of imperial domination. After the revolt of 1857 the Hindus were of no use as partners. They had begun their probe into the economics of the Empire and had built up their own theories of Indian poverty and drain. They set up their own political platform. They initiated their own politics of agitation. A clamorous humanity of this sort was no good as partners.

It is in this condition that a revolution in alignment took place in India. The rulers rebuffed by the Hindus turned their face to the Muslims. The Muslim mind had just emerged out of a shock of a defeat in 1857-58. From their defeat they drew their own lesson. They learnt that their salvation lay in accepting the West. They also learnt that science, technology and reason were the hallmarks of the modern world and they were backward because they had refused to accept them. They now came to terms with the West. This was a boon for the Empire. A robust mankind, a community of powerful subjects of the Empire, began to emerge from the sinking animation of the medieval world. This was a gift of the events of 1857-58 which the Empire was quick to grasp. This came at a time when the British Empire was heading for a global domination. A social base was created that assured a colossal manpower support to the Empire.

A transforming era both for the British Empire in India and the Muslim community of south Asia had set in. This was the aftermath of the revolt of 1857. The man, who presided over this transforming era was the destiny's anointed man of Muslim reformation. He was Syed Ahmed Khan, the man who initiated the Muslim dialogue with the West. It was he who by doing this laid pragmatic wisdom as the new basis for a renaissance, although belated but fruitful. What

[2]"Sarvepalli Gopal, *Jawaharlal Nehru : A Biography, Volume One : 1889-1947,* Delhi, Oxford University Press, 1975, p.13.

[3]The letter was written to Northbrook dated 15 October, 1872. It is available in Northbrook papers, India Office Library, Mss.

Rammohan Roy did for the Hindus, Syed Ahmed Khan did for the Muslims. In the life of a nation seldom comes the time when the man and the moment meet. The Muslim destiny now positioned Syed Ahmed Khan in such a juncture. The destiny's tryst with the Empire now set in.

If the revolt of 1857 had been successful it would have not only overturned the British Empire in India but also would have stopped the British agenda for global domination. This the revolt had failed to do. Speaking of the trends of economic growth in the aftermath of the revolt Sarvepalli Gopal writes : "Efficient administration was all that seemed to be required in order to maintain India within the empire in the interests of the British. They led the world in trade and manufacture, and India fitted smoothly into this pattern of world domination. Railways were laid down, with great profit to British investors and manufacturers but with little advantage to economic growth in India. There was a decline in the production of foodgrains and an incentive to grow cotton and jute, which were required by the factories in Britain, and indigo and opium, which sold at high prices abroad. India's export surplus was utilized to balance Britain's deficits with Europe and the United States; but British capital was mostly invested in 'white settler' countries. The banks of India were largely foreign and made no effort to attract Indian capital and direct it to the promotion of Indian industry. The refusal to permit industrialization on any major scale not only arrested progress but distorted the existing economy by increasing the pressure on land, with all the attendant evils of rural indebtedness, absentee landlordism and a large increase in landless labour and seasonal unemployment. The annual *per capita* income in 1857 has been officially estimated at about £2; and nearly 29 millions are thought to have died of starvation in the years from 1854 to 1901".[4]

The aftermath of the revolt of 1857 had thus three distinctive trends of development : first, the consolidation of the British rule in India as a necessary step towards an economic domination of the world; second, the Muslim tryst with the Empire and third, a very

[4]Sarvepalli Gopal, *op.cit.*,p.13.

profound collapse of the partnership between the imperial British state in India and the Hindu community at large. Overriding all these there was in the administration a basic distrust for the Indians and through all tiers of upper echelon of rulers there was an unwillingness to share power with them. "It was taken for granted", writes Sarvepalli Gopal, "that efficiency in administration meant that it would be, at any level that mattered, untouched by Indian hands. Education in the English language had been introduced in schools, and in 1857, the year that the revolt broke out, universities were established in the three leading towns of Calcutta, Bombay and Madras. But the products of these institutions were recruited to no higher posts than those of clerks. Entry by competitive examination into the higher official ranks was in theory open to Indians, but was made on practice almost impossible. All the senior appointments in the civil service were closed to Indians; and in the army, of course, there were no Indian officers at all. Indians were not permitted even to enlist in the volunteer corps."[5] The aftermath of the revolt of 1857 was thus marked by a calculated tightening up of the British monopoly of power. Why then did the British require a special relation with the Muslims ? Certainly there was no intention on the part of the rulers to share administrative power with them. The motive was otherwise. The vibrant Muslims were to be used as the shield of the Empire against the blows of a rising nationalism.

The aftermath of the revolt of 1857-58 thus saw the Indian Muslims in a new partnership with their masters. A community-specific approach to partnership was also buttressed by a class-specific approach. Attempts were made to rope the Indian Princes and the territorial aristocracy of the land into this network of partnership. It was a new experiment. Next to the army and the bureaucracy the feudal aristocracy was the nearest kin who could be cajoled into partnership. All these were required because after the revolt of 1857-58 the British power-monopoly needed a social base. "Yet the unbroken monopoly of power", writes Sarvepalli Gopal, "had to be maintained in a vast country distant from the ultimate seat of Authority, and by a civil service and troops which were numerically insignificant in comparison to those over whom they ruled. The revolt left with most British a legacy of hatred for Indians

[5]Sarvepalli Gopal, *op.cit.* pp.13-14.

as well as an acceptance of the expediency of buttressing their rule with Indian support, it this could be obtained without compromise of their control."[6]

Thus the imperial predilection towards power-monopoly and control came to a sharp focus after the extinction of the revolt of 1857-58. The benevolence underlying the Queen's Proclamation and the ruthless monopoly of power that formatted the imperial strategies of rule made the Empire a moving balance of two antithetical forces. It was in this situation that the Empire needed new areas of support. But where would the support come from? "The obvious answer", writes Gopal, "seemed to lie in an arrangement with the feudal classes. There were the 662 Indian Princes, with their principalities scattered over the country. Some, like Hyderabad, were as large as an Indian province, others were no more than small estates. But all these Princes had in common a total dependence on the British, who allowed them, in return for loyalty, to the *zamindars* of Bengal, the *talukdars* of the United Provinces and the landlords in other parts of the country. The revenue payable by them to the Government had been settled either in perpetuity or for long terms. It was on these men, whose economic interests were tied to those of the colonial system, that the British relied. It was from their ranks that nominees were chosen for the powerless legislative councils. Other empty, loud-sounding forms were also created to bind the conservative elements of Indian society to the empire without devolving any power of even influence."[7]

The feudal aristocracy was not a reliable reed to depend upon. It was not adept to changes and hence it could not be a reliable partner in the Empire's new career under the Crown. The ethos of a transforming era needed more enlightened and dynamic social elements that could carry the message of the new age. The Aligarh College fitted in with the spirit of the University age that had ushered itself in and the first Aligarh generation had already been at the threshold of a career of confidence the age had bestowed on them. A resurrected community which the upcountry Muslims seemed to be at this time

[6]Sarvepalli Gopal, *op. cit.,* p.14.
[7]*Ibid.* p. 14.

provided a pliant base for new imperial take-off. The pragmatic wisdom of the British had also its other whispers that advised the British mind to turn for a while to the English educated Hindu intelligentsia.[8] But the Hindus had developed a clamorous soul and a spirit of agitation.[9] The year the Muslim delegation met the Viceroy at Simla in 1906 the Bengal partition was already one year old. This event had given Indian freedom movement a new turn. Agitation now became an institutionalized part of national politics. A demon, politics of agitation, was unwittingly released from the bottle and it was to be curbed and contained. The beginning of this process was marked by the Viceroy's meeting with the Muslim delegation at Simla and it matured through another colossal event namely the Morley-Minto Reform of 1909 which gave the Muslims of India the right to form a separate electorate. In the immediate aftermath of the revolt the communal harmony between the Hindus and the Muslims did not suffer any disruption. In

[8] "There was, however, another class in India, the small, growing, elite of Indians educated in the English language. By 1885 they were not more than about 50,000. Some of them went into official service; but the majority the lawyers, the doctors and the journalists, familiar with English political literature, were eager for wider avenues of public work. They were not revolutionaries, asserted their loyalty, and sought only greater opportunities of official employment, administrative reform, facilities for trade and a measure of elections to the legislative councils. For a time, in the years after 1880 when Gladstone was Prime Minister, an attempt was made to rely on this educated sector rather than on the upper classes. But even in the short term the attempt did not succeed. Local self-government never took root, while the effort to win middle-class support for the central government was broken by the weakness of the authorities and the fierce hostility of the British community in India. The only result was a further quickening of political awareness and the formation of various associations, culminating with the establishment of the Indian National Congress in 1885."— Sarvepalli Gopal, *op.cit.,* p.14.

[9] Surendranath Banerjea in Bengal, basically an Anglophile, was driven out of administrative service about this time for no fault of his own. Effecting a junction with Anandamohan Bose, the great Indian Mathematician who just returned from England, he initiated an age of politics in the country. He toured the length and breadth of the country and spread fire through his speech. This is how the age of agitational politics emerged in India.

many cases the two communities maintained their inner organic ties.[10] By the time the partition of Bengal took place Indian nationalism seemed to be quite in an advanced stage of its growth and development but it was till then not imbricated by the concepts of its pejorative other—'communalism'. One may broadly say that the last flavour of the communal unity between the Hindus and the Muslims which was so conspicuous in building up the glamour of the revolt of 1857-58 did not altogether fade till the year of the Bengal partition. In 1909 the imperial axe fell and the bonds of harmony between the two communities became snapped. What happened in 1909 was the opposite of all that happened in 1857. Then—at the time when the revolt burst out—the Hindus merged their entity with those of the Muslims, upheld the Mughal emperor as their legitimate ruler and fought for the restoration of an empire which they thought was essentially theirs. This merger was dissected by the Imperial masters so much so that ultimately the Hindus were made to be seen as a 'nation' and the Muslims with their religion and *qaum* were reduced to almost a marginalized status of the 'other'. In Bengal in 1905 the Hindus were split and in the territorial division of East Bengal and Assam they were made a minority to be dominated by the majority population of Muslims who were mostly peasant and hence a lowly and a backward segment of Indian humanity. In 1909 the Morley-Minto reforms encapsulated the minority status of the Indian Muslims and thus provided the base on which a two-nation theory could be anchored. In 1905 the Bengali race was split; in 1909 the entire nation in India was divided. This division was too precautious because the Muslim mind was not wholly prepared for this division. They were suddenly confronted with a difficult choice. Should they live by faith, or should they live by patriotism—their

[10]The patron-client relations which marked very old bonds between the two communities continued. Here is an example of this : "The fortunes of the Nehrus had for generations been tied to Muslim patrons. There is no evidence for saying that in the early eighteenth century, Farrukhsiyar, the Mogul emperor, had invited Raj Kaul to join his court at Delhi. All that we do know is that Raj Kaul came to Delhi, and gradually the Kauls assumed the double-barrelled name of Kaul-Nehrus, because, it is said, their house was situated on the banks of a canal (*nahar* in Urdu). Then, after the revolt of 1858, and the final collapse of the Mogul, the Kaul-Nehrus moved to Agra."— Gopal, *op.cit.*, p.17.

commitment to the nation and the territorial state of Hindustan? Those who preferred living by faith eventually opted for a new state which would contain a one-faith nation. This led to the birth of Pakistan. The saner and sober elements among the Muslims lived by patriotism, got themselves identified with nationalism and contributed to the strength of Indian freedom movement. It was they who along with the progressive elements among the Hindus and other religious communities blasted off the self-gratifying core of *Hinduttva* and made Indian diversity a paradigm unbeaten by revolutions of time. In any case the Imperial conspiracy played its role. The Indian nation was divided and the British rule was prolonged.

In 1857 the Muslim identity was assertive. With the help of the Hindus the Muslims wanted to restore their own *raj*. This was the *raj* in which a communal partnership had always provided the inner bonds of an unity. The Mughal empire of Hindustan was essentially this—a partnership in which a ruler's majesty presided over the fusion of subordinate identities and differences of caste, creed, religion and clan faded in a system of functional collaboration of dissimilar elements. To uphold the dignity of such an unity the Muslims in 1857 staked their lives and career. The legacy of this was set aside in 1909 and the Muslim identity was dragged into a dilemma from which it never recovered. After 1909 the Muslims were no longer assertive vis-a-vis the state. They no longer challenged the sovereignty of the British *raj*. As a community they laid down their arms. They did not know what their career ahead would be like. Their existence was defined in terms of faith which meant that their immediate loyalty became a split loyalty—one to their faith and the other to British *raj*. This loyalty-split became one curse from which the Muslim mind never recovered in future. Once a Muslim state was created in Pakistan a new split became imminent. Now it was again a torn loyalty that afflicted Pakistan—a split between loyalty to faith and loyalty to language. This split widened with the progress of time and Pakistan itself became partitioned on the question of language. Seceding from Pakistan a new state Bangladesh emerged in 1971. Loyalty to faith on political matters was an error. Seduced by the promises of British rule in India a community of Muslims forgot the legacies of 1857 and stepped blindfold into this error. History changed its course. The unity of 1857 became irrevocably lost.

5

Was The Revolt of 1857– A *Jihad* ?

One important standpoint from which the Revolt of 1857 can be discussed is the standpoint of Muslim psyche. The community psyche of the Muslims in India prior to 1857 was a compound of many factors. Their wretchedness under British rule, their loss of power as a ruling race, their non-acceptance of Western values – all became a focus of grievance for a community squeezed against the margin of life. For Muslims battered under British rule a *jihad* against the tyranny of the *Farangis* would be a common form of reaction. Modern research unearths how the idea of *jihad* moved some sections of the Muslims in India during the time of the revolt of 1857.

Our window to the *jihad* aspect of the Revolt has been opened by Ayesha Jalal. She writes : "The sense of hopelessness was to become a recurrent theme in much of the Urdu poetry and prose written by Muslims after the formal loss of sovereignty. There were Muslims [Muslim] voices other than Ghalib's who were given to perceiving the turn of events from a more communitarian point of view. Momin Khan Momin for instance responded to the 1857 revolt by urging Muslims to wage a *jihad* against the British as a religious duty."[1]

[1] Ayesha Jalal, *Self and Sovereignty: Individual and Community in South Asian Islam since 1850*, Oxford University Press, 2001, p.33.

Jihad means a communitarian approach to events but its philosophy was intensely imbued with a sense of religion. Thus Maulvi Liaquat Ali Khan of Allahabad, Ayesha Jalal notes, acted as "one of the key-players in the revolt" and he rallied Muslim weavers in northern India against the Company's rule. His message was this :

> "Fill Hind with Islam in such a way O Shah
> That there be no voice other than 'Allah' 'Allah'." [2a]

During the early years of Islam when an empire was being built in its name *jihad* was synonymous with a religious war [2b]. When a call for *jihad* was given the sentiment was certainly nothing other than religious. Religious bonds often act as more powerful pace-setters than political ambitions and here a minority of rebels belonging to the Muslim community was actuated by traditional beliefs inherent in Islam. But any attempt to infuse religious sentiments into an apparently political and civil movement had its own limitations. Could Islamic ethos operate on the non-Muslim people who participated in the revolt ? It was here that the call for a *jihad* suffered its setback. Ayesha Jalal writes : "Yet the explicit use of religion in the Muslim call to arms was not without its limitations. Muslims were not alone in revolting against the Company. The importance of non-Muslim participation in the success of the rebellion militated against any attempt to couch the appeal in exclusive Muslim terms. Indeed the famous Azimgarh Proclamation of August 1857, which raised the standard of revolt, was addressed to both Muslims and Hindus. Moreover, the prospect of the restoration of the Shia state in Awadh put the idea of a religious *jihad* at a serious discount for many *maulvis* of the Sunni ilk".[3] The rebels, it should be noted that was fighting against a political state and not against anybody of mankind or any principle of rule. In such cases *jihad* could not be

[2a] *Ibid.*

[2b] "In time, the early raids evolved into larger battles which eventually began to take on the character of a religious war (*jihad*) against infidel or enemy population"– Benjamin Walker, *Foundations of Islam : The Making of a World Faith*, Rupa & Co., (First published in Great Britain 1998 by Peter Owen Publishers) Paperback, 2002, p.321.

[3] Ayesha Jalal, *Op.Cit.*, p.33.

a specific ideology the rebels could rally around. *Jihad*, in the true sense of the term, was a battle against unbelief undertaken for the spread of a true faith.[4] The *jihadist*, (the *mujahids*, in Islamic terminology), were not sure as to what they were fighting against or what they were fighting for. As a result they fell out on the traditional Shia-Sunni differences in the interpretation of *jihad* and its immediate application. Ayesha Jalal notes the poignancy of the Sunni-Shia differences in the matter :

"In any case the Muslim *ulema* of both the Sunni and Shia varieties were unable to agree whether the revolt was a *jihad*. A declaration of *jihad* would make it mandatory for all Muslims to participate in it as a religious duty. Pragmatism in many instances proved to be the better part of the Islamic valour of India's Muslims. The *fatwas* issued are a colourful medley of quite different points of views. In the opinion of some *ulema* there were no grounds for *jihad* so long as Muslims enjoyed religious freedom under Company *raj*. The leading Shia *alim* of Lucknow, Syed Muhammad, ruled out a *jihad* since nobody qualified as *Imam* and went so far as to instruct his followers not to support the rebels. This earned him a pension from the British administration and is another illustration of the practical consideration which influenced the posture of many Muslims during the course of the revolt. His counterparts among the Sunni *ulema* quibbled over the issue of whether there could be an *Imam* who was not of the Quraish tribe. These issues were never resolved....".[5]

Could there be any ground for the Muslims to interpret the revolt in strictly religious terms ? As a matter of fact the Hindus had better reasons to look at the British rule with a tinge of religious melancholy. "The impalpable pressure", writes Percival Spear, "of Western ideas was making itself felt upon Hindu society as a whole".[6] These ideas

[4]"The term *jihad*, 'striving' in the cause of God (5.39), which is enjoined in several passages in the Koran, is commonly interpreted as signifying a holy war against the infidel. The 'striver' (mujahid) is one who participates in such a war, and his purpose is the conversion of unbelievers, the extermination of unbelief, and the spread of the faith" –Benjamin Walker, *Op.Cit*, p.324.

[5]Ayesha Jalal, *Op. Cit.*, p. 33-34.

[6]*The Oxford History of India by the Late Vincent Smith*, Third Edition, Edited by Percival Spear, part III, Rewritten by Percival Spear, Oxford, 1961 reprint of 1958 edition, p.665.

had reformed and almost revolutionized the Hindu society. It would have been in the logic of things if the Hindus had given a call for a *dharmayuddhha*. But the call for a *jihad* came from the Muslims. Spear is of opinion that religious discontent was "stronger and more widespread in Hindu than in Muslim society, but they were by no means absent from the latter as well. Muslim *maulvis* had lost their favoured position in the criminal courts. Muslims in general preferred British to Hindu rule, but only so long as tradition was respected; and they preferred their own to either. So orthodox opinion was rendered uneasy by such activities as Western education and Christian missions and such innovations as railways and telegraphs just as the Hindus were. The annexation of Oudh meant the imposition of infidel rule on the faithful. Shias were outraged by the fall of the King of Oudh, and Sunnis distressed by the steady denigration of the Mughal emperor. It was no accident that one of the leaders in Oudh was the Maulvis of Fyzabad. To the Muslim orthodox Victorian reformers were but old infidels writ large".[7]

Thus the affected sensibilities of the Muslims created a milieu in which the call for *jihad* seemed to be a pertinent form of mobilization. But *jihad* in history had never been a general form of war and it was always a context-specific event.[8] A call for *jihad* was given by the Prophet on the eve of the battle of Badr. The report goes thus : "The two armies reached Badr and camped on opposite sides. The whole night they rested. The Prophet (SA), however, spent the night in prayer.[9]

[7] *Ibid.*

[8] *Jihad* "May express a struggle against one's evil inclinations, an exertion to convert unbelievers, or a struggle for the moral betterment of the Islamic community." - John L. Esposito, *The Oxford Dictionary of Islam*, Oxford University Press, 2003, p. i60.

[9] "The Prophet (SA) prayed all the night, weeping and repeating these words:
'O Allah, Shouldst thou allow this small band of Believers to perish this day, no one Will be left on earth to worship thee.'
Allah responded, "Soon shall the enemy be routed out and will then turn and flee' :- Al-Quran, LIV : 45" — Syed Manal Shah Alquadri, *Islamic Terrorism*, Quadria Academy, Kolkata, 2004, p.73.

And early in the morning he called his men for the 'Fajr' prayer, which having been said, he delivered a rousing sermon on the subject of jihad". "Then the battle was joined".[10]

This was how the first *jihad* in history was fought.[11] If we trace the genesis of *jihad* from the battle of Badr, it becomes clear that religious motive and the motive of self-defense lay at the root of it. Commentators on Islam has no hesitation in saying that "*Jihad* means waging religious war ..."[12] "The sufferings, persecutions and tortures at the hands of their enemies for the sake of their faith was no less a *jihad* for the Muslims at Mecca than their fighting in defence of Islam at Medina. Every effort made to spread the truth is *Jihad-e-Akbar*, the great *jihad*".[13] However, Badr only set the trend of *jihad* in Islam and the trend continued later. Thus a commentator observes : "In time, the early raids evolved into larger battles which eventually began to take on the character of a religious war (*jihad*) against infidel or enemy populations"[14].

Given the above the question arises, was there any *jihad* in India in the past ? This question we ask in order to determine whether the *jihad* of 1857 was unique of its kind in Indian history. It has been said on the authority of Iqtidar Alam Khan that Akbar the Great followed a double policy of adjustment and war in the conquest and consolidation of his empire. His *Suhl-I Kull* or *peace with all* was his policy of adjustment. His war with some of the Rajput states like Chitor was

[10] *Ibid.*

[11] Syed Manal Shah Alquadri writes: "the first *jihad* in Islam was fought at Badr. It was not a fight of aggression but was forced upon the Prophet(SA), whose sacred duty then became to protect Islam from the evil intent of the infidels of Mecca. A *jihad* is always fought in defence of Islam. He Quran says: 'And God did certainly assist you at Badr when you were weak; be careful of your duty to God then, that you may give thanks' "(Al-Quran III: 122)– Alquadri, *Op. Cit.,* p.74.

[12] See F. Steingars, *Persian-English Dictionary,* London, 1963, p. 880.

[13] Alquadri, *Op. Cit.,* p. 142.

[14] Benjamin Walker, *Op. Cit.,* p. 321.

a religious war-*jihad*[15]. Thus *jihad* to Akbar was an ideology of political engagement, temporary, target-specific and limited. This should be contrasted with the broad call for *jihad* as a religious warfare against a community of non-believers, the Hindus. Satish Chandra observes : "Nevertheless, the 'ulama expected the sultans [of Delhi] to act as the champions of Islam by suppressing *bid'at* and the open practice of things forbidden by the *Shari'a.* They also expected them to wage a constant *jihad* against the Hindus, to degrade and humiliate them, and not permit them to make an open display of idolatrous practices".[16] This advocacy for *jihad* was different from Akbar's exercise of it under impulses derived from the dynamics of empire-building. Iqtidar Alam was giving the political ideology of military engagement of the Mughal state. Satish Chandra was giving the sociology of political engagement during the early Muslim rule in India. But in both cases the idea of *jihad* had a strong religious undertone because it was directed against the infidels. Also in both cases it was a state-level attempt to execute Islamic ideas sharpened with a motive of advance and a charged mission of conquest. In 1857, the motive of conquest was not present and the general will of the Muslims did not favour very much the restoration of Muslim rule in India. By 1857, the Muslims in India did not have the strength and adequate political power with which they could mobilize themselves for a *jihad.* Moreover the evolution of *Sufism* through centuries had softened Indian Islam and the fire of *jihad* lost its medieval flames. Alongwith *jihad* Islam also gave rise to a new philosophy of retreat. One such philosophy was

[15]Richard M. Eaton (ed.), *India's Islamic Traditions,711-1750* (Oxford in India readings: Themes in Indian History) Oxford University Press, New Delhi, 2003, p. 118." But upon resorting to the use of force against Rajput opponents, as he did at Chitor (1568, Akbar issued a 'proclamation of victory' (*Fatnamah*) exulting in his having waged jihad against infidelity." - *Ibid.*

[16]Satish Chandra, "Jizya and the State in India during the Seventeenth Century", in Richard M. Eaton (ed.), *Op. Cit.* p.137.

preached by the *Chisti Sufi* movement called the Indian *Mahdawiyah.*[17] The social philosophy of political engagement that was revealed in the *Mahdawiyah* movement only shows the internal softening of Indian Islam in course of transforming age. Derryl N. MacLean gives lucidly the *Mahdawiyah* transformation of Indian Islam with *jihad* as the mellowing force within. He writes :

"On the other hand, the emphasis placed by the Mahdi on the inner life of his followers could be used in support of a quietist stance. The vast majority of the *Mahdi* traditions rélate directly to personal conduct and intensified group ritual, primarily on a radical *Chisti* pattern. Only one of the twenty chapters of the first major compilation of the Mahdi's sayings, the *Insaf-nama* of Miyan Wali, concerns *jihad.* The remainder focus on such matters as the renunciation of the world (*Tark-I Duniya*), the obligations of continual *Dhikr*, the vision of God (didar), and the organization of the institution of hijrah to the da'ira. Indeed, by elevating hijrah over *jihad* as the crucial duty of true believers at the millennium, the *Mahdi* could even be seen as advocating an ethic of retreat, not expansion".[18]

MacLean says that in some cases, "*Hijrat* did lead to *jihad*, political volatility, and a clash with the state. But in other contexts, it did not,

[17]In the course of the Muslim ninth century (fifteenth century AD), a number of millennial movements emerged throughout the Muslim world in anticipation of the tenth century and the impending appearance of a *mahdi* ('rightly-guided one'), a messiah-like figure who, it was widely believed, would herald the events of the end of the world at the close of the first millenium. Most of the movements were ephemeral, and we know of their existence primarily in refutations of the jurists. One, however, did exhibit considerable chronological durability and textual productivity. This movement was the Indian *Mahdawiyah* founded by Saiyid Muhammad Jaunpuri (847-910/1443-1505), a pious religious scholar and Chisti Sufi from Jaunpur in Northern India who claimed to be the long-awaited *Mahdi* in 901/1495. The followers of the Indian *Mahdi* have survived down to the present, in varying conditions of prosperity, in Sindh, Baluchistan, Gujrat, Rajasthan, and the Deccan" — Derryl N. MacLean, "The Sociology of Political Engagement: The Mahdawiyah and the State" in Richard M. Eaton (ed)., *Op. Cit.* p.150.

[18]Derryl N. MacLean, *Op. Cit.,* p.157.

but formed the basis for the Mahdawi retreat inwards and political disengagement as a movement".[19] This concept of retreat from expansion to an inward fulfillment of the self under the guidance of God was a major contribution of Indian Islam to the world Islam at large. Thinking in the context of this indigenisation of Islam in the Indian subcontinent it may be said that *jihad* as a religious war in support of a faith was not a universal phenomenon in Indian Islam. It was always a momentary, event-specific and chance-directed philosophy of war meaningful only in the contexts of military confrontation and social desperation as were found in the various phases of early expansions of Islam. In later years, when the Muslim mind in India mellowed by the defeat of the revolt of 1857 turned to the West with definite overtures of peace *jihad* became redundant concept of battle in a world aggressively closing down upon the Muslims. A time came in later years when Indian Muslims absorbed in their spirit the hospitality of the British *Raj* and *jihad* became unworthy of acceptance in a world where communitarian identities were desperately shading their medieval grabs. A major attempt at the adjustment with realities were made by Sir Syed Ahmad Khan of Aligarh who instilled new ethos in the Muslim quest for identity. In around 1876, his paper the *Aligarh Institute Gazette*[20]. What he was trying to do was to stimulate among the Muslims a sense of national patriotism. He was happy that the Sunnis and the Shias had buries their differences and became one in their support for Turkey. The change he introduced in the concept of Muslim identity was revolutionary. "It may have been easier for Muslims", writes Ayesha Jalal, "to rise above their internal differences on matters concerning co-religionists in Turkey or Persia than to practise unity in religion within India. Remarking on the implications of a declaration of *jihad* by the Sheikhul Islam of Constantinople a few months later, the *Aligarh Institute Gazette* thought it unlikely that Indian Muslims would rush to do battle with infidels. At most they would spread their prayer mats and earnestly urge Allah

[19] *Ibid.*

[20] Sir Syed Ahmad Khan started this paper in 1866. Within a short time this paper became the main spring for regeneration of the Muslims in India.

to come to the assistance of Islam. After all, even the most bigoted Muslim could not deny that "peace and security ... under British rule 'though not free from faults' was 'not to be found in any Muhammedan kingdom on earth'".[21] This was the Muslim sentiment in India only two decades after the Revolt of 1857. How far was the Muslim mind removed from this at the time of the revolt ? Was there a genuine cry for *jihad* against the rule of the East India Company which could find a support from the people ? It has already been pointed out that the *jihad* was basically a mobilization under religious sanction. Therefore, there was difficulty in giving a call for *jihad* in a movement where participants in good number were other than adherents of Islam. In the objective conditions created by the British rule in India it was difficult to satisfy romantic yearnings of any perticular faith. The *ulema* and the faithful might bemoan that India under the Company's *Raj* was no longer a *Dar-ul-Islam* but their support in the society was not large by any measure. Between 1757 and 1857 what was marked in the Muslim mind was an acute sense of the loss of power they suffered under the rule of an English Commercial Company. With this sense of loss ingrained in the Muslim mind *Jihad* could not be a workable strategy of combat. There was no prospect of any positive gain anywhere around for the Muslims if they did not come out from their medieval shell of faith-oriented existence and come to terms with the emerging dimensions of the modern world. Some of the educated Muslims realized that *jihad* in inappropriate conditions would mean taking a leap in the dark. In the past whenever there was a call for a *jihad* there were prospects for gain and without any pre-guarantee for gain *jihad* would be a quixotic exercise of valour. It is true that the Muslims in India had never submitted to the Western concept of seperation of religion from politics but increasingly they found that it was equally difficult for them to negotiate with a western system of governance by ruling this duality out. They might argue that India was not a *dar-ul-islam* in the true sense of the term but they were also powerless to say that it had become a *dar-ul-harb* or an abode of strife. It goes to the credit of Sir Syed Ahmad Khan that he trained

[21]Ayesha Jalal, *Op.Cit.*, p. 61.

a band of educated Muslims, mainly the products of the Aligarh school, who could realize that the spiritual teachings of Islam was not incompatible with the material blessings of the British rule. To them India ruled by the British had become a *Dar-ul-Aman*, an abode of peace, where they could settle down comfortably by taming their aspirations in keeping with the modern age. This was one of the revolutionary turns the Muslim mind had experienced in South Asia in the second half of the nineteenth century. Had they accepted the notion that India was a *Dar-ul-Harb*, a *jihad* would have been obligatory for the Muslims. Alternative to *Jihad* was *Hijrat*, migration to the other lands, an event possible at the time of the Prophet was difficult in the modern world. *Hijrat* was tried in 1921 under the impact of the *Khilafat* Movement when a mass exodus of the Muslims began to take place in the north-west but the experiment eventually failed, partly under Gandhi's influence and partly under the influence of reason and pragmatic considerations.

From all that has been said above it is clear that a call for *jihad* in 1857 was a futile exercise of implementing an Islamic ideology that was destined to fail against a better-armed enemy. In later years, in the forties of the twentieth century there were several occasions when the cry for *jihad* was raised and at least on one occasion Jinnah's advice was to incorporate the scheduled castes among the Hindus in the fold of this holy war.[22] These were spontaneous calls that lacked directions and the inner urge to develop their own momentum from within and as a result none of them proved to be a success. But these calls for *jihad* came when the British withdrawal was imminent when the unity of the Hindus and the Muslims had been shattered to ruins and when the prospect of a Muslim homeland, their *watan*, was already in the air. *Jihad* in history had always been undertaken when success was assured and when success was a distant dream the learned Muslims had always refrained from shedding the blood of their co-religionists in an unsuccessful battle. Two things should be noted about the call for *jihad* in 1857. First, there was no attempt to incorporate the scheduled castes in it thus leaving no example of anomaly in the concept and

[22] Ayesha Jalal, *Op. Cit.*, pp. 411, 422, 454, 459, 491, 494-498, 552.

practice of the holy war of the Muslims in future. In later years when joint meetings of the Muslim League and the scheduled caste organizations tried to extend the scope of the holy war of the Muslims by creating a joint front of resistance to the English, an anomaly became apparent. How would infidels, the scheduled caste, be made partners in a religious war against another sets of infidels, the British ? The anomaly of a Muslim *jihad* had never been more glaring", comments Ayesha Jalal.[23] That apart there was a second aspect in the *jihad* of 1857. It was a split action on the part of the Muslims. The Barelvi *ulema* in Shahranpur district did not allow the Muslims there to support a holy war against the *Raj* of the Company.[24] In 1857 the Hindus and the Muslims were fighting for a common cause and in their battle against the *Raj*, the *sipahis* and the *janta*, the soldiers and the civil population, both rose in a spontaneous movement to drive the *farangis* out of their land. This was a national deluge, a Niagra in the stream of national life, which did not wait for a holy war to be declared by clerics. In such circumstances the call for a Muslim *jihad* became a feeble attempt by the orthodox and the medieval elements in the Muslim society to convert a gigantic event of history into a baseless upsurge of religion motivated by political gains.

Tapti Roy[25], while studying the nature of rising in Bundelkhand found religion as a dominating factor behind the revolt. While saying this she is, however, convinced that it was not a faith-oriented religion. If not propelled by faith the revolt could not be either a Muslim *jihad* or a Hindu *dharmayuddhha*. "Why did the soldier rebel ?" "Without exception, they answered in the idiom of religion"– wrote the historian. This was the verdict she received from British official documents supported by stray pieces of private correspondence. In all these, she

[23]Ayesha Jalal, *Op. Cit.*, p. 498.

[24]"In 1857 the Barelvi *ulema* of *thana* Bhawan in Shahranpur district had decreed against a Muslim *jihad*. This drove a wedge between *thana* Bhawan and Deoband, though they had no serious disagreements on religion" – Ayesha Jalal, *Op. Cit.*, p. 422.

[25]Tapti Roy, *Sepoy Mutiny and the Uprising of 1857 in Bundelkhand*, August, 1991: Occasional Paper No. 129: Centre For Studies in Social Sciences, Calcutta, p. 27.

says, the rebels, "declare their reasons for turning against their masters. While drawing upon their experience as a corporate body for organising actions in the mutiny, soldiers drew upon their wider social traditions when conceiving the struggle in terms of a cause and ideology. The widely shared opinion among the English officers that 'The soldiery had a hard religious panic' was substantially corroborated by the language used in these written addresses sent to mobilize men in the cause of religion. Here the uprising was described not so much as a struggle for political ends as an imperative, a sacred duty, for upholding religion which stood threatened by the English rule. It was a contest for the preservation of faith; therefore, its outcome had to be either the victory or the defeat of religion".[26] In a broad sense, therefore, religion was the context in which a mutiny and a political upheaval were thought of. This was particularly true of the Bundelkhand uprising. There the contemporary British records speak of religion as the only impulse that drove people to insurgency. Political motives, worldly gains and mundane interests formed no part of the purposes and the strategies of the soldiers. This feeling of contemporary British observers find place in some of the modern assessments of the revolt. In the ferment of uprising religion was thus the only sentiment. This provides historians the framework of their understanding.

Modern researches disprove that the motivating values of the Revolt could be a derivative of any ritualistic religion. "We must be careful", writes the historian of the Bundelkhand rising, "not to be misled by the term 'religion'. It appears in that form in the English documents of the period and we, writing in the English language, are forced to use it. In Hindustani, the terms used were *deen* or *dharma*. Religion as the rebels used it to justify their rebellion, did not mean the theological or the ritual principles of a sect or an order. It was used quite consciously to unify, not to divide. And in this sense 'religion' was that which was threatened by English rule, specifically by Christianity. Those who had faith in *deen* or *dharma* had to see the alien Christian religion as heresy and had to resist it in their resistance to the alien religion, Hindus and Mussalmans were brothers".[27]

[26] *Ibid.*

[27] Tapti Roy, *Sepoy Mutiny and the Uprising of 1857 in Bundelkhand*, August, 1991: Occasional Paper No. 129: Centre For Studies in Social Sciences, Calcutta, p. 27.

6

The August Uprisings In The Bombay Presidency

There are two predominant conceptions with regard to the revolt of 1857 - that it was a mutiny and that it was confined within the Bengal Presidency. Recent researches proved these two conceptions to be wrong. We have enough archival records to show[1] that military uprisings did occur in the then Bombay Presidency and the government was shaken by what may be called 'Mutinies' at stations which had no records of uprising in the past. One important example of such uprisings was the mutiny of the 27th Regiment of Native Infantry at Kolhapur.[2] This was a partial mutiny because only a part of the regiment revolted.[3] Nevertheless the government was in turmoil. The mutineers held a strategic place called 'Daga' and there were chances that the mutiny would spread to other parts as well.[4] From the government's side two approaches were made to combat this incident.

[1]Records of the Political Department 1857 preserved in the Maharashtra State Archives, Mumbai have been used in this paper.

[2]Letter to Col. Maughan, Pol. Superintendent, Kolhapur, 17 Aug, 1857. *Political Department 1857 : Deccan Disturbances,* Vol. 25, Letter No. 1329 of 1857. Secret Deptt. Henceforth referred to as *Pol. Deptt., 1857 Deccan Disturbances.*

[3]Letter no. 1330 of 1857, communication to Col. E. Green, Adjutant General of the army, dated 17 Aug 1857, *Pol. Deptt. : Deccan Disturbances.*

[4]Letter no. 1330 of 1857, communication from Col. E. Green, Adjutant General of the army, dated 17 Aug 1857.

First a counter attack was planned on the mutineers and records said that it was successful.[5] Secondly, there was a talk about imposing a martial law in "Southern Konkun".[6] Along with this, there was also an attempt to muzzle the press. All "Vernacular Newspapers published in Bombay" were warned. Similar warnings were sent to the "Papers published at Outstations".[7] The circular which was sent to all northern and southern Maratha territories[8], was a Secret Department directive and it said :

"I am directed by the Right Hon'ble the Governor-in-Council to request that you will have the goodness to warn the Editors of all Native Newspapers published within the limits of your charge, not to make statements in their columns on the subject of alleged mutinies in the Bombay army, without the permission of Government".[9] This was one of the first major attempts at news blackout in colonial India. A vast area covering almost the whole of the Bombay Presidency was brought under the purview of this News blackout. Certainly this was a precautionary measure. But why ? Was there any chance of a general flare-up in the country ? The Magistrate of Satara was advised to keep "a careful watch" on the families of suspects.[10] Did the government have a pre-sentiment about a link between the civilian population and the soldiers that had mutinied ? The civil government was operating under a panic and the military administration was desperately trying to allay the fear of the government. The military administration informed

[5] *Ibid.*

[6] Letter to the Magistrate at Ratnagiri, dated 18 Aug, 1857. Letter no. 1336 of 1857, *Pol. Deptt., Deccan Disturbances,* Vol. 25.

[7] Letter no. 421 of 1857 of Persian Deptt. Memo dated 14 Aug. 1857, "transfer from the Secret Department No. 1265 dated 12 Aug., 1857.

[8] This circular was sent to the Political Agents at Kathiawar Kutch, Muhee Kanta, Rewa Kanta, the collectors of Kolhapur Palilumpur, and to the Magistrates and Collectors of Aurangabad, Broach, Kaira, Khandesh, Surat, Tanna, Ahmednagor, Belgaum, Dharwar, Poona, Ratnagiri, Sholapur and Satara, Entry No. 1341 of 1857, *Pol. Deptt. Deccan Disturbances,* vol. 25)

[9] *Ibid.*

[10] The Secy. Govt. of India to the Magistrate of Satara 18 Aug, 1857, Letter no. 1339 of 1857, *Pol. Deptt., Deccan Disturbances,* Vol. 25.

the secret Deperment of the Government that "The whole of the 27th Regiment at Kolhapore have obeyed with alacrity the orders received, when called upon to act against the Mutineers".[11] In the same despatch we get more pieces of information. We come to know that only 25 to 30 mutineers held their post at 'Daga' and stopped the white army to get into the 'enclosure'. In the skirmish that followed only 14 mutineers succumbed – some were held prisoners and some were killed. Out of disgust the Adjutant General ordered Major Rolland who was in charge of the station, to make over the command to next senior officers, should he consider such a measure to be expedient or necessary and to permit him to proceed to Sattara and Poona....."[12]

From the despatch of the military generals it is clear that the 27th Regiment had split on the question of mutiny. This was at least the impression that the military authorities were trying to drive home with the civil government. But those who mutinied were a very effective core of the Regiment. They held a strategic station which the white army failed to penetrate. From their invincible station at 'Daga' they tried to push into the city of Kolhapur.[13] Lt. Kerr was directed to proceed in that direction with his detachment of horse and to intercept them. But the mutineers were moving fast and they reached "just outside the city before the Detachment of Horse could get out."[14] Eventually the mutineers were overwhelmed under the leadership of Lt. Kerr.

This was apparently a small episode. But the government feared that it would produce repercussions among the civil population. Hence as a precautionary measure a news blackout was effected. As a further measure the government cordoned the Infantry Lines with the police from Thana[15] and a despatch from the Secret Department categorically said that,"His Lordship (The Honorable Governor in Council) does

[11]The Adjutant General of the army to the Secy to Govt., *Secret Deptt., Bombay*, 17 Aug, 1857, *Pol. Deptt., Deccan Disturbances*, Vol. 25.

[12]*Ibid.*

[13]Major Rolland to the Adjutant General, 11 Aug, 1857, *Pol. Deptt., Deccan Disturbances*, Vol. 25, p.98.

[14]*Ibid.*

[15] A Secret Deptt. Letter to the Magistrate of Thana, 18 Aug. 1857, Letter no. 1356, of 1857 *Pol. Deptt., Deccan Disturbances*, Vol. 25.

not consider that it will be avoidable to order the police to vacate th Infantry Lines at the present time.[16] The Governor was expecting reinforcement from outside. In England 10,000 men were ordered t be embarked. Closely following this another 14,000 men were ordere for embarkation. Thus a massive military manpower was mobilize from England.[17] All this was in response to the August uprising i Bombay and the authorities in England could act up to the expectatio of the civil administration there. A record from the Secret Departmen informs us that the orders of embarkation were made when report of the "Mutiny in Bengal" were not known to the authorities i England.[18]

This means that long back a general uprising in India was anticipate in England and preparations were made to meet eventualities in th colony. The police in Bombay was alerted and was kept as a stand by force there. The Deputy Commissioner of Police in Bombay charte out the places best suited for 'Rendezvous' in the event of any seriou disturbance in Bombay.[19] By 'Rendezvous' the police authorities mean the places where the residents could be lodged for safety in case o any disturbance.[20] Additional fire-arms were requisitioned and 100 gun

[16] *Ibid.*

[17] The Minute of the Secret Department dated 25 Sept. 1857, *Pol. Deptt., Decca Disturbances*, Entry no. 3178, p. 122.

[18] *Ibid.*

[19] Entry no. 391 of 1857, p.165. This was a communication from the Secr Deptt. to the Secy. to the Govt. *Pol. Deptt., Deccan Disturbances*, Vol. 25.

[20] These 'rendezvous' were as follows:

For the residents of Kolaba-The Fort.

For those on Malabar Hill, Chowpatty and Girgaun – Government House in Malabar Hill.

For those at the Breach and Tardes – Sir William Yardley's residence.

For the residents at Byculla, Mazagaon and Chinchapoogly – The Sudder Adawlut.

were delivered to the Principal Commissary of Ordnance for safe custody. [21] All these meant that safety measures were geared up to the utmost. The government was under an apprehension that any moment the soldiers would burst out of the Infantry Lines and the police cordon would prove ineffectual.

When this was the situation in Bombay, reports came that the Sepoys in the cantonment of Mount 'Aboo' had mutinied. This was another episode of the August mutiny. Capt. Hall commander at the cantonment informed the Brigadier Major, his superior in command that 50 sepoys mutinied and "attacked the Barrack and my Bunglow, they were driven off leaving one man on the ground and falling some wounded with them." "The whole of the ladies, women and children all", he wrote, "I am happy to say, safe in the school and the whole of the Europeans are here also." [22] This rising at Mount Aboo took place at 8 A.M. on 21 August, 1857. The mutineers hijacked bullocks, carts and whatever transports they found available there. A man called Natha Ajusee who was in the service of a local baker went to deliver his supplies in the army barrack at the hilltop of Aboo. At about 10 o'clock in the morning his bullocks and carts were seized by the mutineers. With the captured vehicles the sepoys rushed down the hill and assembled at a place called Anadra. There they faced a resistance from the European gentlemen. A skirmish followed in which 8 or 10 soldiers and 3 Europeans were killed. In his deposition[23] Natha Ajusee said that, "the road to Aboo from Anadra was shut by the Sowers of the Legion, no one is allowed to come and the Dawk is stopped, the Dawk from Erinpoora which came to Anadra was plundered and the letters torn up by the Sepaees" [24].

[21]Letter to Willam Crawford Esq., Senior Magistrate & Commissioner of Police, dated Bombay 12 August, 1857, *Pol. Deptt., Deccan Disturbances.*

[22]Capt. Hall, Commander at the Cantonment at Aboo to the Brigadier Major, 21 Aug, 1857, *Political Deptt. 1857,* Part II, no. 187, *Secret*: *GUZERAT DISTURBANCES*. Henceforth referred to as *Guzerat Disturbances.*

[23]This deposition was made at Deesa on 23 Aug, 1857 before Lt. J. Black, Acting Political Superintendent at Pahlunpoor.

[24]The deposition of Natha Ajusee *Pol. Deptt., Guzerat Disturbances.* Natha was aged 25 years, by caste cooly (cowley?) and was a resident of the 83rd Regimental Bazar, Deesa.

There were 20 or 25 sowers or cavalry men at Anadra. The sowers of the *thanas* of Muddar, Muggreewaree, Reodur and Wurman left their posts and went to Anadra. Whether they joined the mutineers we do not know. Meanwhile 200 sepoys at Erinpoora chhownee mutinied[25]. The rising of the sepoys took a new turn. The Aboo sepoys and the Erinpoora sepoys now combined and the united force moved in the direction of Serohee. They did not go towards Reodur where they might have confronted the government forces. By the end of the month situations took a bad turn. On 31 August, 1857 Elphinstone the then Governor of Bombay wrote to Col. Durand : "The detachment of the Joudhpur Legion at that place and at Erinpoora have mutinied. At the latter place they have seized the Europeans and have imprisoned them. At Neemuali too a bad feeling has shown itself".[26] From this letter it is clear that after Aboo and Erinpoora the Jodhpur detachments have revolted. The area of mutiny was widening. The government had decidedly failed to keep it localized. In his desperation Elphinstone wrote to Col. Durand : "... the feeling of disaffection is likely to spread over Rajpootana and Malwa. Under these circumstances I advice you to disarm Holkar's Mutinous troops at once before they hear of the disaffection in Rajpootana. At present you may depend upon the 25th N. I. and the 3rd Cavalry, but if you wait until they hear of the Mutiny at Erinpoora, you may not perhaps be able to do so." [27] Situations were drifting very fast. News of uprisings came from Gujrat. Two companies of the 8th Regiment and one company of European artillery with light field battery attached were directed to proceed to Gujrat and that a further reinforcement of one European Regiment "now daily expected from the cape" were to be despatched immediately on its arrival at Bombay.[28] When this was the situation at places the government lost track of the mutineers. Thus they did not know as to which direction the Aboo mutineers moved. Lt. Black, the Political

[25] *Vide* 23.

[26] *Pol. Deptt., Guzerat Disturbances,* Elphinstone to Col. Durand, 31 Aug, 1857.

[27] *Ibid.*

[28] Letter to Major General H. G. Roberts, 2 Sept. 1857, *Guz. Recds.* Entry no. 1598 of 1857.

Superintendent at Pahlumpoor, from whom the government expected news about these mutineers was totally out of information. The mutineers at Aboo did not take the normal routes which the civil authorities had charted and blocked. Lt. Black also had no knowledge whether the mutineers had forged a link with local magnates. Natha in his deposition said that the mutineers made a move towards Rawa Thakur, a local authority of considerable influence.[29]

Under order from the government attempts were made to open the route to Aboo which the mutineers blocked and to explore another route through the "South end of the Mountains". It was speculated that the mutineers proceeded towards Erinpoora. The government immediately took measures to increase its strength around. On scrutiny it was found that the strength of the Iandpoor legion adjacent to Aboo was not more than 200 to 250 men. The government wanted to move from Anadra. Hence it was decided that 50 matchlockmen and 10 horsemen would be requisitioned for posting at Anadra to act under Capt. Hall's order. Lt. Black sent 25 horse to guard Goondree, the last village at Pahlumpoor. Meanwhile reports came that there was a concentration of men "in Thana from the Frontier to Aboo in the disturbed districts of Serohie close by, they were ordered not to go beyond ....."[30] The government was really uncertain about the strength of their defence. A military communication from Mount Aboo reached the Brigade Major at Deesa on 21 August, 1857. It reported that the detachment of the Iandpoor legion then on duty at Aboo consisting of about 50 men mutinied. The European population was sheltered in a school and were thus saved–"no casualties occured except Mr. Lawrence, who has received a flesh wound in the thigh." Situations were certainly not under control. The Brigade Major was informed that the intentions of the mutineers could not be determined and the authorities had no means to ascertain as to where the mutineers were going. [31] The mutineers could not cut off the line of communication

[29]Lt. J. Black to H. L. Anderson. Secy to Govt. of Bombay, Secret Deptt. 23 Aug, 1857, *Guz. Disturbance Recds.*

[30]*Ibid.*

[31]Communication to the Brigade Major Deesa from Aboo, 21 Aug, 1857, *Pol. Deptt., Guzerat Disturbances Recds.*

of the British army and as a result could not destroy the confidence of the government. The army reports betrayed this confidence. "We have a good supply of communication", went on the army report, "and I have sent to all the villages on the Hill to raise the Bheels".[32] Besides military preparations this was the second line of defence. The countryside was roped into the network of military defence. The Bheels were very sturdy people and in them the government found a potential manpower support for cordoning the rebels. But that was not all. Troubles were brewing elsewhere. "The party of the 17th Bombay N. I. here", went on the report, "were found all with their muskets loaded, and have been in consequence disarmed. Should the mutineers return from below we are prepared for them.".[33] These were the preparations made at the hilltop where stations were vacated by rebel sepoys who moved down the hill with the motive to penetrate into the interior. Throughout the month of August these sepoys moved around throwing the government in panic. The government tried to raise the Bheels so that the social base of the rebels could be cut off.

The August uprising in the Bombay Presidency were not a sudden phenomenon. The Raja of Soanth warned the government of army disaffection at least three weeks before the incidents.[34] In a letter to the Acting Political Agent at Rewakanta in July, 1857 the Raja of Rewakanta wrote : "The sepoys openly give out that they will plunder the country and proceed to Delhi - they have taken up a threatening position - The Khants (?) have also become turbulent - a rumour is prevalent that the British Government have lost their *Raj* consequently I have become powerless."[35] The rumour that the British Government had lost its way had been circulating for a long time. This rumour absorbed

[32] *Ibid.*

[33] J. Hall, Captain Commander at Aboo to Act. Pol. Supdt., 21 Aug, 1857.

[34] The 27th N. I. and the Aboo uprising took place between 15th and 21st August, 1857 and the Raja informed the government of the army disaffection on 24 July, 1857.

[35] The Raja of Soanth to the Acting. Pol. Agent at Rewakanta, dated 24 July, 1857, Letter No. 238, *Pol. Deptt. Guz. Disturbance Recds.*

in its fold both the army and the civil population and cut off the base of acceptance of the British rule by the general populace. It was not that the Government were unaware of it. The Government was also scared and hence retaliation was brutal. At Dohud in Rewakanta some suspect rebels were seized and in a Secret Department correspondence they were treated as "persons concerned in treason and armed rebellion in Dohud". No clemency was to be shown to them. Instead of "14 years of transportation", goes a Secret Department note, "such persons should be sentenced to Death, which may be connected to any minor punishment." The note is addressed to a military captain and its author speaks in the idiom of authority that overshadows justice. "I am also desirous." he writes to the Acting Political Agent at Rewakanta,[36] "to inform you that a native prisoner should not be sentenced to transportation for any period short of life".[37]

It should be noted that long before the August uprisings in the Bombay Presidency the Governor General's Council in Calcutta was taking note of the army disaffection all over India and was taking measure to forestall a prospective army revolt in the country. At the beginning of the month of August, 1857 the Government of India sent the following advice to the Government of Bombay : "I am directed to request that the importation by Sea of all Military Stores by Private persons may for the present be prohibited and that the customs and other authorities at every port in the Bombay Presidency may be desired to detain and keep in their possession in a place of safety, all such stores, and not to deliver any of them to the owners or consignees or to any person without an express order from the Government."

"No such order will of course be given unless the Government is

[36]*Guz. Disturb. Recds. Secret Deptt.* Entry no. 1614 Letter to Capt. Buckle, Acting Political Agent at Rewakanta. This letter was in response to Entry no. 411 of the Secret Deptt.

[37]Capt. Buckle was appointed Commissioner under AC XIV of 1857 "for the trial of persons charged with offences against the State" - Letter to Maj. Gen. H. G. Roberts, 7 Sept. 1857, Entry no. 1705 of 1857 Secret Deptt., *Guz. Disturb. Recds.*

satisfied that the stores so delivered are not likely to be used by the enemies of the British Government".

"A law prohibiting the importation of Military stores and authorising their confiscation will shortly be brought before the Legislative Council and a clause if necessary can be added to indemnify public officers for any act done in obedience to these orders."[38] To prohibit importation of military stores by private individuals is one way of disarming the population. The rulers were apprehensive that somewhere behind the notice of the Government a link was forged between the army and the people. Anti-government feeling was running high everywhere in the society. The army was charged with disaffection. Local magnates like the Raja of Soanth(Sawanth?) who acted as buffers between the people and the army had become ineffective. The intelligence of the military administration failed to locate pockets of army intransigence and sepoy disaffection. In this situation a general flare up among the people was not unlikely. It was in this milieu that some important measures were taken up by the Government. They were as follows :

1. Drawing up of a huge military force from England and Mauritius.
2. Disarming of Holkar's troops.
3. Effecting a news blackout.
4. Cordoning of the Infantry Lines with police regiments.
5. Stoppage of the coming of military stores from outside.
6. Decision to inflict death punishment and transportation for life on suspect persons. [39]

[38]Cecil Beadon Esq., Secy to the Govt. of India to W. Hart Esq., Secy. to Govt. of Bombay, 3 Aug. 1857, Entry no. 1196, *Secret Deptt., Guzerat Disturb. Recds*, 1857.
[39]The Hon'ble Company's steamer Assaye arrived this morning from Mauritius bringing a Wing of Her Majesty's 4th Regiment consisting of three hundred and twenty men" - Telegraphic message to Major C. Davidson, Resident at Hyderabad, 18 Sept., 1857, *Pol. Deptt. 1857*, vol. 27, 194. Secret, Part III, *Deccan Disturbances*, Entry no. 1915 of 1857. In this volume there is a sketch map of the places where disturbances were noticed and intercepted letters written in Marathi Language.

7. Imposition of the martial law in the country.
8. Suspect letters were intercepted and were sent "direct to the Oriental Translations (Deptt.) of the Government". [40]
9. Indiscriminate arrest of men charged with offences like "carrying of arms" which were considered "offences against the state". It is important to note that persons under trial were youngmen - as young as sixteen years old. [41]

All these measures were efforts to tighten up the strings of British rule in India. For one hundred years the Indian society had looked at British rule from any point between non-acceptance and revolt. The flare up of 1857 was the outburst of the charged psychology of a nation. The Government harnessed its strength to contain the outburst. It succeeded in the long run to suppress all signs of uprisings either in the army or in the society. The stability of the British rule was retrieved but its credibility was lost.

[40] Letter to E. Impey, Post Master General, Bombay, 19 Sept., Entry no. 1930 of 1857, *Ibid.*

[41] *Pol. Deptt. vol.26(II) 1857*, No. 189 *Secret, Deccan Disturbances.* In these records are included a thick volume of "Proceedings held before John Nugen Rose Esq. Commissioner under the Provisions of Act XIV of 1857, Section VII for the trial of offences against the State, murder &ca".

7

Further on the Revolt in the Bombay Presidency

Historians of earlier generations agree that the Bombay Presidency remained more or less calm during the turbulent years of 1857-58. The official historian of the revolt of 1857, S. N. Sen, observed : "Thus Maharashtra relapsed to its accustomed tranquillity after a feeble demonstration of sporadic discontent. It was really strange that the Peshwa's cause should find so little support in his own home province".[1] This statement of the official historian does not necessarily mean that the Bombay Presidency was free of tensions. It only means that the mutiny tremors there were not as great as those of the North-Western Provinces, Oudh and Rohilkhand. Risings were there in the Bombay Presidency but they were of miniature scale. Sen writes : "The Bombay Presidency witnessed risings at Satara, Kolhapur, Nargund and in the district of Sawant Wadi. It is remarkable that at Satara the call to rise came, not from a Maratha noble, but from a Hindustani Chaprasi. A conspiracy at Bombay was discovered by Forjett, the Police Commissioner, and nipped in the bud".[2] How was it done ? Was the British force competent enough to do this by its own strength ? The answer is broadly 'no'. Forjett himself "testifies to the co-operation he received from Wahabis of high ranks"— declares Sen.[3]

[1]S. N. Sen, *Eighteen Fifty Seven*, (with a Foreword by Maulana Abul Kalam Azad), The Publications Division, Ministry of Information and Broadcasting, Government of India, May 1957, reprinted February, 1958, p. 409.

[2]*Ibid.*

[3]Sen, *op.cit.*, p. 248.

And then this master historian quotes from Forjett's own words to show how the reforming Muslims of west India forged a bond with the English. Here was, therefore, a pocket where the British rule in India found its own redemption. This was one area where a part of the Muslim community did not think that India under the British was a *Dar-ul-harb* (land of the enemies). A grateful Englishman—Forjett—left his own memoir thus : "I was sorry to find that Bombay was not free from Wahabee-phobia; but I am glad to say that I experienced no lack of assistance from Wahabees. The Kajee,—the high priest in Bombay of the Mahomedans,— was a rank Wahabee, but made his services available at any hour of the day or night; so was the soobedar, Mohamed Booden, of the Police, a Wahabee, by whom I was greatly assisted in bringing to light the plot hatched by the sepoys at Sonapoor".[4] Was it an isolated Muslim gesture of co-operation with the English ? Once again the answer would be 'no'. The Wahabis of Bihar had rallied behind the British. The Lieutenant-Governor of Bengal himself declared "Nothing was at any time proved or even alleged against the Wahabis".[5] As a matter of fact an aged Wahabi leader acted as an informer.[6] But the British had no trust for the eastern and up country Muslims and hence the information supplied by an aged Wahabi leader was disregarded. But one point was certain. The liberalism of the Bihar Wahabis at the time of the revolt created the condition in which the Bombay Wahabis could offer themselves as a support to the British rule in India. So was the case with the Wahabis in Punjab.[7]

[4]Quoted by Sen, *Ibid.*

[5]The Minute of the Lieutenant Governor of Bengal on the Mutinies as they affected the Lower Provinces under the Government of Bengal dated 30th September, 1858, p.5.

[6]"In fact information given by one of the aged Wahabi leaders was disregarded"—*Ibid.*, quoted by Sen, *op.cit.*, p. 248.

[7]"It would not have been possible for the Wahabis at Bombay to lend their co-operation to the Commissioner of Police if their leaders in Bihar had decided otherwise"— Sen, *op, cit.,* p. 248. Sen's general observation about the Wahabis in India is worthy of note. "The Wahabis, as a community, did not identify themselves with the revolt. Like many of their countrymen, individual Indian Wahabis might have participated in the revolt of 1857 but if the community as such had decided to cast in their lot with the sepoy leaders, Sir John Lawrence would have found it unsafe to denude the Punjab of European troops and recruit so many Punjabi Muslims to fight for the cause of Britain"— *Ibid.*

The Wahabi's role in Bihar and Bombay was just the opposite of the one they played in northern India "In Northern India", writes Irfan Habib, "the 'Wahabis' were already spreading their net of propaganda about the English being the enemy of the Faith, against whom *jihad* or holy war was enjoined. They actually contributed warriors, called *jihadis,* to the Revolt. Many of these, including persons from amongst 'weavers, artisans and other wage earners', joined Bakht Khan, the rebel commander at Delhi. It was natural that the cry of religion should be employed by the rebels so often; but it is also important to remember that they did their best not to let such sentiments create a division in their own ranks."[8]

Inspite of the Wahabi cooperation with the British the Maratha countries in the west and in the Deccan did not escape the tremors of the time. Here mutiny and a small-scale civil uprising were concurrent phenomena. R. C. Majumdar says that the two prominent mutinies in the Bombay Presidency were at Nagpur and Satara. Both these risings were abortive. "There was a plot at Nagpur" writes he, "and it was reported that the First Cavalry would rise on June 13, 1857, and being joined by citizens, murdered the Christians. But the cavalry was disarmed."[9]

The Satara plot was hatched about the same time. One Ranga Bapuji plotted "to release the prisoners, plunder the treasury, and attack the cantonments".[10] The plot flashed out and the conspirators were held on 12 June, 1857. The leader of the plot fled and his followers were dispersed. These two events revealed broad social perspectives in which both the army and the civil population were clubbed in a milieu of shadowy disaffection. These were broadly the sequel

[8]Irfan Habib, "The coming of 1857" in *Social Scientist,* vol. 26, Number 1-4, Jan-April, 1998, p. 12; also available in *Red the Earth, that year, that year 1857. History of India Series, Sahamat,* 8 Vithalbhai Patel House, Rafi Marg, New Delhi 110 001, 11 May 1997, Red Fort, Delhi, with this *Sahamat* celebrated the 49th-50th years of 1857.

[9]R.C. Majumdar, *The Sepoy Mutiny and the Revolt of 1857*, Firma, K.L. Mukhopadhyay, 1957, second edn., 1963, p.93.

[10]*Ibid.*.

[11]"These troubles were mainly caused by the recent annexation of these two States by the Doctrine of Lapse, as there was strong sympathy for the adopted sons who were deprived of their estates. Besides, the feudatory chiefs at Satara, with a single exception, had no son, and knew that their adopted sons would not be permitted to succeed them. They were, therefore, naturally anxious to overthrow the British Government"— R. C. Majumdar, *Ibid.*

of Dalhousie's *Doctrine of Lapse.*[11]

In Kolhapur there were two revolts—one in August, 1857 and the other in December 1857.[12] In the first revolt the sepoys of Kolhapur mutinied. They plundered the treasure and marched to the city. But the city gates were closed and they could not enter the city. Some of them returned to the lines and some dispersed helter and skelter. They were eventually suppressed, disarmed and executed.[13] In the second uprising the rebels for a moment gained an upper hand. They closed the city gate which was eventually blown open by the British troops. Most of the rebels were seized and executed.[14]

A daring rebellion was that of Baba Sahib, the Chief of Nurgund near Kolhapur. He rebelled on 29 May, 1858 and assassinated Charles Manson, the Political Agent of Southern Maratha country. His rising was suppressed and he was executed. There was an attempt at a mutiny at Ahmedabad and Hyderabad, two places in Sindh. These efforts failed. Another uprising was there at Karachi. It was put down with no effort. Thus on the whole, says Majumdar the Bombay army remained loyal and the Bombay Presidency remained quiet.[15]

[12]R. C. Majumdar gives the two dates as follows— 31 July, 1857 & 5 December, 1857. The date of the first uprising was given by Haraprasad Chattopadhyaya as 1 August, 1857, *The Sepoy Mutiny, 1857. A Social Study and Analysis,* Agents : Bookland Private Ltd. 1 Sankar Ghosh Lane, Kolkata, 1957, p. 19.

[13]R. C. Majumdar, *op.cit,* p. 94.

[14]"It was believed that the rebellion was instigated by the brother of the Kolhapur Raja at the instance of Nana Sahib. There were causes of disaffection which had already provoked an insurrection in 1844..."— Majumdar, *Ibid.* The following words Majumdar quotes *(Ibid)* from Holmes : "the chiefs and smaller landowners of southern Maratha country still smarted from the wounds inflicted upon them from the Enam Commission; to many of them had been denied the privilege of adopting heirs to their estates."

[15]"In general the Bombay army remained loyal, but there were some sepoys who shared the feelings of their comrades in Northern India... on the whole, the Bombay Presidency, though seething with discontent and disaffection, remained quiet"— *Ibid.*

In this historians' chorus of Bombay quietude Haraprasad Chattopadhyaya also mingles his voice. He writes : "The Bombay Presidency was also quiet, but not so quiet as the Madras Presidency. Sepoys of the Bombay Army were not as faithful as those of the Madras Army. On August 1, 1857 the 27th Regiment, Bombay Infantry mutinied at Kolhapur to the south of Bombay on the occasion of 'Buckree Eid'. This caused a ferment in whole of the South Maratha country. Mohammedan conspiracy manifested itself at Poona, Satara, Belgaum, Dharwar, Rutnagherry, Sawantwadi and other places, but the conspiracy was nipped in the bud. The 28th Regiment, Bombay Native Infantry, stationed at Dharwar, and the 29th, posted at Belgaum, also betrayed a tendency towards revolt. But the timely arrival of European troops restored order in those areas by August 1857."[16]

Unlike Sen and Majumdar, Chattopadhyay puts much stress on the Muslim conspiracy in Bombay. He writes : "During the stormy period between 1857 and 1859 certain regiments in Bombay, it is true, rose in mutiny, and the Muslims of certain areas entered into a conspiracy against Government. But the mutinous sepoys were soon brought under control and the conspiracy of the Muslims was frustrated. Two Maulvies, one from Poona and the other from Belgaum, were detected plotting against the Europeans and native Christians of those places. The conspiracy proceeded with a larger plan of blowing up the arsenal at Poona. But the conspiracies failed and the conspirators punished. The conspiracies of the Muslims of certain areas and the risings of a few regiments in Bombay were by no means supported by the population in general, of the province.[17]

From the above it is clear that Haraprasad Chattopadhyaya broadly subscribes to the conspiracy theory of the English historians. To the British administrators who were contemporary to the revolt any uprising among the soldiers was a 'mutiny' and any disobedience among the civil population was a 'conspiracy'. In a general uprising

[16]Haraprasad Chattopadhyaya, *op.cit.,* p.19. At page 195 Chattopadhyaya writes : "Though not as quiet as Madras, the province of Bombay was, on the whole, tranquil during the Mutiny."

[17]Chattopadhyaya, *op.cit,* p. 195.

pre-planning is necessary and to the ruler pre-planning is a conspiracy. Chattopadhyaya was struck by the loyalty of the Parsis to the government and he compares Muslim infidelity with the loyalty of the pro-British people in Bombay. He writes : "The Parsees of Bombay who had 'their worldly interests bound up with the English' remained the most powerful supporters of Government during the Mutiny. To the then Governor of Bombay, Lord Elphinstone, they submitted an address of fidelity, signed by about Four Hundred natives of various castes and creeds. Excepting them, a few Muslims of certain places the civil population of Bombay remained, on the whole, peaceful, and attached to Government."[18] Who among the Muslims, according to Chattopadhyaya, did raise the banner of revolt against the English ? Certainly not the Wahabis ! Chattopadhyaya falls in line with S. N. Sen. He writes : "According to Forjett, the Wahabi Muslims of Bombay were favourably disposed towards Government during the Mutiny." "If Forjett is to be believed, Muslim conspiracy in Bombay was confined to the non-Wahabi Muslim community of the province."[19] Thus a Police Commissioner's verdict became a predominant factor in influencing the opinion of one otherwise very sound historian of the revolt in the country.

According to S. B. Chaudhuri, perhaps the greatest of the centenary historians of the revolt, the tensions in the Bombay Presidency "did not manifest any symptoms of mass rising during this period" of the revolt in India.[20] Two things, according to him, made up the spirit of the revolt. In the first place "the chiefs in some cases were not well disposed to the government." Secondly, "The sepoys manifested a disposition to revolt..." Thus those who had authority and those who had arms were both alienated. Yet the spirit of a general uprising did not manifest in Bombay. S. B. Chaudhuri did not say that the baronial discontent and army disaffection did not combine. He only says that

[18] *Ibid.*

[19] *Ibid,* note.

[20] Sashi Bhusan Chaudhuri, *Civil Rebellion in the Indian Mutinies, (1857-1859),* The World Press Private Ltd., Calcutta, 1957, p. 229.

[21] *Ibid*

"the situation was saved only by skilful management" by the British.[21] It was truly a crisis management in situation where, Chaudhuri says, an outburst could be a legitimate event. "All the elements of discord existed and a plot was even hatched but the attempt of Rango Bapuji to seize the government proved abortive".[22] What was the role of the Muslims there ? Chaudhuri agrees with other historians that it was conspiratorial. He writes : "The Mohammedan population of Belgaum formed a conspiracy which had its ramifications at Kolhapur, Hyderabad and at Poona."[23] The distance between Kolhapur and Belgaum was only sixty miles and ideas travelled quite fast in 1857. Malleson himself admitted that the regiments in these stations— at Poona, Kolhapur, Hyderabad, Belgaum and Dharwar had for a long time been seething under discontent,[24] and they had developed ample communication among them. Thus a time-specific concurrent action from all these stations could not be ruled out. Chaudhuri agrees with Malleson and says that they "were in communication for a simultaneous action. They were secretly supported by the discontented chiefs and openly by the Mahomedans."[25]

The contribution of the Muslims towards building up the ferment of the revolt was significant. In Hyderabad they seemed to be a disaffected community who were kept in check by the exertions of Salar Jang, the able Minister of Nizam Afzaluddaulah." Almost the ferment of a general revolt was created and the ferment spread to the Maratha country. In Hyderabad the revolt took place on 17 July and in Kolhapur the 27th Regiment revolted on 31 July 1857.[26] The link between the two was thus understandable. On the Hyderabad revolt Chaudhuri writes : "Great commotion prevailed calling upon the faithful to murder Europeans, and the green flag was hoisted.

[22]*Ibid*

[23]*Ibid*

[24]*G. B. Malleson, History of the Indian Mutiny 1857-58* (1878, 1879, 1880), vol. iii, pp. 32-33.

[25]Chaudhuri, *op.cit.*, p. 230.

[26]On 1st August according to some other opinions.

[27]Chaudhuri, *op.cit.*, p. 229.

On 17 July, five hundred of the Rohilla troops and four thousand of the people of Hyderabad rose in insurrection but they were sent back reeling by a fire of grape."[27] The spirit that was sought to be suppressed by bullets became an invisible force. On 1 July, 1857 Holkar's troops revolted in Indore and it was suppressed. But the spirit of rising was indomitable. It spread to Hyderabad and from there to the Maratha countries. Chaudhuri informs us that though the Kolhapur rising was "effectively challenged the commotion could not be suppressed." Then he adds : "The rising at Kolhapur soon assumed a formidable character and had considerable strength behind it".[28] This may be called the first major historical recognition that some events of the 1857 Bombay uprisings had assumed serious dimensions. Everything was not simple and plain in the events of uprising in central and western India. Some had roots directed to the past. For example Nagpur, a recently annexed State, did not witness a scene of rebellion at a large scale. Yet the revolt of Narayan Singh of Sonakhan showed that the spirit of rebellion was not absent there altogether. Sonakhan was hilly State situated at the south-western extremity of the district of Nagpur. The zamindars of this State were considered to be small Rajas, all of whom were bitterly hostile to the British. In 1810 military actions were directed against it. When Nagpur was annexed Sonakhan became a pocket of the greatest anti-British feeling in the district. Narayan Singh was sent behind the bar. When the revolt broke out the Raja escaped from the Raipur jail and stirred up widespread disturbance in the interior. The aborigines joined him and many insurgent elements in the society rallied around. This revolt had exercised great stress on the British administration because the ferment of rebellion had spread among the Gonds of the nearby region like Chanda where Rohillas had always remained in a state of revolt. These men did not offer any organised fight to the British. They had their strongholds in the jungles from where they offered desultory fights on the basis of small guerilla warfare techniques.

These events had great repercussions on the Bombay uprisings. In the neighbouring countries the Rohillas, the Gonds and other aborgines had revolted. It was widely feared that the Bhils of the hilly regions

[28]Chaudhuri, *op.cit.*, p. 230.

of the Western Ghat mountains would also show a spirit of disaffection. It was this fear which had gripped the minds of the British administrators during the Kolhapur and other uprisings in Bombay. There was a tradition of a strong anti-British rising in Kolhapur. This had created the context in which the Kolhapur uprising took place. Chaudhuri writes : "The Gadkari rising at Kolhapur in 1844 showed the strong feeling of hostility of the people against the British. In the villages within eight miles of Kolhapur about a thousand men collected with arms to resist the enforcement of the disarming act. They were mostly villagers and not sepoys. On the morning of 6 December, 1857, the rebels entered the town of Kolhapur and took it by surprise."[29] Towards the end of July and the beginning of August, 1857 the 27th Regiment had mutinied in Kolhapur. In four months' time the inhabitants of interior villages rose in arms. In northern India the mutinous sepoys had spread into the villages of various districts and incited people. In many cases the sepoys were persants in uniform and as such the links between military insurgency and popular uprising could be forged. In the Bombay Presidency the administrators did not want such links to be forged. There they wanted to use the Bhils to cordon the mutineers but they fled into the interior. But before any political move is made the government wanted to proceed militarily and crush the back of all uprisings. So without taking any chance mobilization was made against the revolting villagers. "They were soon attacked," writes Chaudhuri," defeated and thirty six of them were executed in the course of a day."[30] The rapidity of the movement showed in what state of amity the British government was on 12 December, 1857, the *Poona Observer* noted that the insurgents were "no better than a set of half-starved villagers and beggars."[31]

This was certainly a revolt of the destitutes. It was a wrong conception that in 1857-58 only the sepoys mutinied and the Rajas

[29] *Ibid*

[30] *Ibid*

[31] Chaudhuri (p. 230) makes a passing reference to this but for details reference may be made to *Overland Bombay Times*, 18th December 1857 and *Hindu Patriot*, 24 December. Malleson in Vol. III of his book *(op.cit.)* refers to this incident (p. 237).

and zamindars revolted. Downtrodden people, men of the interior, children of the soil who had received little benefits of Western civilization and British rule in India found their accustomed life threatened. Fear and anger mingled to produce a compulsive logic for rising. The best example of such risings was Sholrapur. This was a small estate touching the border of Nizam's territory in the district of Gulburga. The ruler of this estate was one Venkatappa Naik whose family had ruled the country for thirty generations. Thus the honour of the whole family was anchored in the status and the stability of the estate. The British had little concern for this. The Head of this family Venkatappa Naik was charged with treason, a crime adjudged in western terms not very meaningful to an eastern baron. However, he was sentenced to transportation which was unheard of in his family. To such a dishonour a man of his status could not submit. He committed suicide. His family and his subjects considered this as an insult inflicted upon the family the estate and its people. Tensions raged[32] everywhere. The entire baronial class of the Maratha country was in a state of shock. Insults and misery were inflicted on them by the Indian Commission. Malleson had described how the populace and chiefs of the Maratha country, the chief of Nargund and the Desais of Kittur were affected by the Inam Commission.[33] The Desais rose twice in revolt against the British in the pre-mutiny period precisely in 1824 and 1829. The legacy of the rising had in fact gone into the tradition of the country.[34] Confusion was in the air. Commotion was in the spirit of the people. In this situation the emissaries

[32]Malleson, vol. II, p. 486 and vol. III, pp. 125-29.

[33]Malleson, *op.cit.*, III, pp. 29-30.

[34]S. B. Chaudhuri, *Civil Disturbances during the British Rule in India (1765-1857)*, 1955, pp. 153-155.

[35]"The people of the southern Maratha country were excited to dangerous discontent by the action of the Inam Commission. The emissaries from Nana Sahib also must have worked there to produce convulsions which indeed took place, and in the country both above and below the ghats, the British authority met with resistance" — S.B. Chaudhuri, *Civil Rebellion in the Indian Mutinies*, p. 230.

from Nana Sahib went into the area with missions of insurgency.[35] It should be noted that the Maratha country had never been very quiet. The Kittur risings took place in 1824 and 1829. Between 1826 and 1829 took place the rising of the Ramosis at Poona. The explosion of the Bhils took place between 1818 and 1831. Then came the disturbances in Cutch between 1815 and 1832. These however, do not exhaust the list of uprisings and disturbances in Bombay and western India. The pre-mutiny years had been very unsettled years for western India. The Gadkari rising at Kolhapur in 1844 came in the wake of the Koli outrages of 1828-30 and 1839. Finally it synchronised with the Koli disturbances which started in 1844 and continued upto 1848.[36] These uprisings satisfied double hatred–a class hatred and a hatred against the foreigners. Pro-British patels were assaulted and in one case was murdered; their money along with government treasury was looted. These uprisings conceded with the formidable outbreak in Savantvadi between 1844 and 1850. This rebellion had created the pre-mutiny fervent of revolt in western India. The insurgents built up links with the 10th Regiment of the Native Infantry. In consequence the government had to impose martial law and adopt stringent measures to suppress the rebellion.

In understanding the 1857 uprisings in the Bombay Presidency these events should be taken into consideration. Kolhapur and Savantvadi on the coast of northern Konkan, it should be noted were not very subdued regions of the Maratha kingdom. They had been turbulent all through history. As late as 1858 the Savantvadi chief Phond Savant headed a formidable rebellion which the British found difficult to subdue. Operating from his base at Goa he arrived at Canara on an avowed political mission namely "to overthrow the government". The entire forest frontier from

[36]The Kolis lived over an wide area in western India, much above and far below the Sahyadri. One of their areas of concentration was the thana district but they could be found in every region between the borders of Cutch and the Western Ghats. One of their first major insurrections took place in 1824 when the Kolis rose in revolt spreading fire and violence over wide area upto the vicinity of Baroda.

Savantvadi to Canara was under the control of the insurgents. Their forest base was in the Darshanigudda hill on the Canara border and from there they carried out their guerilla warfare. They attacked and destroyed police posts and customs houses and important government outposts. Their Darshanigudda stronghold was properly garrisoned and even to the British it seemed impenetrable. On one or two occasions they fought desperate battles with the British forces. Ultimately they were short of resources, men and money and their leaders were either caught or died in battle. Their insurrection was crushed toward the end of 1859.

These events do not show that the Maratha country was essentially quiet during the period of Indian revolt, the two years of 1857-58. Ceaseless fighting had been going on against the British, sometime sporadically, some time in a series throughout the course of the two or three decades preceding the Indian revolt of 1857-58. The last bloody reaction against the British administration in western India was demonstrated by Nargund. This was a small place in the southern Maratha country. It was one state which was affected by the British policy on adoption. Its chief was Baba Sahib whose family had ruled the state for two hundred years. He was denied the right of adoption in his family. His estate was also affected by the activities of the Inam Commission. The result was that his mind was filled with bitterness against the British government. "So he declared" writes Chaudhuri, "war against the British government on 27 May, 1858".[37] Malleson gives a special treatment to this episode.[38] Chaudhuri observes : "Malleson's treatment of this episode would show that the revolt of the Nargund chief brought into existence a national rising in the southern Maratha country".[39] This was because he was joined by Bhim Rao, the chief of Kopaldrug. But this revolt still remained localised and was eventually suppressed by the government. The Raja was tried on

[37]Chaudhuri, *Civil Rebellion in the Indian Mutinies*, p. 231.

[38]Malleson, Vol. III, pp. 238-246. The event was also reported in the *Hindu Patriot*, 29 July, 1858.

[39]*Ibid.*

11 June, 1858 and he was executed the next day. The British government was very much scared. The Savantvadi rebellion of February, 1824 was still fresh in the memory of the people and the Moplah uprising which burst out in September, 1857 had still had in its embers unextinguished. Thus the whole of the southern Maratha country was in turmoil. This turmoil, it is true, was not as flaming as the up-country fire of Gangetic India and this low trajectory of rising the historians took to be signs of a general peace in a Presidency not otherwise marked by too many outbursts, military or civil. Writing as late as 1967 the historian Tara Chand discovered that a host of smaller centres of outbreak in southern-central India created a ring fence around Marahashtra which was then in the Bombay Presidency, Indore, Mandasore, Mhow, Dhar, Anjthera were sites of smaller outbreaks which, observes Tara Chand, "caused great anxiety to the Government, because the region was contiguous with Maharashtra where there was much 'brooding discontent'." In a government record of 1858 this discontent was clearly noted.[40] And Tara Chand lays bare the causes of this discontent. He writes : "Loss of independence, disappearance of Peshwa's rule and degradation of Poona which had been the centre of Maratha power, rankled in the minds of the people."[41] These were all civil causes of the revolt and do not underlie as causes of a military mutiny. The breakdown of Poona as the centre of

[40]Foreign Secret Consultation, Nos. 87-89, 28 January, 1858.

[41]Tara Chand, *History of the Freedom Movement in India,* vol. Two, Publications Division, Ministry of Information and Broadcasting, Government of India, 1967, p. 94.

[42]*Ibid*

[43]*Ibid.* Tara Chand gives the details of another plot in Salora. He writes :

"In Satara, Rango Bapuji Gupte, an old and faithful servant of the house of Shivaji, collected Ramoshi, Mang and Koli recruits and gained some adherents among the Maratha Sardars to oust the new rulers and restore Shahu, the son of Pratap Singh, to the gaddi. Promises of support were obtained from Nana Ramoshi of Kundal, Kashi Raja, Daulat Rao Hari Powar of Karad, Tatya Fadnis of Kolhapur, and others. Shivaram Kulkarni was the moving spirit, and Sitaram, son of Rango Bapuji, was entrusted with general supervision. Man Singh, a Rajput soldier, was chosen as a messenger to obtain support of the sepoy regiments. Unfortunately, the plot was betrayed and the conspirators were put to death."— p. 94. It should be noted that in Bombay there were three Indian regiments all of which are planning to revolt in unison on the occasion of the *Muhurram.* This was one plot in which the Muslims were involved. But the plot fizzled out because of the alertness of Forjett, the Deputy Commissioner of Police in Bombay.

Maratha power was significant for the sensitive Marathas as the breakdown of Awadh had been for the agonizing Muslims of north-central India. In an atmosphere of gloom three more factors added to the sensitivity of the situation. "The confiscation of numerous estates," Tara Chand observes, "at the instance of the Inam Commission, the ban on adoption on the failure of natural heirs to the owners of landed estates and the close relations between the families of Nana Sahib and the Patwardhan chiefs, had created an explosive situation.[42] It was a singular good fortune of the Empire that this situation did not mature into an outburst. Civil rebellion and military mutiny did not get a chance to coagulate. This was one occasion when fortune favoured the Empire for the Indian troops in Asirgarh, Burhampur, Aurangabad, Belgaum, Kolhapur and Bombay were ready for an uprising "and the discontented Muslims plotted a revolt".[43]

From the above it is clear that the Bombay Presidency had all the elements of a general flare-up. But it did not trigger off. The ferment of an uprising was available but the Presidency did not turn as unquiet as any part of north India. There are several reasons for it which can be summed up in the following words of Tara Chand :

"Lack of concerted action on the part of the people and the fact and vigilance of British officers prevented the conflagration from being widespread. The outbreak in the Southern Maratha country remained a minor episode, confined mainly to a few chiefs, landholders and some north Indian sepoys. The Marathas and the Mahars had little in common with the Purbiya soldier and did not respond to the call.

The mercantile community and the small English educated class in Bombay, had no sympathy for the revolutionary cause."[44]

As a result revolution in the Bombay Presidency maintained a low trajectory. But the people's mind was not altogether averse to it.

[44]Tara Chand, *op, cit.,* p.95.

8

The Revolt of 1857 : Points and Counterpoints

The Great Revolt of 1857 has been a centre of discussion ever since its event had started unfolding themselves. Administrative notes, military memoirs, lay appraisals and journalistic debates have built up the entire corpus around which 1857 has come to be assessed. Points and counterpoints are therefore replete in the historiography of the revolt. In a decade in the middle of the 19th century a host of revolts shook the Eurasian landmass. The revolution of 1848 in Europe, the revolt of 1857 in India and the Taiping rebellion in China were the major events that shook the two continents, Europe and Asia. A vast literature has came to be evolved around each of these incidents and none of them can claim to have concluded the debates that had been going on ever since these incidents had taken place. Among these events the revolt of 1857 has a special status in the sense that it took place in a country submerged under a colonial rule. It certainly had shared with the European revolution and the Chinese rebellion a common experience of failure but it had left a greater degree of impression than any of the other contemporary incidents as a deep and well spread violence erupting from below. It at least showed that within the framework of colonial rule the subject people could adjust itself with the tyranny of the ruling top in an antithetical balance of terror. The revolt in a very big sense signified the crisis of consolidation of the British rule in India and the beginning of the eventual colonial defeat and withdrawal.[1]

When the revolt of 1857 broke out the "official British explanation was that the Bengal Native Army alone had mutinied and that any civil disturbances were the natural bi-products of the breakdown of law and order.[2] The British rule in India stood mainly on the successes of British arms and relied for its maintenance mainly on the army. Therefore, the first shock of the revolt was interpreted in terms of the failure of the military machine. Whenever the people in general appeared to be involved in an upsurage the normal British interpretation was that it was a problem of law and order. Reliance on military machinery only shows that an alien empire had failed to build up its own social base on which it could consolidate. Thus events of social tensions were looked at through administrative windows and the whole problem revolved around twin perspectives, either the presence of law and order or their absence. It is not expected that contemporary British writers should look at a major Indian incident of rebellion from any perspective conducive to Indian interest. Admittedly the revolt was at times and in certain areas a sound evidence of the failure of British administration and the collapse of the major organs on which the imperial rule had become accustomed to rest. Naturally there were large efforts on the part of British historians to hide the story of disgrace replete in British failures and to give the meaning of the incident a new turn. It was then evidently considered not as an Indian event but as a British event of heroism on Indian scene, an episode of British eminence,[3] an epic of British imperial experience of India. This military perspective of the revolt was not a universal feeling among contemporary Englishmen. As early as July 1857, "Disraeli flung the questions across the commons whether the British were not standing in the presence of a national revolt."[4] About the same time the

[1]These two expressions have been borrowed from Eric Stokes, *the Peasant Armed, the Indian Rebellion of 1857*, edited by C.A. Bayle, Oxford 1986, Introduction, p.1.

[2]Eric Stokes, *Op.cit.* p-4.

[3]S.B.Chaudhuri, *English Historical Writings on the Indian Mutiny 1857-59*, p.7.

[4]Stokes, *op.cit.* p.4. Also see A.T.Embree (ed.) *1857 in India*, Boston, 1963, pp.4-12.

commander-in-chief of the British army expressed his views where he placed his "fatuous confidence in the fidelity by the Bengal Sepoys".[5] Thus it is clear that the contemporary British mind was not universally afflicted with the concept that the British Empire's main instrument of sustenance had suddenly gone wrong. On the contrary there was also the feeling that the collapse that was apparent was a broad administrative failure to anticipate and understand military dislocations.

Disraeli's contention that the revolt of 1857 was a national revolt could not easily be challenged. The fear of a national uprising was real and its understanding was clear in British mind. Therefore, to get rid of the distressing feeling that the people in general had rejected British administration in India a new effort was harnessed. It was claimed at some quarters that the revolt of 1857 was the follow-up of the mutiny of the army and in this prominent Hindus and Muslims had joined hands in a conspiracy against the British rule. Thus before the revolt of 1857 had died out two very prominent viewpoints, one antithetical to the other, grew up. There was one school that saw in the revolt all unmistakable signs of a 'military mutiny'[5a] while the other saw in it the effects of an undetected conspiracy at the upper layers of the Indian society secretly hatched against the British rule.

One of the earlier exponents of the view that the British empire was facing a military mutiny was Henry Mead.[6] Mead's concept of the 'Sepoy Revolt' was worked out almost concurrently with the revolt itself. The same view seemed to be pounced upon in a book that was

[5] *Calcutta Review,* 1858, vol.30, pp.234, 243.

[5a] The concept of mutiny has received a new turn at the hands of historians in recent times. Thus Michael H. Fisher writes : "the causes and accounts of the events of 1857 are manifold. Whether it be regarded as a 'Mutiny' of Indian Sepoys against their British officers, as a 'Mutiny' of the East India Company against their sovereign, the Mughal or as a 'Revolutionary war' of Indians against the invading British, this conflict raises heated controversy" – *A Clash of Cultures : Awadh, The British and The Mughals,* Delhi, 1987, p.242.

[6] S.B.Chaudhury in his competent work *English Historical Writing on the Indian Mutiny 1857-59* (p.41) points out that "Henry Mead's 'Sepoy revolt' was not the earliest work on the Indian mutiny. A monograph published by Fitzgerald Lee and Radcliffe of Dorsetshire was still earlier."

published from London in 1902 - and was reported to be authored by Sir William Muir.[7] In this book further attempts were made to whip up revolt and its author seemed to convince his readers that "the character of the affair is that of military mutiny - a struggle between the Government and the soldiers, not between the govenment and the people."[8] The whole British effort towards building up the mutiny theory of the revolt thus took nearly fifty years to coalesce into a full fledged and mature programme of historical exercise. It started at a time when the Indian revolt itself did not mature as a subject that may become an integral part of history as an academic subject. It matured with the time that synchronised with the beginning of Indian awareness that the revolt could be utilised as a sensitive instrument for a general propaganda to rouse the national sentiment. At least this was the way how men like Savarkar was trying to interpret the revolt from a broad meaningful Indian standpoint.

The whole of the British effort to build the mutiny theory of the revolt grew out of a vituperation for the failure of the British Government to anticipate and handle sensitive administrative problems at the right time and in the right manner. When Mead wrote, he wrote frankly from an anti-government sentiment.[9] This anti-government feeling was rampant in the psychology of the contemporary European mercantile community available in Calcutta. Stokes comments "the military and vociferous European mercantile community at Calcutta had no patience for such views [i.e. those propagated by men like Mead or Muir] placing the blame squarely on Canning, the Governor General, and his officials for their pusillanimous handling of the crises

[7]The title of the book was 'Records of the intelligence department of the government of the north west provinces of India during the mutiny of 1857.' This book was edited by Coldstrean and was published in two volumes from Edinburgh in 1902. It must not be confused with Sir William Muir's work *Agra in the Mutiny 1896.*

[8]W.Muir, *Records of the Intelligence Department of the Government of N.W.Provinces of India during the mutiny of 1857,* London, 1902, vol. I, pp. 31 and 39.

[9]"...Mead was involved in the prejudices of the time and strikes a frankly anti-government note in most of his observations." - S.B.Chaudhury, *op.cit.* p.42.

and for their refusal to recognise the fact that they had a formidable civil rebellion on their hands."[10]

Stokes further pointed out that G.B.Malleson who later completed J.W.Kaye's great *History of the Sepoy War* "was the anonymous spokesman of this school of vituperative criticism" and he quotes a very decisive statement of Malleson : "The crisis came : at first, apparently a mere military mutiny, it speedily changed its character, and became a national insurrection."[11] Malleson observed in categorical terms that the people of Benaras, Azamgarh, Gorakhpur, the whole of the Doab, Allahabad, Kanpur, Meerut, Agra, Rohilkhand and Oudh" shook off our rule and declared against us."[12] This approach to the study of revolt is very significant. If Mead and Muir wanted to whip up a mutiny theory of the revolt, Malleson was equally a competent contemporary pillar on whom the whole structure of the theory of popular revolt came to be rested. Thus it is a laurel to British understanding of Indian history that in an unbiased and realistic approach of the actual events the British historical mind came to be associated with the genesis of revolt theory of the 1857 rebellion. At the back of this of course lay an exasperation of the British mind with the failure of the Indian administration, the Government of Canning and his men in India. Malleson thus reproached the men at the helm of the administration : "But the men who administered the affairs of India refused to admit the existence of events which were clear to all around them; they persisted in governing as though there were no disorder in the civil districts, and feigned to believe that the cultivators of the soil - the class from which the sepoys are selected - were, to a man, in our favour."[13]

Malleson had in his company Mead and the corpus of understanding of the revolt of 1857 they built up was based on this relentless

[10]Eric Stokes, *op.cit.*, p.4-5.

[11]Stokes (*op.cit.*, p.5) has quoted from G.B. Malleson, *The Mutiny of the Bengal Army* (known as 'the Rud Pamphlet'), London, 1858, p.63.

[12]*Ibid.*

[13]Malleson, *op.cit.*, p.63. quoted by Stokes *op.cit.* p.5.

criticism of Canning's government." Mead had his own views about the situation", writes S. B. Chaudhury. His "opposition to Canning's government was unrelenting. In everything and everywhere it was 'too late'.[14] It was this feeling that the government came to its senses too late in assessing either the resentment of the army or the discontent of the people which lay in the foundation of the British historiography of the revolt. As a matter of fact from Wellesley onwards the British Empire in India was relentlessly pushing its frontiers to distant horizons. This phase of ceaseless expansion was mostly over the first half of the 19th century, more precisely with the imperialist expansions of Lord Dalhousie. The story of expansion was the story of outward turmoil. Inwardly the British Empire was quietly slipping into a kind of complacence which only shows that behind all British missions for civilizing India there was unwillingly growing a tendency to import the victorian repose to the Indian subcontinent. If the revolt of 1857 did anything it was this. It shook the pillars of British complacence that had so long been there in the British tendency to build up a majesty on a sense of repose. What hurt the comtemporary British historians was this very rude blow administered by a subject people to the repose of their imperial masters. The kind of shock the British quill expressed over the revolt was the shock of a lion whose majesty was challenged by the insolence of the prey.

Parallel to the concept of military mutiny the British mind also gave birth to a concept of conspiracy of the Hindus and the Muslims. G.B. Malleson in his later one-volume work [15] on the Indian revolt "set out the essential elements of what has become known as the conspiracy theory."[16] Malleson put forward the view that outside and above the Sepoy regiments there was a very competent level of leadership and sufficient evidence existed to prove that the outbreak of 1857 occurred

[14]Choudhury, *op.cit.*, p.43.
[15]G.B.Malleson, *the Indian Mutiny of 1857,* London 1891.
[16]Stokes, *op.cit.* p.5.

as a revolt of a deep seated conspiracy within this level of leadership.[17] Malleson named the leaders of conspirators as Maulvi Ahmadullah of Faizabad, Nana Sahib and the Rani of Jhansi. These leaders, Stokes observes as a comment on Malleson, "had entered into a plot which mifired only in its actual timimg."[18] After naming the chief conspirators Malleson adds "such, then, were the conspirators. The inhabitants of Oudh cirected mainly by the Maulvi and a lady of the Royal House known as the Begum, the inhabitants of the North West provinces, goaded into bitter hostility by the action of the Thomasonian system, and the Rani of Jhansi."[19] Malleson then goes on detailing the conspiracy : "the executive council of this conspiracy had arranged, in the beginning of 1857, to act upon the Sipahis by means of the greased cartridges, upon the inhabitants of the rural districts by the dissemination of chapatis. This dissemination was intended as a warning that the rising was imminent. It was further decided that the rising of the Sipahis should be simultaneous, and more than once the actual date was fixed. Providentially something always happened to prevent the explosion of that day."[20]

Malleson had in his company other contemporaries who very substantially subscribe to the thesis of a pre-meditated design. There were men like J.B. Norton and Alexander Duff and also to some extent Charles Ball. Duff was a respected person among Indian circles and his views were highly appreciated during his time.[21] In a series of

[17]The conspiracy has been analysed threadbare by R.C.Majumdar in his book Sepoy Mutiny etc. Book IV, ch.I, pp.337-382. Malleson's view about the conspiracy is also available in his *History of the Indian Mutiny* (London, 1878-80), vol. II. Of Malleson, R.C.Majumdar writes : "Among the British historians of the mutiny Malleson held the most definite view about the conspiracy and conceived a very clear picture of it in his mind." Majumdar, *op.cit.*, p.337.

[18]Eric Stokes (*op.cit.*, p.5.) makes this observation on the basis of Malleson's one-volume recension of 1891, *The Indian Mutiny of 1857*.

[19]Quoted by R.C. Majumdar from Malleson, *op.cit.*, p.338.

[20]*Ibid.*

[21]Duff's book was published from London (second edition 1858) and was entitled the *Indian Rebellion, its causes and results in a series of letters.*

letters he discussed the causes and results of the Indian Rebellion.[22] Duff was highly "expressionistic and emotional" and Martin observed that his book was full of mistatements and these were calculated to set the British mind 'aflame' against the natives.[23] Thus it is clear that the British mind was not free of bias just as the Indian mind was not in subsequent years. Contemporary English authors were not historians and therefore they could not critically analyse and assess their sources and materials. Bias was allowed to swing the British mind. Passion was allowed to overpower it. Many of the contemporary authors attempted to write in the style of a historian by referring to the work of previous author in the field. But seldom they had in them elements of real historians. A contemporary writer showed an awareness of this and he wrote : "For in writing history, it is necessary to pull up the weeds as to sow the good seed."[24] But unfortunately the weeds were not properly pulled up and hence a proper and objective analysis is rarely available.

The exception to this was Charless Ball's *History of the Indian Mutiny*. He was also a subscriber to the conspiracy theory but the story of the revolt which he described had a big canvass to cover. It is said that he treated the revolt "in the broader context of British imperial history of the victorian age."[25] Ball wrote in his book that he had taken special care in "sifting the husks of fiction from the grains of truth" and declared confidently that his work should be ranked "among the standard history of the era to which they belong."[26] Ball's contention

[22]These are available in the second edition of his book.

[23]R.Montgomery Martin, *The Indian Empire with a full account of the Mutiny of the Bengal Army*, vol.II, pp.274-75.

[24]This statement is available in *History of the Seize of Delhi*, etc. preface, pp.V-VI. It is assumed that book was published in 1861. W.W.Ireland, a member of the Indian Medical Service described himself as the author of the book. But his authorship is still disputed. For a review of the book see *Calcutta Review, 1861*, 37 Notices, pp.III-VII. W.W.Ireland described himself as the author of this book which was on a story of Anglo-Indian life.

[25]S.B.Chaudhuri, *English Historical Writings*, p.68.

[26]Ball, *History of the Indian Mutiny, II*, p.664.

was that the events of 10 May at Meerut formed a prematured outbreak. Yet it was a part of the organised and well concealed plan. If it had succeeded it would have crushed the power of England in India but it had a kind of precipitancy which totally disorganised the plan of insurrection. As a result it demoralised, and eventually broke up the rebellious masses into 'fragments' which the British found easy to subdue and crush.[27] Ball's subscription to the conspiracy theory was certainly not the result of a conscious effort. His main aim was different. He wanted to show how the existence of the British Empire had shaped the Asian world and how India fitted into it. The result of this was that he incorporated as much material as possible from diverse sources and as S.B. Chaudhury says, Ball's history really becomes "invaluable as a storehouse of all sorts of original materials.[28]

In a broad way the exponents of the conspiracy theory did not distinguish between the Hindus and the Mohammedans as participants in the pre-meditated designs of uprisings. Yet there were historians who did believe that the rebellion was essentially the work of the Mohammedans and the Hindus were in general out of it. Commenting on this school of thinking which grew concurrently with the revolt itself Eric Stakes writes : "British officials serving in western districts of the North-Western provinces (that is, in the Doab above Agra, in the Delhi region, and in Rohilkhand) were convinced that while the mass of the population felt contentment with British rule, they had been worked upon by elements of the old Muslim elite, who had conspired to ferment political rebellion."[29] Stokes contention is this that this narrow view of conspiracy is entertained by William Muir and it drew support from a younger civilian Alfred Lyall who served in the Bulandshahr district. As early as 30 August 1857 the young Lyall wrote to his father "the whole insurrection is a great Mohammedan conspiracy and the Sepoys are merely the tools of the Mussulmans.[30] Even the

[27]Ball, *op.cit.,* vol.I, pp.438-39.

[28]S.B.Chaudhuri, *op.cit.,* p.70.

[29]Eric Stokes, *The Peasant Armed,* p.7.

[30]Quoted by Stokes, *op.cit.* p.7.

Commissioner of the Meerut Division[31] seem to have shared the same view that the revolt was essentially due to the machinations of Mussalmans. In his official narrative he mentioned "the happily, unavailing endeavour of the Mohamedan leaders to make the mass of the population join them, and the bitter complaints of the Hindoo mutineers that they have been deeply deceived, all these indicate that, though a spirit of mutiny may have prepared the native army, the real movers were Mohamedans."[32] R. Spankie, the Magistrate of Saharanpur clearly believed that only the Mahomedans were at the root of the uprising. He wrote : "the common brotherhood of all Mohamedans is a very different matter, and I think it would be impossible to deny that they were in heart and soul against us.[33]

Thus it is clear from above obervations that a very powerful and substantial section of the comtemporary British officials sought to ascribe the responsibility of the revolt entirely on the Mahomedans. Even the Commissioner of Patna in a letter to the Government of Bengal, 6 October 1857, informed the government that "the whole of the Calcutta press, apparently without exception have taken up the idea that this is a Mahomedan rebellion, not merely in the sense that the sepoys were worked upon by individual Mahomedans, which may or may not be true, but that the entire Mahomedan community is disaffected and merely waits its opportunity to rise and throw off the British yoke.'[34] It was thus the British official community of India that numistakably put the stigma of general disloyalty on the Mahomedans. This had urged Syed Ahmed Khan to plunge into his operation whereby he wanted to rescue his co-religionists from the stigma thus attached to them by the rulers. Herein will one find the genesis of the pamphlet *Who were the loyal mussulmans ?* It is very important to note that among all the historians who contributed to the concept of a conspiracy among the Mahomedans Ball was the one who could openly go

[31]It comprised the whole of the upper Doab.

[32]Quoted by Stokes (*op.cit.* p.7.) from *Narrative of Events Regarding the Mutiny in India of 1857-58 and the Restoration of Authority*, vol.I, 285, para 430.

[33]Quoted by Stokes, *op.cit.* p.8.

[34]Quoted by Stokes, *op.cit.*, p.8.

beyond the precincts of the theory itself. He could appreciate the fact that the rebellion of soldiers was not uncommon in Asiatic history and at times the revolt seemed to be a general uprising of masses. At moments he apprehended that the entire European element in India would be destroyed in the torrent of rebellion. And in his book he could clearly write that anti-Brirish feeling had created an atmosphere where the rebellion would involve the whole of the people.[35] At a time when the entire official circle was trying to fix up the responsibility of the revolt there was one historian among the English circles who seemed to be concerned more about the internal dynamics of the revolt than its source of origin. Although Ball belonged to the ring of historians who subscried to the conspiracy theory of the revolt he was also the one who could get rid of the narrowness of pampered historiography cramped within the prejudices and fixations of the ruling official mind.

The British historiography harping upon the conspiracy theory only expressed the British viewpoint. The fact which escaped the British mind was that the Mahomedans never launched a *jihad* or a holy war against the British. Examples of holy war in contemporary world was not absent. But unfortunately the social structure of the Indian Islam did not allow the Muslim response to British rule to grow in a very coordinated nature so that all the streams of Muslim discontent at various strata of the society would mingle into a formidable stream of reaction. Those who discovered a conspiracy underlying the revolt of 1857 failed to appreciate the fact that the Indian Revolt was not one movement. It was a concurrence of many. At one end it was a peasant revolt; at the other it was a national uprising. At one it was the uprisings of certain families of Muslim aristocaracy and at other it was just a mutiny of the Hindu sepoys. All these mingled into one and made the revolt a conjunctural phenomenon. No one theory of revolt can provide a straight jacket into which the Indian revolt will fit itself.

[35]Ball, *op.cit.*, vol. I, pp.644-45.

9

A Note on The Historiography of The Revolt of 1857 in Assam

In 1857 Assam, like Bengal, stood at the fringe of a national revolt. Elements of a full-fledged revolt against foreign rule were not absent anywhere in India but the mass-revolt did not mature into a full-scale outburst in many parts of India. Assam rallied with Bengal, Orissa, Madras and to some extent with the Punjab in staying out of the political map of popular upsurge that engulfed a wide part of northern and central India about this time. Classical historians of the revolt of 1857 are one in asserting that the revolt left no impressive mark on Assam. "It would seem from the reports of the government of India",writes Malleson, "that peace in the districts of Assam was not disturbed in 1857."[1] "The great Sepoy Mutiny of 1857". writes Edward Gait in tune with Malleson, "left Assam almost untouched".[2] To suggest that Assam was peaceful during the revolt of 1857 had deeper implications. "The inhabitants, that is to say, Malleson adds, "displayed no sympathy with the mutineers".[3] The people's mandate in 1857 was not anti-British. What happened then in Assam in 1857 was a surface tension – the crest of the society was in turmoil. The layer of the vast mankind below provided the inoffensive base on which the British rule could lay its pillars. People's non-participation in

[1]Kaye and Malleson, *History of the Indian Mutiny,* vol. VI, p.32.
[2]Sir, Edward Gait, *A History of Assam,* 1967 reprint, p.378.
[3]*Vide,* 1

the revolt was thus one angle from which it has been concluded that Assam at the margin of a broad national revolt in 1857. There is another angle of historical observation from which it had been said that Assam's peace was due largely to effective British handling of a situation which was otherwise explosive. Gait is one who brings this view at home : ' The situation was at times by no means free from danger; and the comparative immunity which this part of India enjoyed was due very largely to the watchfulness and resource displayed by the civil and military officers on the spot".[4] Thus so far as the revolt of 1857 is concerned British historiography provide us with two apparently contradictory arguments. Malleson, an earlier author, presents the point that the British rule in Assam was not threatened with danger because the people did not participate in the revolt. Thus here the role of the people has been appreciated and credited has been given to their wisdom. Gait on the other hand says that the situation was not free from danger and the credit of keeping the country peaceful goes to the British administrators present in the country at that time. Where should a historian place his charity – on the people or on the administrators, on the ruled or on the ruler, on those who wanted to overthrow a foreign rule or on those who contained such efforts within limits ? This seemed to be the point that remained at stake in any discussion on Assam's role in the revolt of 1857.

In any case the official views current at the time of the revolt itself seemed to be born out of the experiences of the British administrators present in Assam when the revolt was taking place. Such official views vouchsafe the standpoint taken by historians in the aftermath of the revolt and represent the same dichotomy in administering viewpoints in respect to the revolt. "Thus in a routine intimation to the Government of Bengal the Magistrate of Goalpara wrote in 1857 ....with regard to the feeling of the people here towards government, I can confidently affirm that nothing can be better than that which pervades all classes of community who view with horror and dread the proceeding of the sepoys and earnestly pray for the restoration of peace and order."[5] Thus the tranquility among the people was appreciated in the official

[4]*Vide,* 2

[5]The Magistrate of Goalpara to the Secretary, Government of Bengal, 27 June, 1857, *Parliamentary papers,* vol. 44, part I of 1857-58 papers, No. 364, p. 244.

circles and formed the major substance of talks among administrators in Assam and Bengal about this time. Yet the administration was not willing to barter away all charity to the people. In Halliday's minute on the mutiny we get the beginning of the view which eventually was given the shape of a mature historical observation by Gait. Halliday writes that in Assam "the seeds of rebellion were sown which but for the timely discovery of the plot, the arrest and subsequent execution of the chief conspirators and the secret and timely despatch of European sailors must have resulted in most serious consequences."[6]

From the above observations two points seemed to be settled. First, there was tension in Assam inspite of the people remaining quiet and secondly, the British administration nipped the tension in the bud and thus left for subsequent historians scope for elation and rejoice. This tension point was another source of dichotomy in the historiography of the revolt of 1857 in Assam. British historians want us to believe that the seeds of tensions were imported from outside. This admirably fits in with the proposition that the people were quiet and not anti-British so much so that outsiders introduced tremors in a society otherwise placid and calm. Thus Charles Ball describes the source of tension from the usual British standpoint : "Many of the sepoys of the 1st Assam Battalion came from the neighbourhood of Arrah and were related to the men of the 40th regiment that mutinied at Dinapur; while others of them were from the territory belonging to Koer Singh. When, therefore, the outbreak at Dinapur became known to the men of the 1st Assam Battalion at Dibrugarh, they openly expressed their sympathy with the mutineers and proffered their services to an ex-rajah, Poorundur Singh whom they promised to restore to the authority and state, he had been deprived of by the English, on condition that he would put himself at their head."[7] Ball's

[6]*Minute on the Mutinies as they affected the lower provinces under the Government of Bengal*, 30 September, 1858 by Frederick Halliday.

[7]Charles Ball, *History of the Indian Mutiny*, vol.II, pp.161-162.

observations have been echoed by Edward Gait[8] who is quick to appreciate British mobility in quelling the tension : "Colonel Hannay, the commandant, at once deprived the Hindustani members of the regiment of the opportunity for communication with each other, and for combination, by sending them to the small outlying outposts, while he concentrated in Dibrugarh the loyal Gurkhas and the hillmen attached to the corps."[9] The contention here is that by dispersing the Hindustani sepoys the English neutralized elements of disaffection in Assam. Thus the whole British historiogrphy of the revolt in Assam has been built up without any reference to the involvement of the people in general. The focus was on the sepoys and the accent was on their mutiny. This may be because of the fact that the sepoys were the mainstay of the rebellion elsewhere in India. But unfortunately "in Assam, there was no sepoy of the soil. In Assam Militia, there were a few hundred of Assamese soldiers, wearing Dhuti and 'a strap of ox-hide' over it. These Sancho Panzas with short lances had nothing to do in the rebellion."[10] Therefore those who wanted to give Assam a rightful place in the annals of the revolt of 1857 turned their eyes from the sepoys to the other elements in the society. At least they wanted to prove that the sources of tension were there in Assam itself and for this one does not have to rely on extraneous and imported factors like the presence of the Hindustani sepoys and their discontent. Historians' eyes thus turned inwards and the dichotomy of historical observations about the sources of tension in Assam on the eve of revolt of 1857

[8]"There was a large number of Hindustani sepoys in the 1st Assam Light Infantry, then stationed at Dibrugarh, as well as in a local artillery corps. There was also a considerable, though smaller, number of these upcountry men in the 2nd Assam Light Infantry which was quartered at Gauhati. In September 1857 an uneasy feeling began to display itself among the men of the Dibrugarh regiment, owing to letters received by some of the Hindustani sepoys from Shahabad, where many of them had been recruited; and some of them were found to have entered into a conspiracy with the Saring Raja, a scion of the Ahom royal family who resided at Jorhat".—Edward Gait, *Op.cit.*, p.379.

[9]Gait, *Op. Cit.*, pp.379-80

[10]Mahendra Bora, *1857 in Assam,* 1957, p.1.

was thus complete. Benudhar Sharma[11], Mahendra Bora[12] and some others[13] were the first to turn our attention to what may be called the real causes of whatever upsurge we have in Assam in 1857. When the British historians saw in the revolt of 1857 in Assam a simple extention of sepoy discontent from the core to an end-part of the British Indian empire, these historians aimed at discovering the 'area of commonness' between the upsurge in Assam and the general revolt in Hindustan. At least their aim was not to shrink 'the national upsurge into a sepoy mutiny'.[14] "Like the rest of India, Assam was also fighting for the restoration of *Swadesh* and *Swadharma*", writes Mahendra Bora. Here he introduces an understanding in a frame of reference different from that of earlier writers. Here he breaks the cordon which the British historians set around our thinking – the cordon within which almost all our classical Indian thinkers, R.C.Majumdar, S.N.Sen, H.P.Chattopadhyaya and others beat their wings. The lead which Mahendra Bora and others gave matured steadily and Assam produced her own historian who could boldly assert that Assam's role in the revolt of 1857 should be treated as the closing chapter of a vast story and should never be glossed as an inconspicuous footnote.[15] But contrary to the contentions of Gait," writes S.K.Barpujari, "this great upheaval did not leave Assam untouched".[16] Many years ago C.E. Buckland put forward the view that in Assam "an insurrection

[11]Benudhar Sharma, *Maniram Dewan* (in Assamese), *Satwan Sal* (in Assamese) and *The Rebellion of 1857 vis-a-vis Assam,* Gauhati, 1958.

[12]Mahendra Bora, *1857 in Assam,* Gauhati, 1957.

[13]K.N.Datta, "The 1857 Rebellion in Assam" in *Proceedings of the Indian History Congress,* 1957.

[14]See M. Bora, *Op. Cit.*, p.1.

[15]S.K.Barpujari, "Further Light On The Revolt Of 1857 In Assam" in *Proceedings of the North East India History Association,* Second Session, Dibrugarh, 1981, p.238.

[16]Mahendra Bora writes : When the revolt of Assam is contrasted with that in the rest of India, it does not give a philharmonic impression but sounds like a musical fugue, lilting cadences of the major key being repeated in the minor one. After all, in point of time, Assam's revolt is more a segment of the sunset than of the nocturnal gloom"--Bora, *Op. Cit.,* p.2.

would have broken out damaging not only the tranquility of the province itself but also perilling the safety of the whole of our Eastern Frontier".[17] Recently historians contradict this view and say that insurrections did break out in Assam although they did not take the form of a mutiny. What was forestalled by the British administrators in Assam was the mutiny and not an insurrection. This insurrection took the shape of 'the final attempt to maintain independence' by indigenous rulers and it never broadened into 'a powerful onslaught to wrest the country from the prowling tentacles of the octopus'.[18] It is only from this standpoint that the events of 1857 in Assam become meaningful.

To earlier historians, R.C.Majumdar, S.N.Sen, Haraprasad Chattopadhyaya and others, Assam had a marginal place in the entire story of the revolt of 1857. This was because they took a panoramic view of the whole event and naturaly Assam shrank vis-a-vis the northern and central India, Meerut, Lucknow, Kanpur, Jhansi, Allahabad and Delhi. This was a folly. Assam had seen the British rule only for thirty years while the rest of India had suffered foreign domination for many years more. Yet things drifted very fast[19] and people could feel the squeeze of the British rule. Then Diwan Maniram Dutta memorialised the government in sharp notes : "In the Shastras it is written, that rulers ought to practise righteousness and govern their subjects with justice while studying their welfare. These are not now done, but the very contrary".[20] What the English did contrary to the path of righteousness has been well discussesd by Mahendra Bora. But the point that is often missed is that the aristocracy of Assam tried to correct the situation through constitutional means. When that failed they turned to the alternative means. One R.C. Majumdar's central points in his analysis of the revolt of 1857 is that there was no pre-planned conspiracy in the whole uprising of 1857. He writes : "Thus both

[17]C.E. Buckland, *Bengal under the Lieutenant Governors,* Vol.1, p.153.

[18]Mahendra Bora, *Op.Cit.,* p.2

[19]"In Assam since 1833 events had moved fast"—Tara Chand, *History of the Freedom Movement in India,* Vol. Two, 1967, p.75.

[20]Quoted by Tara Chand, *Op.Cit.,* p.75.

positive and negative evidences alike rule out the posiibility that the great revolt of 1857 was the result of a general conspiracy".[21] There might not be a general all-India conspiracy but local conspiracies were still there and Assam here may be taken as a case in point. Tara Chand highlighted as did many other historians the conspiracy that lay at the root of the Assamese rising in 1857. He writes : "Maniram was in Calcutta when the revolt of 1857 broke out. Angered by the repulses he had received, he resolved to throw in his own lot with the rebels. He addressed letters to the members of the old nobility and they resolved to rise on the eighth day of the moon in 1857, and place Kandarpesvar Singh, grandson of the last King of Assam, on the throne".[22] Thus the rebels were supplied with leadership and a point to rally around. "But the plot was divulged through the carelessness of a messenger and the government took immediate steps to crush it".[23] The modern Indian historiography about the revolt of 1857 in Assam thus lays stress on the concept of this 'plot'. This was not there in earlier historians. Haraprasad Chattopadhyaya, for example, introduces Assam in two places in his work[24] and his conclusion is : "Mutiny could not make headway in Assam".[25] In Assam what happened was not 'mutiny' but a people's movement in an aristocratic plot to retrieve the old regime. This point was missed by all the three leading centenary historians of the revolt of 1857– R.C. Majumder, S. N. Sen and Haraprasad Chattopadhyaya. At one place Sen writes : "In Assam Maniram Datta was hanged and Madhu Mallik, a Bengalee, was sentenced to ten years' imprisonment for holding treasonable correspondence with Kandarpeshwar Singh.."[26] Patriots activities become 'treasonable' only from a viewpoint that is colonial and it would be wrong to think that all historians were captive to this sort of outlook.

[21]R.C.Majumdar, *The Sepoy Mutiny and the Revolt of 1857*, p.380.

[22]Tara Chand, *Op.Cit.*, p.75.

[23]*Ibid.*

[24]Haraprasad Chattopadhyaya, *The Sepoy Mutiny, 1857 : A Social Study and Analysis*, pp.18 and 194.

[25]Haraprasad Chatterjee, *Op.Cit*, p.18.

[26]S.N. Sen, *Eighteen Fifty Seven*, p.408.

"Assam was combed out of patriots"- this is how Tara Chand describes the consequence of the leaking of the plot and in the end he concludes :"...the attempt of the Assamese nobility to regain their independence was crushed".[27] Tara Chand's angle of vision is clear. He was writing the history of the freedom movement in India and therefore, his standpoint must be different from those who analysed '1857' and wrote the history of the 'sepoy mutiny'.

The revolt of 1857 in Assam must be viewed not as a mutiny of the army but as an upsurge of the nobility. Tara Chand's standpoint was essentially this. Mahendra Bora wants to make it an all-class phenomenon. He writes : "A superficial survey gives the impression that 1857 in Assam was a one-man show. But, all classes of society were associated with it. Maniram Dewan and Piyali Barua belonged to the upper tens; Nilkanta Choladhara Phukan and Marangikhowa Gohain were blue blood to the last tips of their fingers; Sheik Farmad Ali was a court-musician and a fine specimen of Assamese Muslim; and Madhuram Koch was a humble tea-garden contractor.[28] Thus the revolt was a multi-class phenomenon. Bora further adds : 'The moneyed class was in search of a king to restore its vanishing glory and the submerged class was in search of a leader, a symbol to express its discontent. Maniram Dewan harmonised both these aspirations".[29] The line of difference between earlier historians and later historians is thus clear. The old line of thinking traces the mutiny-aspect of the revolt. New thinkers find popular involvement in it. One line finds in it no class involvement. Others make it an all-class phenomenon.

The upsurge in Assam in 1857 was certainly limited in time-scale, and also in porformance and participation. But it was never inconsequential, and marginal. What mattered in case of Assam was the motive force which served as the impulse for action. "The memory that they had not submitted even to the authority of the Grand Mughals was green in their minds. Successive political upheavals had, of course, exercised a severe drain on their energies; but they were no deterrent

[27]Tara Chand, *Op. Cit.*

[28]Mahendra Bora, *Op. Cit.,* pp.2-3.

[29]Mahendra Bora, *Op. Cit.,* p.3.

for the Assamese people to rise up and assert themselves".[30] Thus the point is driven home that in 1857 the people of Assam were apparently quiet but they "had not compromised with their spirit of independence" and therefore, nobody dared underrate them".[31] When Benudhar Sharma writes this, his stand is understandable. Assam was not fighting merely against British tyranny and hence what happened in 1857 in Assam was not simply an effort at tyrannycide. It was more than that, it was an aspiration for total liberty translated in a frame of limited time and action. If motivation has any place in the annals of revolt, Assam must have her own role vis-a-vis 1857. It is unfortunate that the spirit of Maniram Dewan who did the remote programming of the revolt of 1857 in Assam, has not yet been properly appreciated in historical circles. Consequently Assam's role has not been understood, Maniram envisaged a plan of total independence in a scheme of things entire Sepoy discontent at Dibrugarh and elsewhere in Assam created the situation but the impulse came really from the plans of the Dewan.[32] Herein lies the importance of Maniram. He must be placed in proper historical perspectives and should be made a subject of proper historical study. So long as this is not done any study of Assam vis-a-vis 1857 will remain incomplete.

[30]Benudhar Sharma, *The Rebellion of 1857 vis-a-vis Assam,* Preface to the Assamese edition, p.vii

[31]Benudhar Sharma, *Op.Cit.*, p.17.

[32]"The Dewan Plans Armed Insurrection"—this is how Benudhar Sharma writes the title of one of his chapters in his book.

10

1857 in Nationalist Thought, Ritual and Memory

Indian national memory is split on the event of 1857. The nationalist school led by Rajani Kanta Gupta and V. D. Savarkar accepts the Indian content of the revolt, the event of 1857. Others led by S. N. Sen and R. C. Majumdar believe that the revolt was short of being national incapable of having the perspective of a total history. Majumdar sees into it a goonda-upsurge and Sen squarely calls it 'counter revolutionary'. The Marxist school is equally split. Marx sees into the revolt a national movement while M. N. Roy calls it a feudal outburst; yet both accepted it as politically revolutionary. In later years S. B. Chaudhuri dug up the national memory through articulated research and showed that the revolt of 1857 had in its background a series of national insurgency. In working this out he successfully coronates 1857 as the year from which the earliest beginning of the Indian Freedom Movement could be dated. Chaudhuri thus falls very much in line with the nationalist thinkers of the nineteenth and early twentieth century. What is significant in the nationalist thinking is that they – Snigdha Sen argues in the case of Rajani Kanta Gupta and Tapti Roy argues in the case of Savarkar – appropriated the narrative structure of the colonial historians and built up powerfully the Indian case vis-a-vis the English historians. Taking cue from the nationalist arguments Indian writers in later years built up an Indian perspective of the revolt in their circumscribed regional narratives. New studies came up showing how the revolt of 1857 affected Assam, Gujrat, Haryana, Chhotanagpur,

Kanpur, Awadh, Malwa, North-Western Provinces and so on. This was a new kind of awarness in which peripheries were linked to the centre so that the total perspective of an Indian event could be perceived in its Indianness. As time went on there emerged tendencies to commemorate 1857 in rituals. One such ritual was initiated in West Bengal where Mangal Pandey was immortalized through the raising of a martyr's column in Calcutta opposite the Writers' Buildings. It is around this structure that the government organises a ceremony on 29 March every year to commemorate the shooting of the first fire against the English at Barrackpur by Mangal Pandey on the same day in the year 1857. What is celebrated in the rituals was the communal unity which was demonstrated in its grand form in the revolt. Thus from national memory 1857 passes into a social form through which the national mind turns back to find its source of inspiration.

If it is asked why the revolt of 1857 failed to grow into a mass movement in Bengal, historians point to two events – the permanent settlement and western education. The first event had given a kind of economic stability to the upper strata of the Bengali society and the second had fostered a psychology among the people to look to the English as the givers of peace and prosperity. This made Bengal an infertile a soil where revolt could germinate. Historians are complacent with this argument and seldom there has been any further research into the fundamental trends of the Bengali mind which kept the people away from revolt. There has been of course a mass of literature saying how the Bengali mind progressed politically but what social trends retarded that progress have not yet been discussed thoroughly. The present chapter is a draft aiming at regrouping the broad ideas in the context of which one can assess why Bengalees failed to stimulate a revolt although the elements which could have been coalesced into the force of revolt were not altogether absent there.

It is a wonder that the revolt of 1857 which began in Bengal failed to stimulate the entire people of that country to its cause. S. N. Sen, the official historian of the revolt wrote : "In Bengal the sepoys rose in many places but nowhere did they experience any sympathy from the local people." [1] This statement is not wholly true but unfortunately till date there has been no great research work to prove this statement as a total lie. Sri Pramodranjan Sengupta has written two books on the Indigo Revolt and the Great Revolt of 1857[2] where he marshalled a mass of information to prove that in Bengal in 1857 or on the eve of that the social and political climate of Bengal was ripe for a general revolt. But why such a revolt did not come into effect he did not explain. No less important than Pramodranjan's books in the Bengali work of Sri Sukumar Mitra [1857 O Bangladesh — 1857 and Bangladesh] where he has explained how the great revolt had influenced and galvanized the Bengali literature of the time. But the point that is missed here is that the spirit of the general man, not to speak of the people of the educated upper strata, was never geared to the spirit of the revolt. If the revolt fails to absorb the attention of the people in a large scale, it is difficult to appreciate how it became a substantial mover in Bengali literature. If there was an Indigo Revolt in Bengal there was likewise a *Nildarpan* [Indigo Mirror, a work by Dinabandhu Mitra]. No such great work was available in Bengal in which the great revolt came to be mirrored. The appearance of Nildarpan was a phenomenon in the history of Bengali literature and it almost synchronised with the event of Indigo Revolt itself. The Indigo Revolt took place in 1859-60 and 'Nildarpan' was published from Dacca in 1860. Unfortunately during one decade preceding or following the great revolt of 1857 there was no major work in Bengali literature in which the revolt was either anticipated or recognized as a serious event of life.

In Bengali literature the period immediately preceding the great revolt was the era of Madhusudan Dutt just as the period immediately following the revolt was that of Bankimchandra Chattopadhyaya. Madhusudan returned to Bengal from Madras where he went in search of a living in 1856. Shivanath Shastri to whom we are indebted for an authentic study of the Bengali society in the nineteenth century wrote : "... (Madhusudan) again escaped back to his country".[3] Madhusudan who was certainly the greatest of the Bengali poets and one of the prime movers of Bengali literature before Rabindranath Tagore, returned to Bengal, baffled, for fortune never smiled on him in Madras. But was this home-coming happy for Madhusudan ? Shivanath writes: "Alas, what a change he saw in the country on his return.... In the arena of new Bengal there appeared a bunch of new leaders whose manners were out of the familiar tune".[4] Situations did change not only for the in-coming poet who was to shape Bengal's cultural destiny but also for the whole of Bengal as such. How did Madhusudan's literary mind address itself to this changed atmosphere of Bengal ? In 1858 was published his *Sharmistha*, and then *Padmavati* – certainly excellent as pieces of superior literature but certainly beyond the rim of consciousness that made the revolt of 1857 a meaningful event of life. The poet's talent eventually progressed with two satires – *Ekei Ki Baley Savyata* [Civilization – Is it this ?] and *Buro Shaliker Ghare Noa* [Idiosyncracy of the old bird]. Meanwhile the great revolt of 1857 and the Indigo Revolt had taken place. Madhusudan wrote *Tilottamasambad Kavya* and the year was 1860 when the *Nildarpan* was published. Madhusudan, the revolutionary poet of Bengal was absorbed in his own romanticism, absorbed in the classical oblivious of the great happenings around. But the heat of the age was too scorching for a romantic poet and in 1862 he escaped the country and sent to England to be educated as Bar-at-law. Thus one of the prime movers of Bengali literature of the time remained conspicuously untouched by the revolutionary ferment of the time.

Madhusudan's age was followed by the age of Bankimchandra. In 1864 was published his *Durgesnandini* and this was followed by his *Kapalkundala* – two extraordinary novels, real gems of Bengali literature, but fatuous as literary mirror for coalesceing social unrest. Thus in the middle of 1860s the excellence of Bengali literature was built squarely on the ignorance of the indifference to the two great happenings of the age – the revolt of 1857 and the Indigo Revolt. The only novel which had focussed the revolutionary spirit of the time was the *Nildarpan* and this as a piece of literature - could never compete with the works of Madhusudan and Bankimchandra. Shivanath Shastri says that the contemporary Bengali mind was enthralled with the grandeur and gravity of Bankimchandra, or, the majesty and magniloquence of Madhusudan but the effect of Dinabandhu, the author of *Nildarpan* was not abegging. Speaking of the effect of *Nildarpan* in 1860 Shivnath wrote: "We all became captive to *Nildarpan*." Shivnath graphically describes how the intelligentsia became excited and riotous after having read *Nildarpan* and how the characters of the novel whipped the sentiments of the readers and made them feel as if they had risen in revolt against the oppressions of the planters. This was the paradox the Bengali mind could not resolve before and after the great revolt of 1857. On the one hand there was a high latitude of romanticism that helped the reading public of Bengal an escape from the torture of unrest to the serenity, repose and beatitude of Madhusudan-Bankimchandra's literature and on the other there was the blood-thrilling novel of Dinabandhu that stirred the excitement of the same mass of people.

The effect of Madhusudan-Bankimchandra was the grafting of a kind of refinement hitherto unknown in the Bengali society. The effect of *Nildarpan* was the germination of a consciousness of social agonies which cannot be equated with any kind of political consciousness that is necessary to trigger off revolution. The refined Bengali mind thus made itself conscious about social destitution and miseries but shrank from reacting against the causes of the miseries politically. The net effect of the romantic movement of Madhu-Bankim was that social miseries came to be romanticised by the Bengali mind instead of being politicalized and Torab, the hero of *Nildarpan*, become nothing but the human symbol of a race, socially charged but politically callous, struggling against an invisible and inexorable fate but being baffled in the long run by the forces of the age.

Thus the point to be noted is that the appreciation of sovial miseries was never politicalized so that the main preoccupation of the Bengali mind ever since Rammohan, or Iswar Chandra Vidyasagar was social emancipation and not political liberation. In later years the members of Young Bengal or the Brahmo-Samaj took up this trend of thinking, plunged themselves in efforts of social welfare and accepted as their targets of invasion superstition, illiteracy, ignorance and destitution of the womanfolk and so on. There were all round efforts to shed the shackles of social inhibitions and introduce radiations of western culture into the gloom that had settled on the springs of animation. The central subject of social reform was woman and the movements for the abolition of the suttee, widow remarriage, abolition of *kulin* polygamy, female education and the like shows that at the back of Bengali mind there had been a great ascendancy of woman. When Madhusudan wrote his 'Captive Lady' he was unwittingly spurred by a sense of sorrow for Indian women, the wretched soul, captive in her own tower of isolation. The refinement which was recently grafted in the Bengali mind helped it to romanticize the socially confined personality of woman. Rammohan had rescued her from the pyre, Vidyasagar had reinstated her in life and now it was left for Bankimchandra to immortalize her as an object of worship. From woman social eyes soon came to be rivetted in the mother in woman and that invisible mother wailing in her own destitutions soon came to be equated with the motherland reeling in her miseries. We have *Bande Mataram* in Bankimchandra's *Anandamath* and a stage was thus reached where the solitary social woman was universalized as an object of worship. This was how the Bengali mind moved during the two or three decades before and after the great revolution of 1857. This mind was not sufficiently politicized and revolution was not supposed to germinate in this inconducive soil of Bengal.

11

The Revolt : The Indian-ness in Indian History

In all discussions of the Revolt of 1857 one aspect of India has been neglected. It is the Indian-ness of India, the quintessence of Indian history. In the post-centenary golden jubilee year of the Revolt we direct our effort to retrieve this lost aspect of Indian history. Keeping in mind how the Indian-ness of Indian history was sabotaged in the past we wrote a book in Bengali thirteen years ago under the title *Mahabidroho O Bharatiya Udasinata* [*The Great Revolt and the Indian Indifference*].[1] After that enormous time has passed–a decade has gone by. During this period the view of historians did not change in a big way. In all discussions of the great revolt the Indian-ness of Indian history has remained unloved. An arrogance and impoliteness have given rise to intellectual predatoriness and this has masked itself by an apparent show of neutral and objective writing of history. A game of destroying images has taken hold of the craft of history writing. A rude and deliberate iconoclasm has overwhelmed sober appreciation of history. To this we draw the attention of readers.

[1] Ranjit Sen & Snigdha Sen, *Mahabidroho O Bharatiya Udasinata*, Progressive Publishers, 37A College Street, Kolkata 700073, 1997. Also read Snigdha Sen, *The Historiography of the Indian Revolt of 1857*, Punthi-Pustak, 136/4B Bidhan Sarani, Kolkata 700004.

In recent years much dust was raised to smear the image of Mangal Pandey. He has been treated as a lone rebel operating under the influence of narcotics. Those who describe him as an 'accidental hero' take shelter behind the accounts of English writers like Forrest and others.[2] On the basis of English writers they say that the trial of Mangal Pandey was just. These historians are simply holding a brief of British justice in India. To them the revolt was a vainglorious exercise that ended in a fiasco of smoke and fire. Many years ago Dadabhai Naoroji, Romesh Dutt, Mahadev Govind Ranade and others had proved the British rule in India to be a sham, unjust in all its basic performances. The Indian poverty, drain of wealth, rural indebtedness, deindustrialization, the fall in the quality and standard of Indian life, incessant famines, unemployment, racialism, disease and disasters etc. had always been considered to be the most apparent and outstanding signs of a brutish governance in India. The Empire's record was of a century old tyranny in India. Mangal Pandey's revolt came against this. His effort was no doubt a single-handed exercise –an output of rage and emotion that commissioned him into a desperate action. We do not know whether it was a planned event or it was a product of impulse. In any case it involved no calculation of self-interest, no thrust for a change in the trajectories of his personal life. What he did he certainly did with courage. He did not allow scruples to bottle up the riots of his soul. A moment's impulse, the influence of narcotics, an urge of religion whatever be the source of his action it was daring in all respects and there was no denying that by his action he triggered fire into the heart of a sensitive time. Sixteen years later in 1875 Vasudeo Balwant Phadke took up arms against the English. Twenty-two years later from Phadke's time, in 1897, Chapekar brothers performed another act of daring when they killed Rand, the English officer in Poona. Eleven years later from

[2] Sir George William Forrest (ed.) *Selections from letters, dispatches and other papers preserved in the Military Department of the Government of India, 1857-58*, 4 vols., Calcutta, 1893, 1912.

Chapekars' revolt, two desperate young men, Khudiram Bose and Prafulla Chaki hurled bombs on two supposed members of the English ruling community. They missed targets but their efforts showed the spirit of a flaming age.[3] Mangal Pandey was made of this spirit of the age. So he had fire in him. Emerging out of a shadowy existence he was the most unblurred human point in which time manifested in its own majesty.

Many years ago British writers painted the character of Nandakumar in black colours. He was a very effective administrator, one of the last great representatives of the power elite of Mughal Bengal. He was a major obstacle to the transfer of power to the English. Naturally in the age of the 'Plassey Plunder' when men of the English East India Company were engaged in making fortunes out of the resources of Bengal, he proved to be their impediment, hence a sore to the English eye.[4] He did not fit in well with the ethos of an unscrupulous age. He thus became the villein of piece who forfeited the right to exist. He therefore died in gallows facing fictitious charges–the first Brahman ever to be hanged under British rule. The history of the event the English wrote in their own colours and that history prevailed ever since. Nandakumar passed to posterity

[3] The use of bomb marked the coming of the modern age in the emergence of revolutionary terrorism in India.

[4] "Nandakumar was regarded by the East India Company's servants as a 'dangerous man not fit to be trusted'. In the course of a long life he had become obnoxious to almost every party in the Company's Government. In 1765 he had to make room for Reza Khan who became the Naib Nazim and Naib Diwan. When Hastings was appointed Governor in 1772 he was asked by the Court of Directors to put Reza Khan on trial. Hastings was instructed in a secret letter to avail himself of the intelligence which Nandakumar might be in a position to supply because 'no scrutable part of the Naib's conduct can have escaped the watchful eye of his jealous and penetrating mind.' But Hastings was not to yield Nandakumar 'any trust or authority which may be turned to his advantage.' "–N. K. Sinha, *The Economic History of Bengal from Plassey to the Permanent Settlement*, Vol. II, Calcutta, 1962, p. 276.

as the specimen of an unwanted Indian, a rebel in the political parade ground of an emerging state power.

This mark of unwantedness was later stamped on many a spirited soul of India from Phadke to Subhas Chandra Bose via Bhagat Singh and others. Now Mangal Pandey suffers the same fate. N. K. Sinha rose in defense of Nandakumar and retrieving facts from High Court records he showed that Nandakumar's fall was the result of deceit and conspiracy.[5] An Indian author writing as late as 1992 tries to rescue Mangal Pandey from the ignominy of historians' misjudgment. She situates him in the perspective that had set the spirit of the age aflame. She speaks of 'Indian disaffection' which separated 'the world of the English as rulers' from 'the world of the Indians as the ruled.'[6] Her conclusion was: "the twain never met."[7] Thirteen years later this approach was set aside[8] and a new attack was hurled on him. He was branded as an 'accidental hero'[9]–a man who rose up in the solitary brightness of a moment. This was the unkindest cut a hero of our national struggle can suffer in the hands of an Indian historian. In 1988 an attempt was made to assess Mangal Pandey in national perspectives.[10] This was long before the modern conspiracy to sabotage Indian perspective of revolt was set in. A part of this essay quoted at the end of this chapter will reveal how Mangal Pandey had to proceed through the glare of criticism and erroneous assessment of

[5] Sinha writes : "The execution of Nandakumar was to Hastings 'dire necessity.' To the Grahams, Vansittart's and Barwells it was essential to their own safety."– p. 283.

[6] Snigdha Sen, *The History of the Indian Revolt of 1857*, Punthi-Pustak, Calcutta, 1992, p. 97.

[7] *Ibid.*

[8] It is vital to note that Snigdha Sen rejected Savarkar's Hinduttva-motivated assessment of Mangal Pandey. See Pages 164 to 169 of her aforesaid book.

[9] Rudrangsu Mukherjee, *Mangal Pandey : Brave Martyr or Accidental Hero* ? Penguin Books, 2005.

[10] "Mangal Pandey" in Ranjit Sen, *Understanding Indian History*, (Firma KLM Private Ltd.), Calcutta, 1988, Ch. VI, pp. 115-127.

historians before he could find a rightful place in the gallery of our national heroes. A hero in history is made of a national perception and he is not born of accident. Can he be an output of a moment's intoxication when in the train of his action bigger things happen ? A charged soul gathers inspiration from situations. Mangal Pandey was a product of situations that operated around him with the momentous force of history. It was this force that produce self-willed agencies of tyrannicide. Mangal Pandey was born with this force in him. He must not be viewed as an isolated being born of nothingness. He was the product of Indian insolence which was whipped up under pressures of fierce racism of the Empire. He was the expression of the sub-continental anger against alien impingement on life and religion. He was the outcome of spiritual ballistics that gives birth to the missile of mind in conditions of distress. Innumerable mutinies had occurred one after another in the past. The nation's memory stored them for posterity. A vast number of sepoy-soldiers were disbanded over time for no fault of their own. Their tragedy was never forgotten. A countless troops of unfortunate peasants fettered in the uniform of sepoys were blown off at the mouth of cannon. Their deathless presence was celebrated in silence. Every failed mutiny of the past was an experiment in uprising. Every disbanded sepoy carried in him the pangs of a despised soul which was the dynamite necessary for an upsurge. Thus the fire was all round. The message of desperation was everywhere. The mutilated parts of a sepoy's blown up body and the ruddy drops of their blood did not allow them to wither. Desperation has its fire. It burns and then it bursts when time matures. For the sepoys time was maturing slowly. The world of the sepoys was not reeling from end to end with *bhang.* They as a whole did not at any time represent the mesmerized world of capitulators. They for the time being concealed in their barracks the sighs of the oppressed. They stifled tears of a tyrannized humanity. Mangal Pandey as an ordinary sepoy was only a part of this seething mankind. But at the end he was different from them. He made partnership with time at the moment of its maturity.

From the above it is clear that the concept of 'accidental hero' is untenable because it is a part of motivated history. Patriotism is a process. Its outburst is sometimes spontaneous, sometimes engineered and it cannot be judged by hurried, out-of-context and ultra-radical strains of historical composition. History is a quest for truth and its transparency must not be blurred by intellectual posing. In studying the events of 1857-58 we try to discover the touch of truth that lies in the recesses of traditional history. Radical interpretations of history we admire not because they carry a bonfire in the terrain of stale mind-sets but because they reveal unknown veracity which remains stored in obscure corners of knowledge. Facts are bedrocks of history and without excavation of new facts glimmers of interpretations fade. In reading the history of the events of 1857-58 what we find in recent years is the causality of facts. Time has come when we discovered new facts to restate the Indian-ness in Indian history. This Indian-ness belongs only to that sense of history which can see a new awakening of one's own roots in Indian uprising, a new thrust towards self-identity. The failure of Indians was not the last word in the great rebellion of 1857. The victory of the British was also not absolute. A new age, ushering in a new life and a new order of things was riding on the chariot of history. A reckless merchanthood, an evangelizing and missionary priesthood, a relentless military statehood and the autocracy of a racist manhood--these were the four basic attributes that were used to build up the system of rule of the Empire. Therefore, the bullet fired by Mangal Pandey sometimes seems to be a symbolic bullet which had been fired into the heart of this obstruction, the rule of the Empire. The invisible trajectory of the bullet flashed through the maze of a corrupt rule and opened the door to the arrival of a new age, a new nation and a new parameter of existence, organization.

In the third edition of the *Oxford History of India* the historian Percival Spear says that from the time of Dalhousie a new age had come to life. It stayed for many years and came to an end with

Curzon. Spear did not clarify the nature of the age. We think that this age was the beginning of the real history of India. The University age was ushered in and the age of patriotic nationalism burst forth. An awakening of life dawned in the universities. An awakening of power dawned at the barracks of the sepoys. Indian nationalism was the confluence of the two. Viewed from this end the sepoys were the active agents of history at its inauguration. The question as to whether their uprising was successful or not in the literal sense, whether they could re-establish the Mughal Empire or not in their ultimate efforts and whether their self-interest superseded their patriotism is unimportant. More important was their rising itself, huge at any scale, sporadic here, united there, now solitary, then in a group, sometimes limited to locality and at other heedless of place and time. Theirs was a movement which broke the still pattern of history, the endless pattern of a complacent rule of a self-obliging empire. It struck megalomania at its face and returned to the Indians the confidence that if desired power could be snatched from the barrel of the gun. The sepoys had shaken up the self-satisfaction of the ruler, had beaten to dust the insolence of racism and had established face to face with the white terror the avenging power of the exploited. This is not a slight matter. Whether the rebel sepoys had any strategy, whether there was a lack of coordination and collaboration amongst the leaders, whether the rank and file of the people helped the sepoys or not and finally whether any spark of fire was seen all over India at all– these questions are not insignificant. But they fade before a bigger question overlapping and over-riding all these–did the people moved by the sway of time perform the first necessary act towards bringing about the death of the world-wide Empire of the British ? If they could then the great revolt was successful. To expose this aspect of success is to highlight the Indian-ness of Indian history. This history we write in compact form in our own words. It shall contain no word of malice, no word of falsehood, no narration tainted with alien wine. It will only speak words of truth which beat in the Indian heart. Then only history can take guard against its own falsifiers.

12

The Revolt : The Indian Indifference

It is a truism in history that the amount of written matter on the great revolt of 1857 in India is much greater by English and non-Indian writers than by Indians. The Indians have mainly written after 1947, more specifically about a hundred years later, after the centenary of the revolt itself. In the meantime foreigners have written much and the volume of their writing is possibly much more than that of the Indians. Why is the revolt so neglected in the historical consciousness of the Indians ? An easy reply to this is perhaps that the literate Indians in the past in general had not acknowledged this event as a part of the acceptable run of their life. Yet it is strange that historical consciousness about the revolt was foremost amongst the people of Bengal where its process was most neglected. Two Bengalis recorded the contemporary reactions of the Indians against the great rebellion in 1859 : Kishorichand Mitra[1] and Sambhuchandra Mukherjee[2]. Both of them wanted to conceal their names under the expression 'Hindu' and tried to prove that the rebellion was the work of the people

[1] Kishori Chand Mitra, *The Mutinies, the Government and People, By a Hindu.*

[2] Sambhu Chandra Mukherjee, *The Mutinies and People, or, A Statement of Native Fidelity Exhibited during the Outbreak of 1857-58.*

other than the Hindus who were basically anti-rebellion. In later times leaders like Rabindranath Tagore and Subhaschandra Bose tried to imagine the Indians as a great nation composed of many peoples–a *Mahajati.* The revolt, which was brought about by the united efforts of the Hindus and the Muslims, has to be viewed from the angle of this great nation if we truly want to write about it and give it a status of significance.

What is meant by the national viewpoint as regards the great revolt can be understood by discussing two books. The first is '*The Indian War of Independence of 1857*' by the courageous Savarkar. Two things are said about this book : First in this book the British viewpoints has been countered for the first time in a major way. Second, the nationalistic viewpoint has been upheld for the first time here with a thrust and poignance appropriate to the spirit of a revolutionary literature. Sashibhusan Chaudhury writes : "All the assumption and prejudices of the British writers were for the first time questioned by Vinayak Damodar Savarkar in his book, '*History of the War of Independence*' the object of which was to 'inspire his people with burning desire to rise again and wage a second, and a successful war to liberate their motherland.' *If the purpose of history is to stir a nation to action Vinayak Damodar Savarkar was a historian.*" (Italics ours). Sashibhusan Chaudhury has called Savarkar's book "dynamic and truly national." Was there an all-Indian viewpoint truly available in this book ? Did Savarkar have the religious tolerance which is a prerequisite for being all-Indian in its character ? Savarkar has other writings also, such as *Hindutva, Hindu-Pad-Padshahi and Six Glorious Epochs of Indian History.* The writer who translated the last book from Marathi to English was S. T. Godbole. He has thus written about Savarkar's historical consciousness : "Savarkar saw the panorama of Indian history in the rise and fall of the Hindus. The [This] concept of history moulded his political thinking and career." Savarkar saw the great rebellion of 1857 from this Hindu perspective. He himself has written in his book *Six Glorious Epochs* (p. 461) : "But I have already written sometime in 1908-1909 a detailed history of the revolutionary war in my book of about five hundred pages named *Indian War of Independence of 1857*. In it I have reviewed that war from the standpoint of the Hindu nation." How the creator of the '*Hindu-Pad-Padshahi*' escape the eyes of a cautious historian like Shri Shashibhusan Chaudhury and became the spokesman of national historical consciousness ?

Now let us come to the discussion of the second book. The name of the book is *Sipahi Juddher Itihas*, (*The History of the Sepoy War*). The author is Rajanikanta Gupta. This is most probably the first fullscale history of the revolt written in Bengali and as a matter of fact in any Indian language. This book was published in parts within the first twenty years of the great revolt. It is surprising that such a book could be written within two decades of the revolt in Bengal--the land which was neutral and uninvolved or superficially

[3] In recent years there has been a move in the country to show that Bengal was not neutral in the revolt and had a part to play in it, however small it was. This viewpoint till date is undocumented and no work of any significance has come out in support of it. There were minor uprisings among the sepoys here and there in Bengal but no great upheaval did rock the peace of the country and the stability of the government. There was immense panic in Calcutta all through and talks circulated in the form of rumour that sepoys would march from Barrackpore to Calcutta. The fear-struck psyche of the English educated laity sheltered unfounded anxieties and eventually no great conflagration took place in Bengal. Whatever little tensions surfaced among the sepoys of Dacca and adjacent areas did not match the events that took place in the Jumna-Gangetic north India. Two things must be noted here. First, Bengal did not contribute a single sepoy in the native army of the Bengal Presidency. As a result the pangs of the sepoys could not ignite flames in the heart of the Bengal rural society. Inspite of this the contagion of mutiny spread in some cantonment areas and army barracks so that the ferment of an uprising did not seem to be altogether absent in Bengal. The nationalist historians considered Bengal to be a placid region in the days of turmoil. This placidity was an exaggeration for Bengal had never been as quiet as some parts of South India during 1857-58. The story of Bengal's participation in the great revolt of 1857 awaits further research in it.

involved in the revolt.[3] On the whole it may be said that *Sepahi Juddher Itihas (1878)* by Rajanikanta and *Desher Katha* (The Country's Memoirs 1904) by Sakharam Ganesh Denskar were the two largest memorials of the country written in Bengali within five decades of the historical uprising. Harishchandra Mukherjee wrote in *The Hindu Patriot* of 6th May 1858 : 'We think that the way in which contemporary people have looked at the event of the great rebellion of 1857 will vary greatly from the completely different viewpoint in which history will regard it.'[4] Rajanikanta Gupta is probably the first who has regarded this history from a different viewpoint. Ramendra Sundar Tribedi, a great Bengali intellectual of the time read this book and wrote : 'It did not satisfy me to read it once. I read it over and over again....the devotion to truth, the devotion to the people, the devotion to the motherland, could be seen manifest in every page of the book.' Truth, people, motherland--make up a full standpoint of history. Those who have read Rajanikanta's book know that the facts presented here have been taken from Kaye's book, the only available source then ready at hand. To borrowed facts he gave a touch of a national sentiment. This was his contribution. We shall naturally be reminded how Dadabhai Naoroji and Romeshchandra Dutt had used British Government documents in their *Poverty and Un-British Rule* etc. and *The Economic History of India* (2 vols.). There was not much of anti-British feeling in their writings. What was present there was a charged national consciousness that unmasked the evils of the British rule in India. It should be noted that all the Englishmen who wrote books about the revolt of 1857 did not write without any feeling of nationalism. Depending, as we do, on the writings of British

[4] Abstracted from the Bengali text *1857 O Bangla Desh* by Sukumar Mitra. For the influence of the revolt on Bengali literature, *see* the Bengali text by Dr. Sankar Prassad Chakraborty, *Bangasahitye Maha Bidroha,* Karuna Prakashani, Kolkata-700009, 2008. It should be noted that in 1888 was published a sensational Bengali Novel *Jhansir Rani* (The Rani of Jhansi) by Chandi Charan Sen. In this is available the story of a transforming time.

historians, we tend to forget this aspect of the British historiography of the revolt of 1857. We copy them and imbibe from them the disdain which they had for the revolt. As a result our national perspective gets lost.

While considering the writings of those who have depended on British historians to write the history of the great revolt, we must be cautious about two factors–one, what information they use; two, what language they take recourse to in interpreting their facts derived from different sources. Let me give an example. Mangal Pandey rebelled on the 29th March of 1857 at Barrackpore. This incident was adopted from the writing of Mr. Holmes by many historians including the doyen of Indian historians Rameshchandra Majumdar. Before accepting facts from him he acknowledged that Holmes was a 'high authority' on the event. Mangal Pandey rebelled against the British almost single-handedly; in the great revolt against the British he tried the first shot. He also tried to excite the other sepoys. Savarkar wrote that, standing in the parade ground, he called his fellow-soldiers saying : "Rise ye brethren, rise. Why do you back, brethren, come, let us rise. I bind you by the oath of our religion. Come, let us rise and attack the treacherous enemies for the sake of our freedom." But when no sepoy answered his call and when a sepoy named Sheikh Paltu caught hold of him and stopped him from killing the British, then only he tried to commit suicide so that he could escape an arrest by the British. Though fallen to the ground, he shot himself. He was wounded, but he did not die. Ramesh Ch. Majumdar has taken this event from the writing of Mr. Holmes, using it within inverted commas. The first hero of the great Indian revolt was now lying on the ground. The one who later on was to be the first Indian martyr at the gallows now lay prostrate on the dust. He has been satirised by Holmes thus–"He [Pandey] fell wounded; but he did not save himself from a felon's death" and Rameshchandra Majumdar has not forgotten to quote this sarcasm in his book. Any Indian would be surprised to read this quote from Holmes in Ramesh Majumdar's book. The word

'Felon' has been defined in the Oxford Dictionary as a 'criminal'. Mangal Pandey's death was criminal's death ? It is strange to see that in the very next sentence Ramesh Ch. Majumdar wrote : "Mangal Pandey fully deserves the honour of the first martyr which posterity has given to him". Is this a historical joke ? The very person who emerges as a 'criminal' when quoted from the writing of a British historian gets such empathy from him in the very next sentence ?

Actually, the whole matter is a question of perspective. In the India of the nineteenth century the father of the Muslim awakening Sir Syed Ahmed Khan was busy with counter-revolutionary works at Bijanor at the time of the uprising of 1857. On 14th December of 1864 he wrote a letter to Mr. Kaye. In it he speaks of the great rebellion thus : "There was no popular outbreak." According to him, three types of people joined the rebellion : "Robbers and dacoits, some of the minor chiefs whose families have fallen into decay, lower classes variously employed"! What was written by a man who was knighted by the British has been echoed by Ramesh Majumdar thus : 'Hopes of personal gain also undoubtedly operated to a large extent among all classes, and were the sole motive of many, notably the goonda elements and those professional classes who were accustomed to live by plunder, such as the Gujars, Ranghars, Jats etc.'[5] However Sir Syed Ahmed Khan and Ramesh Chandra Majumdar may lament for the joining of the rebellion by robbers, dacoits and goondas, it is an undoubted fact that this species of anti-socials have played a major part in many of the rebellions and mutinies of the world. The man who researched the dacoits of the world and became famous on that account was Eric Hobsbawm. I quote from his book : "...Social banditry has an affinity for revolution, being a phenomenon of Social protest".[6] In 1929 most of the Red Army of Mao-Tse-Tung was composed of the fierce elements of the society–in Mao's

[5] The British Paramountcy and the Indian Renaissance, Part-I, p. 497.
[6] Eric Hobsbawm, *Bandits*, p. 98.

language "declassed elements–soldiers, bandits, robbers, beggars and prostitutes".[7] Mao-Tse-Tung has himself stated : "Those people fight most courageously. When led in just manner, they can become a revolutionary force." It is not blameworthy if bandits and robbers take part in a rebellion. After the research of George Rude would anyone dare say that only the people of the established orders rebelled in the French Revolution ? Who were the crowds of the French Revolution ? Were they only the men of the upper estates ?

Actually established people do not easily break laws or rebel and take to violence. In the nineteenth century, nobody expected that people like Raja Radhakanta Dev and the Tagores in Bengal or the scions of the Mysore *Raj* or the *Nawab* of Patiala and others would rebel. Even in Kolkata which was the centre of capitulation, a place of flattering the rulers and fawning on them, the rebellious atmosphere was thick, as can be understood from the statement of Alexander Duff : "...while we are surrounded with enemies from without, there are tens of thousands of them prowling about in the very midst of us." This statement is full of matter for those who think that the people of Bengal were totally nonchalant. The inner burning of the people did not create outward flames but the latent anti-British feelings manifested itself in the second half of the nineteenth century. Who were, for example, those people whom Alexander Duff called the enemy in the midst of the crowd ? Are they only bandits and robbers ? Most probably not. This problem can be solved if we look into the *Hindu Patriot* of 2nd July, 1857. No less a person than Nawab Ali Khan of Chitpur was said to be helping the rebellious sepoys of Barrackpore with money and arms, and the British rulers were fearing that the sepoys would start from Barrackpore and come and take charge of Kolkata. The person who first revolted in Barrackpore was a Brahmin–Mangal Pandey–and those who followed him were mostly Hindus. The fact that a certain Muslim Nawab had

[7] Eric Hobsbawm, *op. cit.*, p. 106.

helped Hindus may seem poisonous to many, but the incident was probably true. Perhaps the impact of the revolt was not as widespread and deep in Bengal as in Awadh but who can deny that the gun-powder of revolt was equally dry and dense here, too ? In any case the atmosphere here was tense although the life was not fashioned by the great events of 1857. In an article on the disturbance at Barrackpore dated 19th February, 1857 *The Friend of India*, clearly states that the people of Barrackpore had turned against the British rule. Kaye and Surendranath Sen both acknowledged the fact that army commanders at Barrackpore preached Christianity amongst the soldiers. Perhaps many other such commanders stationed at various military centres in Bengal used their gun to preach their religion and there is no doubt that their activities enraged the people of the country. Specially, it was not unknown to the English rulers that the Muslim populace had not accepted the British rule and looked at it from any point between rejection and resistance. Before the great revolt of 1857, the British feared that the Muslims would revolt on the day of the Eid, Mohurrum or some such festival day. The British had also feared that through some secret channels of the society an alliance between the sepoys and the Faraizis had been formed. Surendranath Sen himself admitted that two famous personalities of Dhaka, Kalinarayan Choudhury and Mugal Aga Golam Ali, had announced openly that they would financially help the rebelling sepoys.

These facts are not new. After independence, when the Indian historians were writing books on the great revolt of 1857, these facts perhaps were not undiscovered. But probably under the stress of a colonial hangover they did not have the mental attitude to evaluate 1857 rightly in the light of these facts, to remove the nation and national history from the stained and soiled influence of the British viewpoint and present it fairly. Beneath this mental disinterestedness lies a strange indifference towards the nation and one's own country. Perhaps only Rajanikanta Gupta managed to be free from this disinterestedness and contempt. Surendranath Sen has written the official history of the great revolt of 1857. Michael Edwards in his book *Battles of the Indian Mutiny*[8] wrote in praise of this book : "There is no satisfactory modern history of the Mutiny, but that of the Indian historian S. N. Sen, '*Eighteen Fifty Seven*' (New Delhi, 1957), which is valuable for its attempt to free the story from the not unnatural bias of nineteenth century British writers." Does Mr. Edwards want that the Indians would write a history of the mutiny ? Not rebellion, not revolt, but simply mutiny ? Is he disgruntled because there is no satisfactory modern book on the mutiny ? In the first chapter of Mr. Edwards' book the start and the spread of the rebellion has been discussed. The name of this chapter is 'The Devil's Wind'. Therefore the aim of the person who has eulogised Surendranath Sen is clear. The title of the book of the Indian historian who has been praised so much eventually is *Eighteen Fifty Seven.* This title has no poignance, no significance save a digital expression denoting time. This expression indicates an indifference to everything the revolt stands for – mutiny, revolt or rebellion, uprising of the chiefs, participation of the people. Is this a middle way of avoiding the Indian viewpoint and of not refuting the British standpoint ? In English, do we call this viewpoint 'non-committal' ? At least, compared to this Rameshchandra Mazumdar has shown a lot of courage--he has named his book '*The Sepoy Mutiny and the Revolt of 1857.* His writings about the great revolt available in the book published by the Bharatiya Vidyabhavan is also called '*The Mutiny and the Revolt of 1857-58*'. At least mutiny and revolt - the parallel identity of two separate events, of the sepoys and the non-military public - the combatant and non-combatant humanity – could not be denied by him.

No one can deny the fact that the viewpoint of historians is clearly expressed through the titles given to their books by them. The book written on the rebellion of the *Sannyasis* by Jaminimohan Ghosh

[8] Michael Edwards' book was published in 1963. At page 207 he makes this observation.

in 1930 was titled *Sannyasi and Fakir Raiders in Bengal.* Jaminimohan perceived the *sannyasis* and *fakirs* as 'raiders'. Yet the uprising of the *sannyasis* and *fakirs* was a part of a greater movement of Bengal's history. That it was not a 'raid' or attack can be seen clearly if it is compared to the Maratha attack of the mid-eighteenth century. Another book was written later on the *Sannyasi* movement : its title is *The Sannyasi Rebellion*; its author is A. N. Chandra. The uprising of the downtrodden, hungry people against the tyranny of the British rule has been treated from such different and diverse angles by the two historians of our country. Their differences can be understood simply from the titles of their books. The *Sannyasis* broke down the secure base of the British rule in its formative years. Those who were shaded by the umbrella of the British rule would naturally consider these *Sannyasis* 'raiders'. The responsibility of the Indian historian does not end by applying connotative terms to those who try to turn the society upside down. 'Raiders', 'bandits', 'dacoits', 'marauders' and such terms have been applied to those who have been blamed over and over again as destroyers of the British peace. The British historians have not failed in their duty while composing history – they have constantly put the British rulers on alert and indicated the directions from which the empire seemed to be threatened. Behind whatever they wrote about India there was an aim – a mission. No one denies this fact nowadays. Otherwise why did they think so much about the great revolt of 1857 for the past 150 years ? It was the Indians who needed to be conscious about the event, but they were callous and indifferent to the event. The British have discovered the past of our nation, have provided the inspiration and matter for our nineteenth century renaissance, have awakened our love for the Sanskrit and other oriental literature – all these are facts of history and, therefore, true. But behind all these facts there is one question "why" ? The famous Bengali poet Buddhadeb Bose has given the answer to this :

"In fact, the number of books in European languages on Sanskrit are numerous, but equally rare amongst them is any vital literary comment, any insight into the poetry, any attempt to evaluate Sanskrit in the background of world literature....In totality it is true that in the works of the Sanskrit language the whites have not seen any literature like in Greek or Latin, no sensuous flavours, no creativity, -they have seen in it the ingredients of history etc., and a possible method of keeping the Indians servile by getting a clue about the Indian mind. The last remark, it goes without saying, is specially applicable to the English. The famous Wilson made English translation of *Meghdoot*; ....one understands, by reading his very readable notes, that his main aim was to render information about the geography, climate, birds and beasts, and flora of India, and in this topic letting his fellow-Britishers know that the people of India were not barbarians, they even understood the meaning of gratitude... Lieutenant Bouden, who donated the chair of Bouden Professorship to Oxford, clearly stated that he had established this post with the aim for the improvement of the translation of one Bible into the Sanskrit language 'so that his fellow-Britishers could advance in the work of converting the Indians into Christianity'. The first two men holding this post were very conscious and respectful about the founder's aim : the main criterion of appointing Wilson was the translation of some words from the Bible into Sanskrit by him; and Monier Williams did not forget to mention in the preface to his huge and noble book that the translator of the Bible got a lot of help from the first edition of his book. Of course all the writers are not vociferous about the spreading of Christianity, but no Britisher got intellectually involved in Indian matters –whether that was geology, anthropology, architecture, agriculture or grammar – unless he knew in his mind that his work was an integral part of the maintenance and spread of the empire.

–Buddhadeb Bose, *Kalidaser Meghdut*, (Meghdoot of Kalidasa), pp. 3-4.

This responsibility of the British was called by them 'the white man's burden' : The British historians have carried this burden when they wrote the history of the great revolt after the event had taken place. In 1874 – within two decades of the great revolt – the book *The Chuar Rebellion of 1799* by J. C. Price was published. The English historians had applied the nomenclature of 'rebellion' to all the Indian uprising. T. R. E. Holmes called the great revolt a 'civil rebellion'. He is perhaps the first historian who called the great revolt a 'rebellion' instead of a 'mutiny'. Yet the post-independence Indian historians suddenly put aside the terms like 'revolt', 'rebellion' etc. and why they took up words like 'insurrection; 'disturbance', 'unrest', etc. as terms much dearer to their heart cannot be comprehended. Let me give one or two examples :

1. *The Kol Insurrection of Chota-Nagpur* by Dr. Jagdish Chandra Jha.
2. *Unrest against British Rule in Bihar,* 1831-1859 by K. K. Dutta.
3. *The Santal Insurrection* by K. K. Dutta.
4. *Civil Disturbances Under British Rule 1757-1857* by S. B. Chaudhury.

An allegation by Shashibhusan Chaudhury is that in many places the historian Ramesh Majumdar, his teacher, has blindly followed Mr. Holmes.[9] But has he himself been able to come out of the influence of Mr. Holmes ? Holmes called the great revolt of 1857 a 'Civil Rebellion'. The title of Holmes's book is *A History of the Indian Mutiny and of the Disturbances which Accompanied it*! The titles of the two books by Shri Shashibhushan are, in order, *Civil Rebellion in the Indian Mutinies (1857-59)* and *Civil Disturbances During the British Rule in India (1765-1857).* Suprakash Roy while remembering of this last book wrote : "a famous professor and writer of our country has written about the history of the peasants' rebellion (1765-1857) and named the book '*Civil Disturbances*' and, in imitation of the English writers have called the rebellious peasants 'marauders', 'dacoits', 'murderers' and gave them other names. The thought processes of the writers can be recognised

[9] *See* S. B. Chaudhuri's *Theories of the Indian Mutiny*, pp. 10-11.

through such compositions. Their class-character and class-consciousness become clear. They want to write a history of the people, but distort their rebellious character".[10]

The main question, therefore, it seems, is the question of the viewpoint of historians. The great revolt of 1857 has never received any great sympathy from the educated Indians. The events of 1857 to them were a rebellion by sepoys and nothing else. This idea was mainly created by the Indians themselves. This is what Ramesh Chandra Majumdar says. He writes : "So far as available evidence goes, it was the Indians, and not the Englishmen of the time, who unanimously represented or misrepresented the outbreak as essentially a mutiny".[11] This statement is possibly incorrect. Sambhuchandra Mukherjee has written at the beginning of his *Native Fidelity* that it was in the July edition of *London Times* of 1857 that the military character of the great rebellion was first exposed. Sambhu Chandra wrote (p.1) : "It was the first English journal which spoke out upon the military character of the revolt..." Sambhu Chandra further stated that in the edition of April 1858 of the *Edinburgh Review* the uprising was called a 'Military mutiny'. He quotes from the said paper thus : "It was the general goodwill of the population which rendered the suppression of the military mutiny both practicable and beneficial." Was it then by absorbing the utterances made by the British that the Indian historians build up the theory of the sepoy mutiny ? From the Indian viewpoint the historicity of the great revolt boils down in the final analysis to one of 'native fidelity'. It expresses the servileness of the colonized Indian mind. This subservient Indian mind cannot be a guide to the historical intellect of Independent India.

[10] Suprakash Roy, *Bharater Krishak Bidroha O Ganatantrik Sangram* (Peasant Revolt of India and People's Democratic Struggle), 1st Part, p. 9. It is vital to note that S.B. Chaudhuri did not call the rebels marauders, dacoits etc. Such expressions occur in the works of his teacher Ramesh Chandra Majumdar. Suprakash Roy grouped them together.

[11]. R.C. Majumdar, *Sepoy Mutiny* etc., p.385.

While writing about the history of the great revolt of 1857 it is necessary to remember that at least two English historians – J. B. Norton (his book – *Topics for Indian Statesmen*) and Charles Raikes (his book –*Notes on the Revolt in North Western Province of India*) have stated clearly that the uprising of 1857 was actually a revolt on a large scale – not of the sepoys but of the people. Norton's book was printed in 1857, Raikes' book in 1858. Therefore, the opinions about the great uprising that were printed in the contemporary English newspapers were challenged by an alternative opinion provided to the Indians by English historians themselves. *A History of the Indian Mutiny* by T. R. Holmes was printed and published in 1904, almost five decades after the writings of Norton and Raikes. In this book he has clearly called the uprising a 'civil rebellion'. Thus it is seen that for almost five decades after the great revolt the British historians had been calling the events of 1857 a true upsurge by the people. They did not give any credence to the concept of a military mutiny so meticulously put forward by the contemporary newspapers. How the Indian historians suddenly became immersed in the ideas of a 'mutiny' cannot be explained. In the times contemporary to the uprising of 1857 one question was discussed over and over again in England. It is this : 'Is the unrest in India a military upheaval or a national revolt ? Is the behaviour of the soldier an outcome of sudden passion, or is it the outcome of a well-constructed conspiracy ?' Actually the first person to raise this question was Disraeli, and this question is the main point of Marxist thought process about the rebellion of 1857. Marx has raised this question of Disraeli in his own writings and has himself solved the question in this way : "...The present Indian upheaval is not a military upheaval, but a national revolt, of which the sepoys are only the active weapons".[12] The opinions expressed by eminent British historians like Kaye, Maleson, Duff, Ball etc. are practically indistinguishable from that of Disraeli and Marx.

[12] Karl Marx, "The Indian Question" 28 July, 1857 *The First Indian War of Independence, 1857-59.*

Amongst them at least two – Maleson and Duff -- have called the uprising of 1857, in order, 'revolt' and 'rebellion', and this is clear from the titles of their books -- *The Revolt in Central India* and *The Indian Rebellion, its causes and results, in a series of letters.* Alexander Duff's book was published in 1857. Maleson's book in 1908. The third and last part of Kaye's book was published in 1857. The date of publication of the book by Charles Ball is not known. On the whole it is clear that for almost five decades after 1858, the British historians were trying to make readers understand that the uprising of 1857 was not a narrow incident. From the abstracts used by Ramesh Majumdar from the writings of Norton and Duff this fact becomes even more clear. For example, Norton wrote : "It is true that some villagers proved friendly to the English refugees, but the general run of the story is a reverse of this." Taking a quote from a certain American observer, Norton writes : "The present rebellion in Oudh is eminently a National Rebellion". Mr. Duff had written : "It was not a military revolt but a rebellion or revolution which alone can account for the little progress hitherto made in extinguishing it."

Dr. Kalikinkar Dutta in his book *Reflections on the Mutiny* has given some impression as to how the historicity of the great revolt got built up in the consciousness of the people of countries other than those within the British empire. In the contemporary Russian public consciousness the uprising of 1857 was noted as a great rebellion, not as a sepoy mutiny. N. A. Dobrolyubov while writing in the pseudonym of N. Turchinov in September 1857 said that the Indian uprising could not be explained away by any single factor; it lay hidden in the entire history of India.[13] Dobrolyubov called this an unavoidable historical event – 'an event of historical inevitability'. Two statements by Dobrolyubov are full of gravity : one, the Indian populace had rebelled in its entirety of the *bhadralok*, the mentality of the *Babu* community. There was no spirit of rebellion in this mentality. There

[13] In Dobrolyubov's own words the causes lay 'not in one or other influential factor, but in the whole history of India'.

was servility whose symptomatic externalisation was Shambhu Chandra's *Native Fidelity*. The twenty-six years old Mangal Pandey rebelled against the British, and the eighteen years old Sambhu Chandra (he was born in 1839) wrote about the fidelity of the Indians. With unusual maturity this eighteen years old youth gathered the material for his book from almost nineteen newspapers and journals. Just at the same time another Bengali Dakshina Ranjan Mukhopadhyay tried to bring the Awadh landholders back to obedience to the British government. On 26th March of 1861 he established a body named 'Awadh British Indian Association' (according to some historians 'Oudh Taluqdars Association'). Sambhu Chandra was the Secretary to this body for sometimes. He edited the journal of this Association *Samachar Hindustani*. Therefore, his fidelity to the English is unquestionable. The book he writes under the dictates of this fidelity serves as an evidence of servility of the Indians to the English. It contains various accounts of how Indians helpful to the British were rewarded in many ways - starting from gold watches, gold chains, medals, cash rewards, swords, appellations and titles like *Rai Bahadur*, *Raja* etc., extra wages for some months, promotion at work, rights of possession on land, exemption from tax to the granting of *Jagirs* to devoted Indians. Sambhu Chandra discovered these surprising facts after much labour and much mental exercise. He quoted from the *Edinburgh Review* and *The London Times* at the beginning of his book only to show that the uprising of '57 was actually a military uprising by sepoys. If the Indians as a whole had not supported the British, he said, then the latter would not have been able to recapture their lost empire. The satisfaction that Sambhu Chandra felt at this recapturing of lost empire was expressed in the depth of his language : "[*The London Times*] attributed the salvation of the Indian Empire as a dependency of Great Britain to the fidelity, aid, and advice of the people of the country during the insurrection."[14] The viewpoint of a historian is often expressed through his language. Those who have read the writings of Jadunath Sarkar

[14] This excerpt is from R. K. Chakravarty (ed.) *Native Fidelity*.

or Lord Acton cannot deny this. The passion that Sambhu Chandra has shown about 'Native Fidelity' is not without reason. Bruce Norton had criticised, in sharp language, the so-called devotion of the Indians and specially the Bengalis, in his book *Topics for Indian Statesmen* and in his various writings in the journal *Madras Athaeneum*. At this time there was a talk in the English circles that the Bengalis had not adequately come forward to help the ruling forces at the time of their crisis. Sambhu Chandra understood that this allegation was very harmful for the Bengalis and so, to crack down Norton's accusation he wrote the complete text of a book. In the epilogue of that book he wrote : "We are sorry to observe that persons whose antecedents and known habits of thought give them claim to public attention, still acquiesce in the senseless cry raised at the height of the panic days, by a portion of the Calcutta Europeans, better known as the Leaguels, viz, that the quiet people of Bengal were the enemies of the Government, and that whatever loyalty they expressed or evinced was confined to words and never wooed action. Mr. Bruce Norton, we are mortified to find, echoes the same cry. His knowledge of the Indian matters, the just and generous spirit with which he used to treat of Indian subjects in the columns of the *Madras Athaeneum* and his accurate appreciation of the native races, their feelings and virtues indicated in his previous writing on India, fairly led us to hope for justice to the Indians at his hands, especially now when the mists which hitherto shrouded Indian questions, have been cleared away by the light of the sepoy revolution. But we have been disappointed. Mr. Norton, in his recent work entitled *Topics for Indian Statesmen* takes a most unjust view of the part which the people of Bengal played in that momentous drama. He denies that they were sincere in their expressions of loyalty and that they rendered any services to Government in its difficulty. We hope these pages will convince Mr. Norton that neither of his statements regarding the Bangalis is correct."

A long letter was published in the 12th February 1859 issue of the paper, *Indian Field*, blasting Mr. Norton's attempt to debase the

Bengalis in the eyes of the Government. Excerpts from Norton's writing were quoted in this letter. Norton's criticism of the Bengalis was refuted, the hostile attitude of the Government was criticised and the devotion of the Bengalis were praised. The whole thing ran like this.

Norton's statement of criticism : "I see a few nations here and there have offered us their hollow and cheap lip service, but where have they stood forward with their persons and their purses to help us at our extremity ? What instance is there of the Bengalis who insulted the English inhabitants of Calcutta ...They have shared in no peril, they have volunteered no services, they have not lent us their cattle...and expressions of loyalty, after the fall of Delhi, may be as good policy as they are racy of expression. But the truth is that these memorials and addresses (which were put forward by the Bengalees) are the merest sham conceivable."

An excerpt from the letter in praise of the Bengalis : "...as regards the loyalty of the Bangalees, we have no hesitation in asserting that Mr. Norton is entirely wrong : they did come forward with their cattle, and if they had not we should not have been able to have procured one single hackery in spite of fifty Impressment Acts."

The accusation against the English and other Europeans : "What did the Calcutta Europeans do ? Their loyalty of course cannot be questioned. Did they come forward with their carriage-horses for the guns, or their spare hacks for the cavalry : we never heard that they did, although they talked considerably about doing so".[15]

This letter helps in a special way to understand the Bengali society and the psyche of the Bengali race in times contemporary to the great revolt. Mr. Norton and many other Englishmen like him did not believe that the Bengalies were at a distance from the rebellion.

[15] *See* R. K. Chakravarty (ed.) *Native Fidelity*, pp. 173-74 and Promod Ranjan Sengupta, *Neel Bidroha O Bangali Samaj* (the Indigo Revolt and the Bengali Society).

The English also had a doubt about the unquestionable devotion of the Bengalis to the British cause. In that case how did Indian historians over the last hundred and fifty years take it for granted that there was no atmosphere for rebellion at all in Bengal ? It is clear from their writings that historians like Duff, Norton and others did not look upon the Indians of the time of the great revolt with much respect. The contemporary intellectual Bengalis became busy either refuting the opinions of Duff and Norton, or following the cry of contemporary English papers and magazines to call the uprising a mutiny of the sepoys. In all this, the general Indian viewpoint got lost.

From Sambhu Chandra to Syed Ahmed, all the Indian historians were successful in upholding the theory of collaboration with the English. The result of this was that in the later generations the idea became rooted in the people's minds that side by side with the sepoy mutiny and the people's revolt there was active collaboration taking place. In later years the British marked this collaboration as a service of a race of devoted servants. The Indians were the sepoys in the British army. These sepoys fought against the British. Again at a later time it was these sepoys who helped to let the British Empire survive. Not only the gun-bearing sepoys, but the general Indians at large had given every possible service including immense physical labour to the English army. They served the army and the officials in every way and built up a system of support without which the external success of the British would not have been achieved. The glitters of the prosperous British Empire was fuelled by the drops of the Indian blood. Perhaps the British were not ungrateful. Therefore, they in later years remembered the devotion of these ignorant, dim and dumb servants and said : ' The reforms that followed the mutiny left one factor basically unchanged : the British still depended for this power upon native soldiers. In fact, they could not have defeated the rebels without them. Before Delhi, for example, out of 11,200 effectives, no fewer than 7,900 were Indians. Even if the British had not had the service of loyal sepoys, they could not have moved an inch without the vast army of non-combatants -- of whom there were 20 to every white soldier. Indians cooked the food, Indians brought water, and Indians carried the wounded away from the battlefield. Though the British could not do without the native portion of their Indian army, and despise its gallant performance in the two world wars, never again would they wholly trust it."[16]

The matter of regret is this that inspite of rendering all the service of devoted servants, the Indians could not win the hearts of the British. When they could not, they turned about. The collaboration did not survive any more. Michael Edwards writes very sorrowfully : "The next rebellion was to come from neither the soldiers nor the princes, but from the middle classes who, in 1857, supported the British and though their revolt took longer it was they who 90 years after the Mutiny were to be successful in making Britain give up her Indian empire."[17]

Even if the newly awakened middle class supported the English in the great uprising of 1857, what role did the other classes within the people take ? What role did the tribes like Gujars, Ranghars etc. play ? Sambhu Chandra called them 'professional plunderers'.[18] Ramesh Ch. Majumdar referred to them as 'The goonda elements and those professional classes who were accustomed to live by plunder'.[19] Actually the settled classes of the society had always thought of the under-privileged people as lowly and terrible. An attack by these under privileged ones had shaken up the self-complacency of the well-established people of the upper ranks. This is clear in Sambhu Chandra's accounts : "It converted the crusade of the sepoys against

[16] Michael Edwards, *Battles of the Indian Mutiny*, 1963, p. 202.

[17] Michael Edwards, *op. cit.*, p. 197.

[18] *Native Fidelity*, p.27.

[19] Ramesh Chandra Majumdar in *The British Paramountcy and the Indian Renaissance*, Part I, p. 497.

Europeans and Christians into a crusade against the wealth and property of the landholders.[20] Did the revolt against foreign rule suddenly take on the characteristic of a class war ? No historian of India did touch on this point.

If the above discussion is accepted, then two questions appear with profound dimensions : 1. Did only the feudal lords and their vassals take part in the rebellion ? 2. Who were they who opposed the rebellion -- were they only the middle class -- the Indian bourgeoisie ? Until these two questions are fully answered it is impossible to discuss the genuine nature of the great rebellion of 1857. The resources that the present writer has can motivate a discussion of the first question, but not the second. Therefore this chapter will end with the discussion of the first question only.

Manabendra Nath Roy has given a very short yet sharp answer to the first question. He wrote that the rebellion of 1857 was a reaction of the Indian feudal system against commercial capitalism. The flames of reaction from Indian feudalism were lit up for the last time in 1857 before it was finally extinguished. He wrote : "The last vestiges of feudal power were shattered by the failure of the revolution of 1857, which is known as the Sepoy Mutiny. The revolution of 1857 was nothing but the last effort of the dethroned feudal potentates to regain their power. It was a struggle between the worn-out feudal system and the newly introduced commercial capitalism for political supremacy".[21]

Manabendra Nath was thinking of the Talukdars or landholders of Awadh and the rebellion of some royal personages who had lost their power. No doubt Manabendra Nath knew a lot of what he was writing about but perhaps two facts did not reflect in his consciousness : one, the people who were gathered behind the landholders of Awadh were all marginal men – middling, and landless

[20] *Native Fidelity*, p. 27.

[21] M. N. Roy, *India in Transition*, p. 20.

peasants and people off their classes. Two, the Jagirdars of Punjab had also been stripped of their property, but they had not rebelled. Therefore the loss off property that Manabendra Nath is hinting at through the expression "dethroned" is not sufficient to explain the people's uprising in 1857. In this context, we put forward another view, the opinion of Jagdish Raj : "The taluqdars and the small cultivators both took part in the rising. It has been argued that the taluqdars were discontented with the land policy of Dalhousie and so rebelled. But as Innes (*Lucknow and Oudh in the Mutiny*) points out, the taluqdars did not join in the Mutiny until September (1857). Moreover, it is hard to see why, when the jagirdars of the Punjab failed to rebel, though stripped off their possessions, the taluqdars of Oudh, who had been but lightly hit and had been reassured about the Government's intentions by Sir Henry Lawrence, should have risen. In the event, the taluqdars, while they could, remained passively friendly to the British officials. It was the belief that the British cause was hopeless that led the taluqdars openly to rebel".[22]

It is not correct to say that only the feudal lords rebelled. In some places, for example, in Awadh, the feudal lords and peasants rebelled together against the English. In some areas the marginal men, the Gujars and Ranghars rebelled against the landlords. The two rebellions blended together inseparably. How many Indian historians have explained that the class revolts and revolts for Independence had been carried out simultaneously and at many places were concurrent and overlapping phenomena. Was it correct when Manabendra Nath described the great rebellion of 1857 as the last attempt of the dethroned royalty to maintain its power ? Was the revolutioin at any level only the last attempt to maintain power ? At least in Manabendra's writings the alternative use of the word 'revolution' instead of 'revolt' or 'rebellion' will be noted by conscious readers. What was really a 'revolution' – the attempt to possess power

[22] Jagadish Raj, *The Mutiny and British Land Policy in North India 1856-1886*, p. 170

only ? The author is silent on this point. Given this any, a sensitive historian today is faced with the questions : what was really a revolution in the context of the time – the revolts of the chiefs or the uprisings of the peasants ? The mutiny of soldiers and the support they got from the people or the surfacing of the denizens of law-breaking societies to curve out a new way of life ? Or was it the ultimate collapse of a gigantic upsurge contrasted against the collaboration of the gentry that was revolutionary ? Neither Manabendranath nor others did answer these questions.

It is clear from the above discussion that there is little exaggeration or hyperbole in the history written about the great revolution. Truly speaking what exists around its study were gaps and lacuna. Those who have researched the great rebellion have mainly viewed the ground from the sky. In their writings the main characters are the nobility, the privileged and titled people, the taluqdars and men in their retinue. The topic of their writings have been Bahadur Shah II, or Nana Saheb, Rani of Jhansi, Tantia Tope or some such prominent personalities. Perhaps no one except Shashibhusan Chaudhuri has been able to descend from the sky to the grassroot level of the soil. At least the way in which Shashibhusan has explained the background of the Indian uprising from a hundred years before the great rebellion is unique in its own way. But unfortunately he did not use his unique research faculties to explain the rebellion at its source. Instead of doing that he wrote books on the English historians and diverted his trend of research towards historiography. Somewhere there persists an indifference of the Indian historians to the great Indian uprising of 1857. O'Malley, in his *District Gazetteer, Bankura* (p.41) says that at the time of the great revolt the threat of an uprising by the Santhals and the Chuars at Bankura kept the British in a state of mental unrest. Mr. Kaye in his book (second part, p. 11) has given the news of the revolt at Kolkata. It is said in O'Malley's *District Gazetteer, Nadia* (p.32) that getting the news of revolt at Behrampur, the entire Jessore Division had been filled with an atmosphere of unrest. Mr. Norton openly criticised that the Bengalies had not helped the English at the time of the great rebellion. Not only Norton, but many English historians acknowledge the fact that in 1857-58, it was not at all easy for the government to get transport, resource, labour from Bengal. Bengal certainly did not rise in revolt. But there were signs of a disjuncture in the pattern of collaboration that had so long formed the primary theme of life in relations between the Empire and its subjects. In this disjunctures sensible historians should try to find Bengal's role marked by a tangential involvement in the revolt.

13

The Bengali Psyche and the Revolt

It seems strange that in 1857 the uprising in the army started in Bengal but it did not overcast the province itself. The official historian of the revolt Surendra Nath Sen writes that though the sepoys rebelled in various places of Bengal the local populace did not support it. Till to-day this statement has not been challenged in a big way and no research work has come out to prove it totally false. Promode Ranjan Sengupta has proved with undeniable evidence that there was an atmosphere of rebellion in Bengal. But why a full-fledged outburst did not take place he did not explain. Sukumar Mitra has shown that the influence of the great rebellion left its mark on the contemporary Bengali literature. But he too has not been able to prove adequately as to how the country where a general rebellion could not totally influence public consciousness had enough powerful influence on its literature. Just as there was the Indigo rebellion in Bengal so we got *Nildarpan* (the Mirror of the Blue). But no such major work of literature had been composed in Bengali literature which can claim to have mirrored the great rebellion. *Nildarpan* was composed just at the time when the Indigo rebellion took place. This rebellion occurred in 1859-60 and *Nildarpan* was published from Dhaka in 1860. But neither before nor after the great revolt, not even within a decade of it, was any book composed in Bengali literature that may be said to have contained in a big way the shadow of this historical event.

In Bengali literature, the revolt synchronised with the period of

Michael Madhusudan Dutt and Bankim Chandra Chattopadhyay. Mudhusudan returned to his country from Madras in 1856. It was his home-coming – as if he had fled back home. In the words of Shivnath Shastri : "…..(he) again ran back to his country." A failure in an alien land, he returned to his own land and Shivnath Shastri has these words for Mudhusudan : "But alas on returning to his country what a change did he see ! ...In the stage of the New Bengal a new set of leaders had arrived; their behaviours were of a different kind." In this changed atmosphere, what did Madhusudan write ? Varied were his writings, starting from the play *Sharmistha* in 1858 to *Padamabati, Ekei Ki Baley Sabhyata* (Is it a civilization we call ?) to *Buro Shaliker Gharey Ro* (Idiosyncracies of an old *Shalik*. *Shalik* is a bird). In the meantime the '57 revolt and the Indigo rebellion had become events of the past. Mudhusudan wrote "Tilottama Sambhab Kavya" – in 1860, the year in which Dinabandhu's *Nildarpan* was published. To a romantic poet the contemporary times were very harsh. In 1862 he "set out for England in order to be a barrister". So wrote Shivnath. Then came the age of Bankim Chandra. In 1864 *Durgeshnandini* (Daughter of the Lord of the Castle) was published. After that came *Kapalkundala* – "the brush that had painted the visually attractive softness of *Durgeshnandini* now created successfully the serious mood of *Kapalkundala*. People were filled with wonder." This was the simple and rare mental attitude of the Bengali, the attitude which mixes strangeness and beauty to create the illusion of romanticism. This then was the post '57 dream-world of Madhusudan and Bankim Chandra. How much of the rebellious Bengal did exist in the middle of the 1860s – the decade of Bankim's influences noted by Shivnath Shastri ? Rather, the influence of Dinabandhu, Shivnath observes, shows the atmosphere of rebellion visible in Bengal at the outset of 1860s : "...the play *Nildarpan* appeared in the end part of 1860. It was as if suddenly there was a meteoric fall in the field of Bengali society. Who presented this play and from where, nobody had any knowledge. Whether this play followed the show rules of ancient plays, could not be judged as there was no time for it; there was no time available to find out whether the incidents were all true. *Nildarpan* simply enveloped our consciousness. Torap grabbed our love. Our blood became heated at Kshetramoni's sorrow; we started thinking that if only we could get Mr. Rague once, then, even if we had no weapons we would have torn him up into pieces with our teeth." (*Ramtanu Lahiri*, etc., p.224).

The consciousness that grew for indigo, was not a political consciousness but a social consciousness. The social consciousness that had started from the time of Rammohan Roy had kept Bengal in its grip for almost five decades. Social progress and economic establishment – these were then the main aims of the Bengali middle class. That is why the Bengali middle class wanted understanding and co-operation with the British - in a word 'collaboration'. The social movement of 19th century Bengal had been built on the model of the English, under their patronage with their collaboration. The Bengali middle class believed that this collaboration would help to establish their economic stability. The political consciousness that was the inner cause of the great rebellion of 1857 was contradictory to this philosophy of self-establishment. Consequently the Bengali middle class of that time did not have the courage to integrate itself to the cause of an upheaval. Therefore, to prove that the Bengalis had no role in the rebellion, in the year 1858 two Bengalis - Kishori Chand Mitra and Shambhu Chandra Mukhopadhyay (according to other opinions Krishna Das Pal) - behind the pseudonym 'Hindu' wrote two books, whose objective was to prove that the Hindu Bengali middle class was in no way involved with the rebellion. Was then the great rebellion of 1857 the work of the Muslims alone? Why then the pseudonym 'Hindu'? The mentality that the Hindus were aloof from the rebellion was not only contemporary, many later Hindus could not be free of that attitude. On the other hand, the Muslims tried to prove that the great rebellion of '57 was actually the work of anti-social, lower class people. In this view the leadership was given to the Muslim educated society by Sayed Ahmed Khan, the leader of the U.P. intelligentsia. To protect themselves from the fury of the rulers who were wounded and angered by the rebellion the Hindus appealed to the ruling power : "It is well known, Your Excellency's Lordship, that we, the Bangalees, are a cowardly people" (Charles Ball, *History of Indian Mutiny*, vol. I, p. 612). Between those who vociferously begged the pardon of the ruling power, and those who stayed silent and inactive as spectators, there was basically no difference.

However much we may deny it today, to the contemporaries it was not unknown that on the whole the Bengalis were a race of collaborators. "The Bengalis are the right hand of the English – the key to their lockers, the diamond on their ring, the salt in their cooking" – and probably somewhat more than that – "The Bengalis are the spies and the secret counsellors of the English". (Quoted in Sukumar Mitra's *1857 O Bangladesh*, p. 23). A certain Bengali has unhesitatingly admitted this. The great rebels of North India knew this and so their slogan was "Beat, catch, tie up Bengalis". The Bengali middle class could not avoid the fear of persecution in the hands of the up-country people. It was therefore difficult for them to side with the rebels. They had gathered in them a sense of superiority and its exuberance acquired from Western education. With superiority came impetuosity. From impetuosity was born an impatience towards fetters and an urge to break down traditional ways of life. This was a special characteristic of the Bengali mental attitude in the middle of the nineteenth century. Rammohan, Vidyasagar, and the men of the *Young Bengal* tried to break down the traditional and conservative social norms of life in Bengal. This attempt was made by the members of the Brahmo Samaj too. In literature there was the eagerness to break away from the fetters of refined but rigid Sanskrit syntaxes that governed Vidyasagar's sophisticated language. There was also the anxiety to turn away from the rustic, crude and unsophisticated language of Pyarichand Mitra and Radhanath Sikdar. Or else the attempt was to go to the use of blank verse by breaking up the inflexible structures of Sanskrit rhymes that fashioned Bengali verses. All this was the reflection of the social impatience of being fettered. But unfortunately, this anti-fetter consciousness of Bengal was applied to one agendum only, namely, from start to finish the freedom of women. There was the eager plea to revive and rehabilitate the down-trodden captive feminine identity, the 'Captive Lady' so to say. Through the *sutee*, the widow-remarriage, movements against *kulin* polygamy and many other movements this single agendum was implemented. This plea was made by men with the co-operation of the English in an attempt to re-establish their social fortune and refashion their drab family life. The Permanent Settlement established peace and Western education promoted aspiration in the social psyche. Anarchy being expunged from social life effective conditions were created for the Renaissance. Consequently like the Renaissance poet Dante the Renaissance-struck Bengali manhood wanted the Beatrice of Bengal, who would overcome the stereotypes of garden house, *nautch*-girls, the charms of mistresses, the trash culture of Iswar Gupta, and feminine frolics to become a real woman whose touch would satisfy the scorched mind of the male. Could the regenerated Bengali manhood remain confined only in the fort of the flesh,–Could remain dazed in the feminine sensuousness ? What woman did he long for once he broke the bodily fetters of a soul-less woman ? In the entire social consciousness of Bengal there was this plea for a new woman – the idyll not of femininity but of womanhood. The *Leelavatis* or the frolic companions of the past now yielded place to the *Padmavatis*, the lotus playmates held in admiration and love in this age; the dolls of the interior, the housewives of that bygone age now became the *Sharmisthas*, the accomplished women of this age. This consciousness of the transforming woman in the inner self became more impressive in the later years. "What the mother was like, and what has she become ?" Bankim Chandra in his novel *Anandamath* thus tried to implant this image of a transforming motherland in the mind of the people. The transforming woman suddenly becomes an icon of worship – the mother. The adored figure of a woman in Bengali literature and philosophy was now mixed and blended into the consciousness of the nation, the end result of which was *Bande Mataram* which was both a philosophy and slogan. The woman who was the target of men's lust and an object of his enjoyment was brought back from the jaws of death by Rammohan, and Vidyasagar rehabilitated her in life. Bankim Chandra transformed her popular form into the idyll of contemplation, an object of the ideal search. This ideal force became an inexorable quest in the context of the time eternal *Mahakal* and so became the 'Mahakali' worshipped by revolutionists. This is the neat summary of the transformed social consciousness of the nineteenth century Bengali male psyche.

The emancipation of women is a desired and progressive movement for any country. Perhaps its felicity could have been preserved by doing away with the exaggerations. But the emotion of the educated Bengali fell like a cataract and overcast all social consciousness so that the logic of this movement was lost. This trend of feminism was increasing a short time before the great revolt of '57. In the month of *Agrahayan* of 1856 a friend of Iswarchandra Vidyasagar, Shrishchandra Bidyaratna, married a widow. Undoubtedly the mind of the educated Bengali became immersed in the thoughts of changing society and stayed out of politics. At the same time as feminism increased the sensuous Bengali leapt into a dramatic movement. "At that time (1856-57) there was a famous theatre belonging to the English in the city. Many educated and wealthy people of the country went there to see the acting. After seeing it, they would bemoan the fact that there was no such theatre belonging to us (i.e. the natives)" (*Ramtanu Lahiri,* etc., p. 233). "In the meantime in the year 1854 the 'Oriental Theatre' was established at the Oriental Seminary building. There the educated society of the country took to an abundance of English acting. Acting at the theatre became an obsession. The boys and youths of schools made their own groups and started small presentations of Macbeth and other performances" (*Ramtanu Lahiri,* etc., p. 203,. All renderings into English ours). Before the great revolt of '57 this was the second urge that made the Bengalis anti-politics. In 1857, the year of the great revolt a wealthy man of Simla Chhatubabu patronised the enactment of the play 'Sakuntala' by Kalidasa. After this under the patronage of the royal family of Paikpara a theatre was established at Belgachhia. The Bengali, so long enmeshed in the drudgery of social reforms, now got an exposure to entertainment. The Bengali became even more anti-politics.

The person who influenced the Bengalis just before 1857 was the poet Iswar Chandra Gupta. Shivnath Shastri has noted what his influence was : "Gradually poets who imitated Iswar Chandra made their appearances in the country; and a new age started in Bengalis literature. Just as today young, old, men, women whoever writes poetry does it in the style of Rabindranath, similarly whoever held the pen to write poetry would, consciously or unconsciously, mould it after Iswar Chandra. In the twinkling of an eye, there emerged his disciples, their followers, branches and tributaries that together imitated Iswar Chandra and formed a community of poets. Amongst those disciples the composer Sudhiranjan, Dinabandhu Mitra, Harimohan Sen, Rangalal Bandopadhyay and Manomohan Bose had obtained fame and prosperity at later time." (*Ramtanu Lahiri,* etc., pp. 207-8). Such a figure as Iswar Chandra Gupta published a paper named *Pashanda Piran* (the taming of the rogue) shortly before the great revolt. Shivnath said about *Pashanda Piran* : "The work of that *Pashanda Piran* became mainly to revile and to carry out a poet's war with *Rasaraj*, a paper published by Gourishankar Tarkavagish, the editor of the paper *Bhaskar.* At that time there were battles of poets on a regular basis in the cultural arena of Bengal and to carry that war into the field of literature was the main aim of these two papers. We feel ashamed to remember how uncultured, unmannerly the statements and reports they were. Due to this such an uncultured stream was unleashed in Bengali literature, as in bad taste cannot be seen in the story of any other country." (*Ramtanu Lahiri,* etc., p. 208). "It is fortunate that the people of the country rebuked this immediately. There was a negative reaction everywhere. The battle of the poets stopped." (*Ibid.,* p. 227). Perhaps because of this negative reaction in their hearts, at this time "The educated people felt an aversion to read Bengali newspapers or write in Bengali. Those amongst them who wanted to publish newspapers, did so in English". *(Ibid.)* The main point is that Bengali newspapers of that age did not have enough maturity to deal in political discussions. Whatever maturity existed belonged only to English newspapers. How many people knew English ? And they had accepted the establishment of orders provided by the English as heavenly peace. Those who became vocal about the Indigo tyranny were not writing being moved by the plight of the peasants. Actually they had an exaggerated idea about the concept of British justice. They felt that this British justice was being endangered by the atrocities of the *Indigo sahebs.* When Burke criticised Hastings he had this concept of British justice before his eyes. Dadabhai Naoroji also acknowledged this British justice when he wrote his *Poverty and un-British Rule in India.* So there is no way in which we should think that the Bengalis excited about Indigo were very politically conscious.

It is seen from the above discussion that amongst all the attitudes seen just before the great upheaval, none can be clearly termed political. The Bengali middle class, specially the D'Rozio group, were commended on for their political and social outlooks in the '*Englishman*' in May 1836. It was memorable statement indeed. "In matters of Political, they are all radicals, and are followers of Benthamite principles.... They think that toleration ought to be practised by every Government....with respect to the question relating to political economy they all belong to the school of Adam Smith." Had political consciousness created any awareness in the public mind on the eve of the Revolt ? If there had been an urge for politics then how did Keshab Chandra Sen, a graduate from the Hindu College in 1856 and an undisputed leader of the Bengali youth in the decade of the 1870s involve himself in social reforms and progressive feminist movements instead of taking to politics as his career ? Actually it does not seem that political consciousness came to Bengal before the decade of the 1870s. In trying to analyse how that political consciousness came and due to whose influence it came, Shivnath Shastri writes : "In 1874 on one hand Ananda Mohan Bose returned from England; on the other hand at the time or slightly later Surendra Mohan (Nath) Bandopadhyay came and settled in Calcutta after being retrenched from work. They both started working amongst the students. Thousands upon thousands of youth ran forth to hear their words, and the desire for uplift and patriotism became great in myriad hearts; it was as if the youths turned their backs upon the Brahmo Samaj and turned their faces towards politics and the betterment of the nation" (*Ramtanu Lahiri,* etc., p. 274). The Bengali middle class had not turned their faces towards 'politics and the betterment of the nation' two decades before this. Movements of feminism, enthusiasm about the theatre, an excess of anti-political thoughts and a return to the past in literature or a tendency to go against contemporary incidents in the way in which '*Nildarpan*' was consciously contemporary – all this had created a mental atmosphere in Bengal which prevented the immediate and direct effect of the great revolt from falling on Bengal of the time. Bengal was truly apolitical when the revolt took place. It, therefore, was indifferent to the passing blast which the revolt was.

14

The Sepoy Aspect of the Revolt

The revolt of 1857 is a past event in Indian History. But its memory is living in Indian consciousness. This is because it occurred over almost half of the Indian subcontinent. In its spread, depth and mass involvement such a huge rebellion had not occurred any time before. In this sense it was a millennial event in Indian history. The area where this event took place is the entire north and central part of India. If we draw a tangential line from Assam to Maharashtra through Bengal, the north of that line could with certainty be identified with the field of this rebellion. It has not been decided through research how much of the waves of rebellion reached the south of that line.

People's uprisings and mutinies of soldiers do not often go together. When they go they do become formidable. Mutinies had rare antecedents in pre-colonial India. But under the colonial rule there were too many of them. The Mutinies of '57 had their immediate precursor in the Barrackpore mutiny of 1824. The latter mutiny had its ancestor in the south – the Vellore mutiny of 1806. This mutiny like any other mutiny in colonial India was also a social rebellion for it expressed the anger of a segment of the society – peasants in uniform. Hence this mutiny was not at all a small event. The Indian sepoys were frightened because new rules were formed in the army.

They were seized with an unknown fear – the fear of losing their caste and religion. They had other provocation too. Some members of the exiled royal family of Mysore were held nearby. At this the Indian sepoys got enraged. Their national feeling stirred up. They rebelled. English historians do not admit the significance of this mutiny. William Bentinck was then the Governor of Madras. He had to resign on account of his failure to handle the mutiny. This shows how great the mutiny was. A Governor surrendered his power under its impact. No Governor resigned after the sepoy mutiny of 1857. But together with the uprising of the people it swept away the rule of the East India Company itself. The uprising of the people showed that the content of the British rule was corrupt while the mutiny of soldiers showed that its foundation was weak. Since the sepoy mutiny had shattered the base of the Company's rule we feel that our primary concern should be to understand the sepoy aspect of the sepoy mutiny. The real force of the 1857 revolt came from the sepoys.

In 1857 the total strength of soldiers of the East India Company in India was 2,38,000. Of these 38000 were European soldiers – the rest were all Indian. Each Presidency had its own army. Amongst them, so goes the English opinion – only the soldiers of the Bengal Presidency staged the uprising. Percival Spear said : "Each Presidency had its own army and it was only that of Bengal which was seriously affected". The tone suggests that if one Presidency had a movement the tremor of that did not reach other Presidencies. We must remember that much before the sepoy mutiny of Bengal Presidency in 1857, there was the mutiny of the Madras Presidency in 1806. The Madras Presidency thus gave the lead to the Bengal Presidency in a major army uprising. Any way, the Bengal soldiers – in Government parlance the Bengal Army – had a soldier strength of 1,51,000 of which 23000 were European soldiers. Of this strength of European army a large section – at least 1300 soldiers – were then in Punjab, beside the Sutlej river. This means, says Percival Spear, that between Meerut and Bengal there was no European army (that belonged to the Bengal Presidency) – only some soldiers were there at Dinapur and Patna. Because of the Crimean and the Persian Wars these soldiers had been withdrawn from the Indian territory. Almost all English historians in recent years have presented this picture of military vacuum in the whole of North India. The aim of this is to serve one purpose – to prove that the uprising of '57 was staged in a military vacuum, where there was no European defence. So there is nothing to say much in praise about the efforts of the Indian sepoys.

We must remember that there are various stages in the explanations of history. Behind the direct analysis lie many indirect and unpronounced insinuations. The talk of lack of defence of north India in the primary stage of the revolt is one such insinuation. If such insinuations are allowed to carry on to any length the gravity of the great event then fades in readers' mind. When Percival Spear revised *The Oxford History of India* of Vincent Smith and set himself to re-write it in the third edition, he accomplished this work of effacing the seriousness of the '57 uprisings. This he did with great skill. He was not the only one skillful in this. There are two other historians who formed partnership with him – Edward Thompson and G. T. Garratt (The title of their book is *Rise and Fulfilment of British Rule in India*). They sought to expunge from their writings the seriousness of all the events of 1857 so that the mutiny of the sepoys and the revolt of the people are left with no significance at all. They say that difficult fights were staged during the years of 1857-58 – some were exciting and horrible. But they were all on a small scale. This was the domestic affair of the English, very circumscribed and scattered. No English port was attacked, no foreign power was involved. On the contrary much help was received from foreigners. Afghanistan, under the leadership of Dost Mohammad, remained neutral. Nepal allowed the Gurkhas to join the army and the British defence army became powerful by a generous addition of Gurkhas to the force. Also, a Nepalese force under the leadership of Nepalese

Minister Jung Bahadur had joined Sir Colin Campbell near Lucknow. None of the border tribes had rebelled – they were keeping a watch as to what the result of the sepoy rebellion would be internally. Most importantly, within the British Empire this rebellion spread to less than one third of its area -- over two thirds of the area, that is the greater part of the Empire had not been touched by the rebellion.

These are all observations made by British historians who have been named above. Their aim is to show the rebellion of '57 in a less powerful light. No incident in history can be totally unstained bright. The sepoy rebellion of '57 was similarly not so. But there was in this rebellion something else – a speed which was intolerant of limitations. It cannot be denied that this sepoy uprising was strengthened by the gathering of various levels of people from society. Thompson and Garratt have admitted that at the time of the rebellion the ruler of Persia had sent an emissary to Bahadur Shah II at Delhi. The historian Ramesh Chandra Majumdar who saw this rebellion as devoid of significance could not however deny that ultimately this rebellion became uncontrollably sweeping at places where the huge participation of the people took place. If someone calls the uprising of '57 merely a sepoy mutiny instead of great rebellion of the people, even then the glory of this event does not fade. When we use the term sepoy rebellion we tend to forget that the Indian sepoys were mainly peasants, the agriculture-oriented humanity of villages. Much before the revolt of '57, during the whole span of the second half of the eighteenth century peasant rebellions pervaded the Indian landscape. We must understand the revolt of 1857 against the background of these peasant uprisings.

The three English historians named above had not attached much importance to the uprising of the sepoys. Their point is that out of three regional armies only one army rebelled. It is doubtful whether even one fourth of the total army took up arms against the British Empire. From the report that we get of Delhi and elsewhere, it is seen that as soon as the rebellion started, many sepoys of the rebel army ran away to the villages. Those who joined the uprising raised the banner of rebellion at Meerut. Then the sepoys raised the cry "Onward to Delhi" and journey towards Delhi started. At that time in the whole of India there was not 40,000 active British forces. Just before the start of the rebellion, the total of British soldiers in India was 45,552. Amongst them were the non-combatant services and the invalids. Besides them there were the Indian forces whose total strength was 2,32,224. The bulk of these were the sepoys. When Havelock started on his march to capture Lucknow, under him there were only 2000 soldiers. Clive stood on the field of Plassey with more soldiers than this. The English forces were mostly absent, or even if present, they were in very small numbers and were totally unprepared. This means that -- the sepoys operated in vacuum.

This view of English historians should be read along with the views of Premangsu Bandopadhyay. His book is *Tulsi Leaves and the Ganges Water : The Slogan of the First Sepoy Mutiny at Barrackpore 1824*. There he has shown that within the first hundred years of colonial rule in India there were intermittent sepoy rebellions which created a tradition of restlessness and revolt among Indian soldiers. That tradition, he says, is as follows :

From 1764 to 1892 The Small Rebellions within the Northern and Southern Sepoys of the Company

Year	Place	Indian force
1764	Barrackpore 9M	Bengal Native Infantry
1788*	Pallam Kotta	Madras Native Infantry
1781	Vizagapatnam	Madras Native Infantry
1784	Ami	Madras Native Infantry
1785	Arcot	Madras Native Infantry
1796	Madras	Madras Native Infantry
1797	Walahazabad	Madras Native Infantry
1812	Quilon	Madras Native Infantry

*1788 comes before 1781 in the tables given in the source book.

It is to be noted that the sepoy revolt of 1806 in Vellore has not been given a place in this table. Because according to Bandopadhyay that was the first large scale rebellion in South India – "the first major mutiny.......in South India". This theory is totally opposite to the opinion presented by Percival Spear. Not only that, in Barrackpore also there were some more small rebellions after 1764 which Bandopadhyay has referred to as "other minor mutinies". We must remember that in the armed forces of the British Empire the revolt of the native soldiers was not an Indian phenomenon only. From the research of the historian James (L. James, *Mutiny in the British Armed Forces 1797-1956*, London, 1987) we get to know that in India and Africa there had been repeated revolts by soldiers in the regions ruled by the British and racial enmity -- the arrogance of colour and the audacity of rule – were the reasons for these rebellions. Everywhere these rebellions by soldiers were mercilessly suppressed and beaten to dust. As a result there were terrible bloodshed, humanity was cut up into pieces by the sharp edge of tyranny. This was followed by the unfailing and gracious consolation given by British justice. In India and outside repeatedly through the failed mutinies of soldiers was revealed the violent side of British rule, which has been referred to by historians as "The autocratic white supremacy over the native troops". Nimai Sadhan Bose, in a researched book *Racism, Struggle for Equality and Indian Nationalism* said that the greatest factor behind the rise of nationalism was racism of the British. Premangsu Bandopadhyay wrote that racism and the self-assumed importance on the part of the white men were the main reason for the deterioration of the relationship between the Company and the sepoys. Yet the English historians have been saying for centuries that the sepoys had rebelled because they shrank from the act of biting with their teeth cartridges which had the fat of cows and pigs, and also from fear of crossing the *Kalapani* (i.e. making sea voyages, and losing their castes.) They wanted to avoid going to foreign lands to fight the aliens in uncertain fields. None of those who have researched on the history of the sepoys – Barat, Mason, Heathcote and others –

mentioned racism as the cause of the sepoy rebellion.* Religion was certainly at the surface of all tensions of the sepoys. Racism was at the fathomless interior of the sepoy agony – an invisible bottomless excitement it was. Therefore, the inner trembling of every rebellion spread from place to place. The influence of the Vellore rebellion of 1806 reached Nandidurga and Bangalore. Under its influence the next year 450 Muslims rebelled in Pallamuta, Wallazahabad and Sankaradurga. The news spread in the English circles that these sepoys rebelled in fear of losing their religion. The Governor of Madras, William Bentinck himself wrote to the Court of Directors to let them know that this was a rumour, a wrong idea raised on false alarm and erroneous information. The idea of British justice that it was full of truth, humanity and right judgement was imposed in the minds of respectable Indians by the English rulers. But that was a wrong concept, a hollow pride based on falsehood. The fascination for British justice had aroused respect in the elite class, not in the minds of the masses. The common people looked at the British rule from any point between non-acceptance and rejection. This is proved by the prevalence of social banditry in India during the whole of the British rule. A book written many years ago (Ranjit Sen, *Social Banditry in Bengal 1757-1793 : A Study in Primary Resistance*, 1988) makes this point clear. The British justice to many was an illusive thing. In a recent research it has been shown that there was not a vestige of British justice in the behaviour of the army chiefs. The Indian sepoys had to live in an inhuman, strange, claustrophobic atmosphere. The natural tendency of the sepoys was to escape from these situations where life was an experience of closing animation. Who can say that in 1870 at Midnapore, or in 1825 in Rangpur the very small sepoy revolts that occurred, were not local explosions against the inhuman roughness of the English army chiefs ?

*Cf. A. Barat, *The Bengal Native Infantry : Its Organisation and Discipline 1796-1852* ; P. Mason, *A Matter of Honour : An Account of the Indian Army, Its Offices and Men* ; A. Heathcote, *The Indian Army 1822-1922.*

In the first phase of expansion of the Empire, native armed forces were used over and over again to oppose native powers. This was catastrophic. Recent researches have unearthed innumerable literature, mostly local and regional in different Indian languages, which shows the plight of the sepoys who had to fight their brethren as their enemies. They had to fight against people of their own country. They had been employed in killing their own men in their own land. As a result of this a pressure was created in the minds of the sepoys. A riot was stirred up in the blood flowing through their veins. The fire of agony in their mind did not die. This memory was handed down to their children. Captain John William writes in his book (*A Historical Account of the Rise and Progress of the Bengal Native Infantry from its Formation in 1757 to 1796*, London, 1817) that when in 1789 Warren Hastings directed his army against the Raja of Benares, Chait Singh, then a deep dissatisfaction and excitement were seen amongst the Indian soldiers. What he wrote is a very topical and meaningful statement for any soldier in India. He wrote : "... at this time not only the military character of the native soldiers was put to the severest test, it is to be remembered that the trial of their fidelity and duty as soldiers had to contend with the most powerful personal feeling, arising out of the occasion of being employed in arms against their connection and friends, in the heart of their own country, and in putting down the authority and adherence of a prince or a ruler who in the previous government of his country was universally extolled for beneficence and hospitality, moderation and justice."

What a terrible picture! The soldiers were used in their own country, against their own race, in the task of killing their own people – forced inhuman performances indeed at the behest of the empire. Thus were assessed their martial character, their fidelity, their sense of responsibility as soldiers – that is the logicality of letting the active soldiers retain their places. Those whom they had so far known as their *Raja* or ruler, those under whom their ancestors bowed their heads, were now placed before the sepoys as targets of their attack.

From their ancestors the sepoys had imbibed some social and political beliefs that had become stable in their consciousness. Such beliefs were now totally shattered. The Indian soldiers were standing amidst the ruins of their belief and they were sinking into a hopelessness from which there was little escape for them. In their mind, therefore, age after age was buried the landmines of disbelief. That is why explosions burst over and over again culminating in 1857.

There was an allegation from army chiefs that sepoys were a set of unwilling soldiers who did not remain attached to their stations. They wanted to return to their villages all the time. This was because they married early and kept their wives and children in villages. Powerful ties of kinship held them back. Consequently they became restless with their desire to go back to the villages every now and then. They did not have the army discipline. There was much conflict amongst them due to differences of caste and creed and so they did not have unity and coherence. None of the these allegations are apparently false. But the falsity of the whole thing lies deeper and elsewhere – in saying that they were reluctant to work and that there was a mentality of desertion among them. From the rebellion of a regiment in 1766 in the newly constructed Bengal army to the great revolt of 1857 – it was a long period of slightly less than one century during which there were so many sepoy revolts, small and large. The government of the country had the idea that there was no military discipline in the army and no fidelity of the soldiers to the army chiefs. The arrogance amongst the native soldiers was rampant. At the time of Lord Dalhousie there was a conflict about this between the higher army commanders and the executive government, and as a result the British Commander had to resign. After resigning, the British Commander Napier stated clearly that there was discontent like gunpowder stored in the hearts of the sepoys. There was no dearth of clear proof of that. In 1852 when the 38th regiment were ordered to go to Burma they refused to go there. All these facts were sent to England to the higher authorities. They attached no importance to this. Or else they wanted to hide the matter of sepoy discontent for that would have brought disgrace on them. Many white officers of the army knew the depth of the sepoy dissatisfaction. But fearing the recrimination of the higher officers, they kept silent. Russell noted in his Diary : "an officer would be presented, hunted down, ruined who dared to tell the truth" (Russell, *My Diary in India*, i, p. 267). Lord Dalhousie himself knew about the sepoy discontent in detail but he avoided it and made the allegation that there was no discipline amongst the Indian armed forces, top to bottom. Anarchy grasped all – from officers to ordinary sepoy. He believed that the problem would be solved if the number of white soldiers was increased and the sepoy soldiers were reduced in size. He wrote a letter to the President of the Board of Control in England where he said : "The discipline of the army, from top to bottom, officers and men alike, is scandalous" (Lee Warner, *Life of the Marquess of Dalhousie*, ii, ch, viii). And some officers believed that the experience of large scale rebellion was absent in the Indian army after it had been re-built on new lines. So even if there was sepoy dissatisfaction, it would never explode in a big way – "The absence of serious disaffection in the Indian army after its re-organisation has obscured the extreme disaffection with which most officers, especially of the British army, viewed the state of the Company's forces. This could not be expressed openly"*. Amongst the British army chiefs there were anxiety and also self-complacency. This anxiety reached its zenith within four months of the revolt when, even it was only for a month, the English authorities thought that they would not be able to return to India any more. When afterwards the rebellion faded, the uprising failed, then those authorities could get their confidence back. With confidence came complacence. The English felt that the Indians could organise uprisings, but they could not take those uprisings to fulfilment.

It cannot be said that all the sepoys belonging to the Bengal Army were anti-British. Actually there was such discrepancies in the structure of the Bengal Army as disturbed its inner unity and brought

* Thompson and Garratt, *op. cit.*, p. 438 note

restlessness within it. Though it was called the Bengal Army none of the sepoys within it were recruited from Bengal. People from Ayodhya, the North West Provinces, Punjab and other regions would be employed in this force. In 1857, from Ayodhya only 40,000 were '*dwija*' – in contemporary British documents 'twice-born', that is in social terms *Brahmans*. They were looked upon with respect by the army chiefs, and took small benefits from them. This led to jealousy in the minds of Muslims and people of other castes. We need to remember that on the 29th March of 1857 when Mangal Pandey fired the first bullet in revolt against the English then a Muslim named Sheikh Paltu caught hold of him because of which his attempt to commit suicide failed and he became a captive in the hands of the British. Of course there was no communalism in this, – a jealousy towards a *Brahman* might have been there. Respect for the '*dwija*' person had spoiled the right of the sepoys to have equal share in dignity. This became an obstacle to military discipline. Though the *Brahman* sepoys stayed at the same barracks as the other sepoys, they considered themselves to be very different from the others. As a result the unity of the sepoys was disturbed and that eventually hit at the military skill of the sepoys. There are many reasons why sepoys did not ultimately succeed in the sepoy revolt though they participated in great numbers – one reason undoubtedly being the lack of ease amongst the sepoys as to caste and creed. The British could not streamline the caste and communal differences in the army and sepoys remained attached to all patterns of traditional village kinships.

They could not accept progressive forces emanating from the developments of science and statecraft and being peasants had no incentive to do that. Two conservative factors about the Bengal army are often stated by historians, because of which its framework was never perfect – one, respect towards the '*dwija*' sepoys, and two, the custom of promotion on the basis of seniority. In the Bombay or Madras forces, there was no rigidity or conservatism about these two factors. Because the *Brahmans* of north India joined the Bengal army, the nature of this army was conservative. The sepoys who were there in the Bengal army till 1857 were scions of the old sepoys, their remnants and direct descendents and people belonging to their villages. By old sepoys is meant those sepoys who were quickly employed by the government at the time of the expansion of the Empire. Such recruitment took place in order to bring fear to the neighbouring countries. They were kept within the rough framework of the army. They were the outcome of the initial and primary experimentation of the Company to form an army with available Indian manpower. There had been almost no attempt to revise the system. So the aptness of these armies in the work of defending an expanding Empire, was becoming out of date. For example, the vegetarian, caste-conscious *Brahman* sepoys of Ayodhya – the sublime *Ram*-worshipping devotees – belonging to the Bengal army had been a host of medley people steeped in their traditional, old-world life whom the British government did not give any touch of modernity. They naturally did not have the skill or mentality to go for different kinds of warfare required by the expansion of the Empire. Thus to suppress the powerful tribals of the north west, to defend the restless border there, to garrison distant and insolubrious parts of India, to protect the progress of the empire towards the Sindh or Baluchistan, to proceed to the congesting atmosphere of jungle-infested and damp territories like the unknown country of Burma – were not to their efficiency. Nor was it to their liking. They were ill-paid and ill-treated people terrorized from the top and denied of status from within. They had no incentive to engage themselves to hardwork and sacrifice their life in far-off countries. Yet it was they who had to go over and over again to foreign lands where they failed to connect with different atmospheres and lifestyles ; and failed to live their lives with the minimum ease required for sustaining human existence. Therefore naturally they were very reluctant to go to foreign places. In the first stages of the Company's rule this reluctance was overcome in two ways – by tempting them, and by frightening them. Encouraging the growth of fear in the minds of the sepoys was a regular technique with the British army officers. This can be explained by referring to two incidents of the eighteenth century.

The first incident took place at Barrackpore in January 1789. Then there was a discontent going on amongst the sepoys of the Regiment there. The authorities of the Company suffered an anxiety that this discontent could turn into a rebellion. Cornwallis was the Governor General at that time. All that he did was to make effort to prevent the discontent bursting into an open rebellion. Naturally he failed to remove the discontent of the sepoys. Just at that time news came from Bencoolen, a foreign outpost of the Company, situated to the north west of the Sumatra coast, that sepoys from Barrackpore had to be sent there on an emergency basis. He ordered that the 1st, 30th and 32nd Battalions of the 4th Brigade of Barrackpore be sent overseas to the Sumatra Island. The sepoys were tempted by the promise that they would each get an extra allowance of ten rupees and when they returned home they would be referred for promotion. Captain John William* said that after getting the money and the promotion as per promise the sepoys boarded the ship and returned to Calcutta in December of that year. On this journey no sepoy died. This incident proves that the talks of objection of the sepoys to cross the sea which were reported by the English officers and written with so much exaggeration by the English historians were totally false. The feeling of race and religion would have been secondary to the sepoys if they had adequate financial incentives to work. If the sepoys were received with dignity and trust, if affection and care had been spared for them, if their rights had been made certain, if no enmity had been shown towards them, then there would have been no rebellion in their attitude to the English. The journey of the Indian sepoys to Sumatra in a formative stage of the British rule proves this. This is the result of Professor Premangshu Bandopadhyay's most recent and excellent research on the subject. It had reversed the trend of revolt-

* John William, *op. cit.,* pp. 216-221

historiography set by British historians which dominated the field for the last one hundred and fifty years.

Now let us come to the second event. It happened in 1795. That year it became suddenly necessary for the Company to send the Bengal sepoys abroad. A talk was going on about sending a group of sepoys to Amboyana and Malacca. Since there was a lack of actual eombat personalities there the Indian sepoys from Barrackpore were summoned. The South Indian sepoys quartered at Madras had then gone to fight at Ceylon. So perforce, the sepoys of Barrackpore were called. The authorities in the army knew that the mind of the sepoys were in bad shape. Therefore, without any delay, the 15th Bengal Native Infantry Regiment was sent to Mindapore. It was decided that they would be trained there and then sent overseas. The trouble arose when this body of sepoys rebelled in their uniform in an armed state on the parade ground. They firmly announced that they would not go to foreign lands to fight without adequate incentives. The army chiefs present there ordered them to surrender their arms. In the first excitement of rebellion the sepoys refused to do so. Immediately the white sepoys under Capt. Bradley were called in and he rapidly came in a force. With them came some small sized cannon which were called field guns. It was decided to blow off the sepoys in the mouth of the cannon. The cannon fired accordingly. The sepoys were unprepared. They suddenly faced death. They did not know what to do. They started running away here and there in fear of their lives. Immediately they were seized, shackled and punished. A few of them died at the mouth of the cannon. That battalion was immediately disbanded. The sepoys were also dismissed. All military insignias were snatched from them. They were stripped off their uniforms. All over the field a reign of terror descended. In this situation the next order came. The 29th Bengal Native Infantry Regiment would have to be ready for departure. They would go and fight in foreign lands. No protest now came from the terrified sepoys. The native army of Barrackpore set out for Malacca.

Given this, our question is : Did the sepoys rebel in fear of losing their castes on crossing the sea ? The answer would be 'no'. In 1803-4 in the Bay of Bengal and in the Indian Ocean French pirates had to be suppressed in order to make the sea-trading of the Company safe, and for this purpose the sepoys of Barrackpore were again sent overseas. They gathered from Fatehgarh, Kanpur, Allahabad, Danapur, Behrampur (Baharampur of Bengal), Kissangunj, Gaya, Midnapore, Chittagong and other places and put into the Barrackpore cantonment. This mixed native force made no objection to their compulsive overseas voyages. Again between 1810 and 1812 a great number of Indian sepoys were packed off from Bombay, Madras, Calcutta and despatched to Java, Mauritius and other places. In Java with the help of the Indian soldiers a huge amount of French and Dutch weapons and appurtenances were grabbed. This success of the British arms there was essentially the success of the Indian sepoys – their labour, their courage, their sacrifice and their dedication to the English cause with which they had identified themselves. The entire British fight against the French at Mauritius in 1810 was done with the Indian military man-power. Never did the Indians raise any objection against this misuse of Indian mankind – no word was uttered against sea-voyage to foreign lands. Did the Indian sepoys receive adequate pay for this - any additional incentive that would compensate their sacrifice and make room for others to emulate this ? The answer had never been in the affirmative. For the same work the labour of the white sodiers was considered more valuable than that of the Indian sepoys who left their fields of agriculture, their home and hearth in the lure of a better life. They were tempted, allured and finally forced to submit to the commands of their superiors. But at the end they found themselves duped and deprived of the benefits of their service. A miserable humanity – they were ill-fated and ill-treated by their masters whose indifference to the sepoy cause had become endemic in the military administration of the Company.

After the Java war a huge amount of movable property – all of it looted goods – came into the hands of the English. This was the booty of war referred to in English documents and English books as 'prize property'. To bring away that property the native sepoys were engaged and made to work – the English documents say – like "Bullocks and Buffaloes". Yet there was a conspiracy to deprive the sepoys of their quota of "prize wealth". Arrangements were made to distribute the entire wealth amongst the Royal Navy, the white military officers and the white soldiers. Later on, due to the graceful interference of Lord Minto a small sum was decided to be awarded to the native sepoys. Yet ten years after the Java war it was found that numerous native sepoys did not get even the slightest percentage of this "prize wealth" – in fact they did not get their other dues – the promised money and even their pensions. The sepoys fought against this deprivation, against this waste of manpower, against this misuse of native military strength and finally against this denial of justice. The families of those sepoys who were killed in the Java war did not get any of the money due to them. In this way the Indian sepoys were being pushed into a distress that seemed to be increasing with time. The sepoys were mostly from peasant families of village gentry. The distress of the sepoys in the foreign lands left terrible repercussion on their families. Their unhappiness would create endless pain in the minds of their kins. In the disgruntled minds of the people gathered the gunpowder of anger. The new force wherever it was raised carried this memory of indescribable pain. In the Indo-Burmese War the Indian soldiers had to fight in dense, tiger-infested forests with diseases and epidemics all around and they went without food, cloth, medicine, money and even weapons. The peasant sepoys knew that to work in the English army was to enter a death-trap. The sepoys who went from Barrackpore to fight at the Arakan lands mostly died. Consequently anger and unhappiness yawned in the army. It was not that the commanders could not hear the murmurs of this mental unrest. They neglected the murmurs just as they neglected the sepoys and their well-being.

What was the pay of these sepoys who gave their lives for the expansion and protection of the British Empire? Haraprasad Chattopadhyay, through his research, (*The Sepoy Mutiny, 1857 : A Social Study and Analysis*) made the first social and economic analysis of the events of 1857 and showed how the sepoys had to spend their days in indescribable misfortune. The sepoys of the Infantry joined the army of the Company at a pay of 7 Rupees per month. After working for sixteen years they had an increment of one Rupee. After working for twenty years the increment was two Rupees. At the end of their work at old age their pay would be monthly nine Rupees. The sepoys in the cavalry would get twenty-seven Rupees at the start. Their increment would be one Rupee after six years, two Rupees after ten years, three Rupees after fifteen years. From their pay fifteen Rupees would be deducted every month for the upkeep of the horses. Apart from this two Rupees ten Annas would be deducted from their pay every month for sundry expenses – expenses for their uniform, their tent equipments, the repair of their guns and swords, their haircut and shaves, laundry, cleanliness etc. That is, the Company's authorities did not bear any expense for their well-being and livelihood. All expenses were borne by themselves. With this salary the sepoys could not eat nutritious food. And a large part of their salary had to be sent home to their families. Consequently the sepoys of the forces spent their days in a continuous state of poverty.

Their poverty was a cause for their endless misery.

It is strange that the Indian sepoys kept themselves quiet year after year in this situation. Many English commanders were highly moved by their fidelity, their service to the authorities, their courage and skill on the battlefield, their capacity to bear pain quietly, their patience, their low or non-existent wants. But patience has its limits. Fidelity cannot be eternal and submission to poverty and lifeless existence cannot be endless. Long term deprivation ultimately searches its way for release. That was what happened in the case of the sepoys. With the persecution of caste and religion was mixed two factors

– the poverty of the sepoys and the racial discrimination of the English authorities. The great rebellion of 1857 was an explosion of the human nature – the spark of fire from discontent that had gathered behind all collaborations at high up levels of Indo-British give and take.

Appendix - 1
Events According to Chronology

1857

29 March

Mangal Pandey, the sepoy of 34 Native Infantry of the Bengal army, rose into revolt at the time of the military parade at Barrackpore.

8th April

Mangal Pandey was hanged at Barrackpore.

9 May

85 Sepoy were court-martialled because they had refused to touch fat-smeared catridges. They were sentenced to ten years of rigorous imprisonment.

10 May

Three Regiments rebelled in Meerut. The rebels freed the imprisoned sepoys and set out for Delhi.

11 May

The rebel sepoys captured Delhi and the Mughal Emperor of that time, Bahadur Shah Zaffar was declared to be the Emperor.

13-31 May

The rebellion spread to Ferozepur, Mujaffarnagar, Aligarh, Noushera, Etwa, Mainpuri, Rurki, Etta, Nasirabad, Mathura, Lucknow, Bareilly and Shahjahanpur.

1-5 June

The rebellion spread to Moradabad, Badaun, Ajamgarh, Sitapur, Neemak, Benaras, Kanpur and Jhansi.

6 June

The siege of Kanpur by Nana Saheb started.

9-13 June

Rebellion started in Dariabad, Fatehpur, Nouganj, Gwalior and Fatehgarh.

1 July

The rebellion spread to Hathras and Indore.

12 July

The army of Nana Saheb fought at Fatehgarh under the leadership of Jwala Prasad and Tikka Singh and surrendered.

16 July

A fight took place at Kanpur. The force of Nana Saheb retreated and went away to Bithur.

27 July

Kunwar Singh captured Ara.

3 August

The Sepoys moved away from Ara under the pressure of the English army.

13 August

Kunwar Singh was defeated at Jagdishpur.

16 August

Tantia Topi was defeated at Bithur.

17th August

Sir Colin Campbell was appointed the Chief Commander of the British Army.

14 September

The British army blew away the Kashmir Gate of Delhi by cannon fire.

19 September

The British army captured the Lahore Gate and the attached defence Barricade.

20 September

The British army re-captured Delhi.

21 September

Bahadur Shah Jaffar surrendered himself to the British in front of Humayun's Tomb.

22 September

Major Hudson imprisoned the sons of Bahadur Shah Zafar and mercilessly killed them. This is one of the world's most atrocious examples of the massacre of innocent people.

23 October

The British Army broke through Sikandar Bag and captured Lucknow.

26th October

Tantia Topi was defeated by the British army beside the Pandu river.

27 October

Tantia Topi drove the British army out of Kanpur and captured Kanpur.

6th December

The British Commander Campbell drove Tantia Topi out of Kanpur upon which he joined with the Rani Lakshmibai of Jhansi.

9 December

The Battle of Kalpi took place. Tantia Topi backed out.

1858

5 March

Mehendi Hossain and the Rajas of Gonda and Chardah attacked the British army camp at Chanda.

21 March

The British Army brought back Lucknow totally under their control. The rebel army of the sepoys were driven away from there.

22 March

Kunwar Singh captured Ajamgarh.

1 April

Tantia Topi, advancing to the support of Lakshmibai with 2200 soldiers was stopped and defeated by the British army on the banks of the Betwa river.

3-5 April

The British Army stormed into Jhansi and captured the Jhansi Fort. The Rani of Jhansi, Lakshmibai fled. Kunwar Singh defeated the British army for the second time at Ajamgarh.

23 April

Kunwar Singh defeated the British army at Jagdishpur. At this repeated defeat of the British at his hands the Indian rebellion took a new turn.

26 April

Kunwar Singh died.

6 May

The British army captured Bareilly from the hands of Bahadur Khan.

11 May

The British Army blockaded Shahjahanpur. At that time the defence of Shahjahanpur was conducted by Moulabi Ahmedullah Shah.

22 May

The Second Battle of Kalpi took place. In this war the rebel force was led by the Rani of Jhansi, Lakshmibai, the Nawab of Banda and Rao Sahab (Nana Saheb's nephew).

24 May

Kalpi fell at the hands of the British.

1 June

The Rani of Jhansi, Lakshmibai, Rao Saheb and the Nawab of Banda defeated the ruler of Gwalior, Sindhia. They imprisoned Sindhia and announced Nana Saheb as the Peshwa.

17 June

The British army laid siege of Gwalior. While fighting against the British army in the Gwalior war the Rani of Jhansi died. Tantia Topi fled.

20 June

The British troops re-captured Gwalior.

2 August

The rule of East India Company ended and the British Crown took over the Indian Empire.

14 August

The Battle of Kotra (Udaypur) took place. Tantia Topi was defeated.

17-19 October

Jagdishpur came under the siege of the British army. This place was then being defended by Kunwar Singh's brother Amar Singh. He was defeated by the British army at a place named Nenadi.

1859

21 January

The Battle of Sikhar took place. Tantia Topi was defeated.

7 April

By the betrayal of Raja Man Singh, Tantia Topi became a prisoner at the hands of the English.

18 April

Tantia Topi was hanged. A powerful chapter of the great rebellion came to an end.

October – 4 December

By organizing a mammoth search in north Ayodhya and Nepal for people belonging to the rebel army, the British soldiers imprisoned at least 4000 sepoys and myriad of common men. All of them were severely punished. This is one of the rarest examples of state vendetta in the history of the world.

Appendix - 2

The Centres of Regional Uprising before the great revolt of 1857-58

1. Hazara
2. North Western Frontier Province or N.W.F.P.
3. Rawalpindi
4. Bannu
5. Punjab

6. Hissar
7. Rohtak
8. Roorki
9. Rampur
10. Bareilly
11. Pilibhit
12. Bhiwani
13. Rewari
14. Marwara
15. Rohilkhand
16. Ayodhya
17. Garakhpur
18. Shahjahanpur
19. Kalpi
20. Bundelkhand
21. Benaras
22. Patna
23. Bhagalpur
24. Purnia
25. Birbhum
26. Manbhum
27. Dishpur
28. Bankura
29. Bishnupur
30. Midnapur
31. Hazaribag
32. Ranchi
33. Sagar
34. Rewakanta
35. Malwa
36. Palamou
37. Chhotanagpur
38. Arbos
39. Shadia
40. Singpas
41. Akash
42. Jorhat
43. Naga Hills
44. Khasi Hills
45. Dhaka
46. Tripura
47. Noakhali
48. Sambalpur
49. Nagpur
50. Khurda
51. Cuttack
52. Pipli
53. Puri
54. Kamsur
55. Ganjam
56. Surat
57. Thana
58. Puna
59. Bijapur
60. Kolhapur
61. Belgaon
62. Badami
63. Kittar
64. Bidnor
65. Mysore
66. Kottayam
67. Madurai
68. Shivganga
69. Karnool
70. Vellore
71. Ramnathpuram

Appendix - 3

The distance from Calcutta, the British seat of power, to places where revolts took place

Place	Distance by Miles	Place	Distance by Miles
Agra	839	Ferozepur	1181
Allahabad	498	Fatehgarh	703
Ara	406	Faizabad	576
Aurangabad	963	Gwalior	772
Barrackpore	16	Indore	1030
Bareilly	910	Lahore	1356
Benares	428	Lucknow	649
Bithur	712	Meerut	1008
Kanpur	700	Mau	1018
Delhi	976	Nimak	850
Dinapur	411	Sialkot	1291
		Ambala	1108

(Courtesy *1857 Droh Kal*)

Appendix - 4

Dates of Blockades

The siege of Kanpur by Nana Saheb : 6 June 1857

The siege of Delhi by Sir H. Barnard : 8 June 1857

The siege of Lucknow by Nana Saheb : 4 August 1857

The total re-capture of Delhi by the British army

: 20 September 1857.

(Courtesy *1857 Droh Kal*)

Appendix - 5

The Dates of the Main Killings

10 May 1857	:	at Merrut
11 May 1857	:	at Delhi
31 May 1857	:	at Lucknow
31 May 1857	:	at Bareilly
3 June 1857	:	at Nimak
4 June 1857	:	at Benares
5 June 1857	:	at Allahabad
7 June 1857	:	at Faizabad
27 June 1857	:	at Kanpur
20 July 1857	:	at Lahore

(Courtesy *1857 Droh Kal*)

Bibliography - 1

Two books that may be read for different historical opinions are :

Ainslee T. Embree (ed.) — *1857 in India : Mutiny or War of Independence,* Boston, 1963.

In this book opinions of historians contemporary and later times are given.

C. H. Philips (ed.) — *Historians of India, Pakistan and Ceylon,* London, 1961.

In this book the essay entitled "Writings on the Mutiny" by Surendranath Sen is a very necessary work. For general school and college students and also for absolutely initial learning and for primary reading on the great revolt, the necessary books are : Percival Spear, *India : Modern History* (Ann Arbor, 1961), R. C. Majumdar et. al., *Advanced History of India,* (London, 1956) and E. J. Thompson and G. T. Garrett, *Rise and Fulfilment of British Rule in India* (London, 1934 and Allahabad, 1958).

Those who want to go in for more advanced research should see the Government papers, the despatches from the Government of India to various places or and also those received by it, the papers, letters etc. that were involved with these despatches, the depositions of civil servants or rulers and the situation during their rule, notes on how the rebellion was suppressed, the description and documents etc. pertaining to that. All this can be found in *Parliamentary Papers.* These documents are classified into various volumes. The necessary volumes for 1857 are XXIX and XXX. For 1857-58 the volumes that will be needed are three : xlii, xliii, xliv; for 1859 are needed xviii, xxiii, xxv and xxxvii, for 1860 there is one volume – I, the volume for 1863 is X.

Those who want to see more Government papers outside of these will see Sir George Forrest, *Selections from the Letters, Despatches, and other State Papers of the Government of India, 1857-58* (4 vols. Calcutta, 1893-1912). Collection of documents like this have been published from India and Pakistan. After 1947, the great rebellion of 1857 as seen from the viewpoint of these nations can be judged by the following books which have been published, one from India, another from Pakistan : S.A.A. Rizvi and M.L. Bhargava (ed.) *Freedom Struggle in Uttar Pradesh* (4 vols. Uttar Pradesh : 1957-59) and *A History of the Freedom Movement (Being the Story of the Muslim Struggle for the Freedom of Hind-Pakistan* (Karachi, 1957).

Some Military autobiographies were written about the great revolt. These were written much after the uprisings although their subjects were the uprisings themselves. In them one will find important descriptions of events and incidental and scattered letters. They are very important. These books are noted here : Lord Roberts, *Forty-One Years in India* (2 vols. London, 1924) [This person was a very youngman in 1857. Later he became the Commander-in-chief of the Indian Army.] A very important book was written by a young Lieutenant, V. D. Majendie. His book is *Up among the Pandies* (London, 1859). General George Jacob's book *Western India before and during the Mutinies* is a book full of information and is needed for the understanding of the perspectives of the revolt. Both the books contain examples of how the British looked at their commanders and the men under them.

L. J. Trotter's *Life of John Nicholson* (London, 1898) -- *Bayard of India, A Study of General Sir James Outram* (Edinburgh, 1903) is an important book. In these two books the two English commanders have been transformed into heroes with heavenly auras. Embree, in commenting upon this, has said : "While these and other biographies have a hero-worshipping tone unpleasing to modern tastes, they provide much useful material" [*op. cit,* p. 100]. These books should not be considered to be dependable histories. These are based on eulogy, and are general parts of the songs of praise of the English in the Eastern country.

In recent times a few books have been written about the great revolt in the English language which have caused a turmoil in the history minds of the students of India. The titles of a few of such books are given below :

William Dalrymple, *The Last Mughal* : *The Fall of a Dynasty,* Delhi, 1857, Penguin/Viking, New Delhi, 2006.

Tapati Roy, *Raj of the Rani,* Penguin Books, New Delhi, 2006.

Rudrangsu Mukherjee, *Mangal Pandey : Brave Martyr or Accidental Hero ?* Penguin Books, New Delhi, 2005.

Premangsu Kumar Bandopadhyay, *Tulsi Leaves and the Ganges Water : The Slogan of the First Sepoy Mutiny at Barrackpore 1824,* K. P. Bagchi & Company, Kolkata, 2003.

The books referred to above are each important in its own way. Amongst them the shortest is Rudrangsu Mukherjee's book -- small in size -- all in all a hundred pages. This is not a researched book. The writer has admitted that. His own feelings about Mangal Pandey have been written here. But he has admirably used historian's tools. Therefore it has become at the end a piece of new research itself. It can be called interpretative history. The writer's adverse comments on Mangal Pandey had hurt Indian public consciousness and so there was a lot of discussion about this book in papers, magazines and the electronic media. Tapti Roy's book has fulfilled a vacant aspect of the great rebellion. This is a serious research on the Rani of Jhansi, Lakshmibai. The book by Mr. Dalrymple is a unique creation. Much before the publication of this book in 1958 was published the fact-filled research of Syed Mahdi Husain on the great rebellion and Bahadur Shah Zaffar, which was acknowledged to be a unique book. The title of the book is, Syed Mahdi Husain, *Bahadur Shah Zafar and the War of 1857 in Delhi.* The book was reprinted in 2006 by Aakar Books. The preface to this new print has been written by Mushirul Hasan. This book is totally different from Dalrymple's book. Dalrymple wanted to show the fall of a royal dynasty in his book, but his actual aim is to show the collapse of the Indo-Islamic civilisation in the Indian sub-continent. Premangsu Bandopadhyay's book is important for it unfolds a specific Indian point of view. He has gathered together various facts from the various archives of England and has written a book which is entirely a new Indian perspective in the writing of the history of the sepoy uprising.

Recently a book has been published from the Asiatic Society of Kolkata – Subhas Ranjan Chakraborty (ed.) *Uprising of 1857, Perspectives and Peripheries,* 2009. It is a very readable book. In it the essays of 14 writers including the editor have been collected. This is better than many of the books of its kind published recently. We must remember that currently many essays and collections regarding the great revolt are being printed. In most cases it is seen that these essays are the outcome of superficial research. Their aim is to create a viewpoint or a perspective. But facts necessary to form a viewpoint are absent in them. Digging for facts is a laborious job. Not many walk that path. The writing of foreign writers is so vigorous for this reason. They may write with a certain purpose, but usually they do not write without going into wide and analytic research and excavation of facts.

A dependable overall research on the historiography of the great rebellion is Snigdha Sen's *Historiography of the Indian Revolt of 1857,* Punthi-Pustak, Calcutta, 1992. This book was a piece of predominant research. We must remember that in the centenary of the great revolt Ramesh Chandra Majumdar, Shashibhusan Chaudhury and Haraprasad Chattopadhyay wrote a kind of full-fledged history of the revolt. That sort of total history has not been written in the hundred and fiftieth year of the great rebellion. The doors of many archives have been opened in the last few years, many new facts and source materials have been unearthed and opened to the researchers, but one does not see the laborious eagerness of gathering information amongst young historians any more.

The historians do not devote their attention to the heroes of the great rebellion. Professor Anunoy Bandopadhyay has written a book about them. It is – Prof. Anunoy Bandopadhyay, *Unmourned Heroes of the Indian Mutiny (1857-1859),* (Ashabari Publication, 24 Thakur Ramkrishna Lane, Howrah - 711104, Phone 2667-9442, Pustak Bipani, Kolkata, 700 009), 2003. The heroes referred to in this book are – Raja Jaylal Singh, Mehndi Hasan – The Rebel Nizam of Allahabad, Sultanpur, Raja Man Singh of Shahganj, Rana Beni Madho of

Shankarpur, Rao Sahib – the Nana's Deputy. This book has been written from the nationalist viewpoint.

Sipahi Bidroher Dersho Bachhar – Phirey Dekha. The writer of this booklet is Jahar Santra. It has been published from the Ghatal Municipality in 2007. This is an example of writing history in local levels. A big example of the attempt is the book *Palasi Thekey Maha Bidroha.* It has been edited by four people Samir Kumar Patra, Shekhar Bhowmik, Arindam Chakraborty and Sourabh Maity. The book has been published as the joint enterprise of the History Department, Mahishadal Raj College, East Midnapore, India, in 2009. The appendix of this book contains 'some documents and literature regarding the great rebellion preserved in the West Bengal Archive'. – This is an excellent book published in the hundred and fiftieth year of the great rebellion. It is edited by Aniruddha Roy : *Prasanga : Mahabidroha 1857-1858*, National Book Agency Pvt. Ltd., Kolkata, 2008. Here the writings of fifteen writers, past and present, have been collected.

There is much controversy amongst historians as to how much the great rebellion can be called a national rebellion. Ramesh Majumdar himself had not agreed to call it national. It must be remembered that unless there is love for one's own nation and people, and opposition, discontent and hatred to a foreign rule, the fire of rebellion is not lit in people's minds. The national consciousness that emerged after the revolt of 1857 could not have accrued in one day. How that preparation came, how the necessary chemistry was supplied into the social consciousness is very important. To know that, the folowing book have to be read :

Rajat Kanta Roy, *The Felt Community : Commonality and Mentality before the Emergence of Indian Nationalism,* New Delhi, 2003.

With it can be read another writing by Rajat Kanta Roy – "*Race, Religion and Realm*" [M. Hasan and N. Gupta, *Indian's Colonial Encounter,* New Delhi, 1993].

The work that was most important to do in the hundred and fiftieth anniversary of the great rebellion was a full-scale discussion on the historical facts of the great revolt through which the Indian viewpoint would be clarified. The introductory attempt at this will be found in Ranjit Sen and Snigdha Sen's *Mahabidroha O Bharatiya Udasinata* (in Bengali) and in the *Historiography of the Revolt of 1857* by Snigdha Sen. Sekhar Bandopadhyay has brought out an edition on the Indian Uprising in which he has attempted to understand the historical facts of the great events in a new way. The book edited by him is *1857 : Essays From Economic and Political Weekly*, Orient Longman in association with Sameeksha Trust, Hyderabad, 2008. The important point is not the writing about historical facts but it is the discussion on the Indian side of the great event. For that a dependable bibliography is necessary. The Council of Historical Research in Delhi came forward at the beginning of the 1970s to do this work. Attaching himself to their work scheme, Kalyan Kumar Sengupta wrote in 1975 : *Recent Writings on the Revolt of 1857 : A Survey*, New Delhi, 1975. This book is a brief product of an investigative research. Four years after this was published another book full of research and deep understanding of the historiography of the revolt was published. This was S.B. Chaudhuri, *English Historical Writings on the Indian Mutiny 1857-1859*, World Press Private Ltd., Calcutta, 1979. In this book there is an exhaustive list of English writers who exercised their mind on the revolt of 1857. There is also the mention in it of innumerable books published in the Indian languages. This book of 668 pages has a survey of the English understanding of the revolt and, together with it, it has clarified the Indian viewpoint also. This is indeed an unique research. 19 years after this book, in 1998 a new book was published from Haryana - Vipin Jain, *The Indian Mutiny of 1857 : An Annotated and Illustrated Bibliography*, Vintage Books, Gurgaon, Haryana, 1998. In this book he has given a list of 1,172 printed books published in the European languages and with that has referred to 369 essays, 108 stories, novels and fiction published in various papers and magazines. Even after this eleven years have passed, there has been no stock-taking of new discussions.

In the meantime various new types of writings on the great revolt have appeared, such as the following :

Gautam Chakravorty, *The Indian Mutiny and British Imaginations*, Cambridge University Press, Cambridge, 2005.

Saul David, *The Indian Mutiny, 1857*, Viking, London, 2002.

Dr. Kaushik Roy, 'Company Bahadur against the Pandies' in *Jadavpur University Journal of History*, vols. 19-20, 2001.

Anisha Shekhar Mukherji, *The Red Fort of Shahjahanabad*, New Delhi, 2003.

Ayesha Jalal, *Self and Sovereignty : Individual and Community in South Asian Islam since 1850*, New Delhi, 2001.

There have been writings on the horrors of great revolt. One or two such books are mentioned below.

Rudrangsu Mukherjee, *Spectre of Violence : The 1857 Kanpur Massacres*, Viking, New Delhi, 1998.

Rudrangsu Mukherjee, "Satan let loose upon Earth : The Kanpur Massacres in India in the Revolt of 1857" in *Past and Present*, 128.

Andrew Ward, *Our Bones are Scattered : The Cawnpore Massacres and the Indian Mutiny of 1857*, Henry Halt and Co., New York, 1996.

Not exactly the great uprising, but the India before and after the uprising is the subject of a long essay by Acharya Prafulla Chandra Roy. It was originally published in 1886. It has been reprinted and published as follows : Acharya Prafulla Chandra Roy, *India Before and After the Mutiny*, Readers Service Edition, Kolkata, 2007.

One rather large book on the revolt of 1857 is preserved in the Kolkata National Library -- the book is Chicks, *Annals of the Indian Rebellion, Part I-II* (The catalogue number of book is S. C. 954, An 72). This was printed in 1859, the printers were Sanders, Cones And Co., of 23, Lalbazar. Unusual incidents of the great rebellion are described here.

There is an excellent list of books published on the great revolt of 1857 upto its centenary year which is available in the book by S. N. Sen, *Eighteen Fifty-Seven.* There are references to many books, papers and magazines in the 1957 and 1958 editions of *Journal of Indian History*. At the conclusion of Ainslee T. Embree's *1857 in India : Mutiny or War of Independence*? At the end of this work there is an extensive discussion of books on the uprising. Many old and classical writings or excerpts from them are being arranged in a new way and being presented to the readers. The readers do not even get to know what the sources of those writings are. One should be cautious in accepting such outputs as always authentic. Recently there is a mention of Kanpur in many writings. The reader should know that the original book on Kanpur is by George Otto Trevelyan, *Cawnpore*, London, MacMillan, 1865. To know the whole history of the great revolt one should read a classical book by an English writer who has written his book from the English viewpoint. This is one of the best books on the revolt. It is written by T. Rice Holmes, *A History of the Indian Mutiny*, London, MacMillan, 1913. The book was first published in 1883 and from then onwards this it influenced the opinions of historians. Ramesh Majumdar himself depended on this book at many places in his writings on the great revolt.

On the hundred and fiftieth year of the great uprising, of the books published in the Bengali language, the most sizable book is Sabyasachi Bhattacharya (ed.) *1857 Drohakal*, Bengal Association, Delhi and Victoria Memorial Hall, Kolkata. It has been published from Bangabhavan, 3, Hailey Road, New Delhi 110001. This book comprises the writings of 52 writers. In this book which is a little more than 430 pages there is not much digging up of new facts. But an attempt has been made to think of the great events of 1857 in a new way. This is however, a massive production of contemporary Bengali intellect. In it there were some writings which are translations from the original English. But the writings are unique. Apart from this book the following books should also be read.

Michael Edwards, *Red Years : The Indian Rebellion of 1857*, London, 1973.

Charles Ball, *The History of Indian Mutiny*, Vol. I, London, 1858.

Pratul Gupta, *Nana Sahib and the Rising at Kanpur*, Oxford, 1963.

Colonel Julien R. J. Joshelin, *The History of the Royal and Indian Artillery in the Mutiny of 1857*, London, 1915.

J. G. Brown, *The Pubjab and Delhi in 1857*, Subhi Publication, Delhi (Reprint) 1999, Vol. II.

Moinul Haq, "The Great Revolution of 1857" in Hakin Muhammad Said et. al. (ed.) *Road to Pakistan*, 1990.

Bibliography-2

Some Books on 'Sepoy Mutiny' in The Collection of The Asiatic Society's Library

No.	Call No.	Author	Title	Place/Year
1.	954.0317 A245d	Adye, Jon, Lt. Col.	The Defence of Cownpore, by the Troops Under the Orders of Maj. General Charles A. Windham in Nov 1857.	London : 1858
2.	954.05 B187h Vol. 1-2	Ball, Charles	The History of the Indian Mutiny, Vol.1-2	London
3.	923.5540317 B215u	Bandyopadhyay, Arumoy	Unmourned Heroes of the Sepoy Mutiny	Kolkata : 2003
4.	Banga 891.443 H973b	Banerjee, Brojendra Nath (ed.)	Hutom Penchar Naksha	Kolkata : 3rd Ed. 1391
5.	923.554 B255 l	Barker, G.D	Letters from Persia and India 1857-1859	London : 1915
6.	954.05 B714O	Bonham, John, Col.	Oude in 1857 Some Memories of the Indian Mutiny	London : 1928
7.	954.05 C445h	Chambers, W & R	The History of the Indian Revolt and of the Expedition to Persia, China and Japan 1856-78	London : 1859
8.	954.0317 C45s	Chattopadhyay, Haraprasad	The Sepoy Mutiny, 1857	Calcutta : 1957
9.	954.0317 C552t	Chaudhuri, Sashi Bhusan	Theories of the Indian Mutiny (1857-59)	Calcutta : 1965

10. 954.05 C496eng.	Chaudhuri, Sashi Bhusan	English Historical Writings on the Indian Mutiny 1857-1859	Calcutta: 1979
11. 954.1620317 M992c	Choudhury, Sujit	The Mutiny Period in Cachar	Silchar: 1981
12. 915.4 C559t Vol. 1	Chunder, Bholanath	Travels of a Hindoo Vol. 1	London: 1869
13. 954.05 C699s	Collier, Richard	The Sound of Fury	1963
14. 954.05 D234 k.a	Datta, K. K.	Biography of Kunwar Singh & Amar Singh	Patna: 1957
15. 954.0317 D979r	Datta, Kalikinkar	Reflections on the Mutiny	Calcutta: 1967
16. 954.0317 D251i	David, Saul	The Indian Mutiny 1857	London: 2002
17. 954.05 D272s	Dawson, Lionel	Squires and Sepoys 1857-1858	London: 1960
18. 954.0317 D634I	Dobrolyubov, Nikolai; tr.From Russian by Hanish C. Gupta	The Indian National Uprising of 1857: A Contemporary Russian Account	Calcutta: 1988
19. 954.05 D814cr	Duberly, H.	Campaigning Experiences in Rajpootana and Central India	London: 1859
20. —	Duff, Alexander, Rev.	The Indian Rebellion; Its Causes and Results	London: 1858
21. 954.0317 E26p	Edwards, William	Personal Adventures During the Indian Rebellion in Rohilcund, Futhe Ghur and Oude.	London: 2nd ed. 1858

No.	Call No.	Author	Title	Place/Year
22.	954.05 F695r	Forbes-Mitchell	Reminiscences of the Great Mutiny 1857-59	London : 1910
23.	954.0317 F546t	Fitchett, W.H.	The Tale of the Great Mutiny	London : 1901 Rep. 1924
24.	954.0317 F728h	Forrest, G. W.	A History of the Indian Mutiny Vol. 2-3	London : 1904
25.	954.0317 S464f. Vol. 1-2	Forrest, G. W.	Selections from the Letters Dispatches and Other State Papers.... Vol. 1-2	Calcutta : 1893
26.	954.05 C344g Vol.2	Grant, James	Cassel's Illustrated History of India Vol. 2	London : 1891
27.	823.554 G787 l	Greathed, H.H.	Letters written during the Siege of Delhi	London : 1858
28.	954.0317 H624g	Hibbert, Christopher	The Great Mutiny India 1857	London : 1978
29.	954.05 H753h m	Holmes, T. Rice	History of the Indian Mutiny	London : 1898
30.	954.05 H968b	Husain, Mahdi	Bahadur Shah II	Delhi : 1958
31.	954.05 H976n	Hutchinson, G.	Narrative of the Mutinies in Oude.	Calcutta : 1859
32.	954.05 I39m	Imperial Record Dept.	Press List of Mutiny Papers 1857	Calcutta : 1921
33.	954.05 I51s	Inglis, J.	The Siege of Lucknow : A Diary.	London : 1892
34.	954.0317 I58s	Innes, McLeod Lt. Gen.	The Sepoy Revolt : A Critical Narrative	London : 1897
35.	954.05 I58L O	Innes, McLeod	Lucknow & Oude in the Mutiny	London : 1895

36. 954.0317 J63h	Jocelyn, Julian R. Col.	The History of the Royal and Indian Artillery in the Mutiny of 1857	London : 1915
37. 821.9 J77r.	Jones, Ernest	The Revolt of Hindostan or the New World	Calcutta : 1957
38. 954.05 J83r.e.	Joshi, P. C. (ed.)	Rebellion 1857 : A Symposium	New Delhi : 1957
39. 954.05 J88o	Joyce, Michael	Ordeal at Lucknow Defence of the Residency	London : 1938
40. 954.05 K23h Vol. 1	Kaye, John William	A History of the Sepoy War in India 1857-1858, Vol. 1	London : 1870
41. 954.0317 L438r	Leason, James	The Red Fort.	London : 1956
42. 923.2540317 M156m	Mackenzie, A. R. D., Col.	Mutiny Memoirs : Being Personal Reminiscences of the Great Revolt of 1857	Allahabad : 1891
43. 954.05 M234m	Majumdar, R.C.	The Sepoy Mutiny and the Revolt of 1857	Calcutta : 1957
44. 954.0317 M252i	Malleson, G. B.	The Indian Mutiny of 1857	London : 1912
45. 923.540317 M447m Vol. 1	Maude, Francis Cornwallis	Memories of the Mutiny Vol. 1	London : 1894
46. 954.05 M479s	Mead, Henry	The Sepoy Revolt	London : 1857
47. 954.06 M565t.n.	Metcalfe, Charles T.	Two Native Narratives of the Mutiny in Delhi tr. From the Originals	1974
48. 954.0317 M678n	Mishra, Anand Swarup	Nana Saheb Peshwa and the Fight for Freedom.	Lucknow : 1961

49. 923.5540317 P189m	Misra, Amaresh	Mangal Pandey : The True Story of an Indian Revolutionary	New Delhi : 2005
50. 954.0317 I39r.v.	Muir, William	Records of the Intelligence Dept. of the Govt. of N. W. Provinces of India During the Mutiny of 1857	Edinburgh : 1902
51. 954.0317 M953a	Mukherjee, Rudrangshu	Awadh in Revolt 1857-1858	Calcutta : 1984
52. 954.074 N277c	National Library, Calcutta	1857 Centenary Exhibition of Printed Books, Documents & Illustrations.	Calcutta : 1957
53. 954 N787i Vol. 2	Nolan, E.H.	Illustrated History of the British Empire in India, Vol. 2	London
54. 954.05 O54h	O'Malley, L.S.S.	History of Bengal Bihar & Orissa Under British Rule.	Calcutta : 1925
55. 954.035 O55s	Omissi, David	The Sepoy and the Raj : The Indian Army, 1860-1940	London : 1994
56. 923.55479 T219p	Pal, Dharm	Tatya Tope	New Delhi : 1955
57. 954.05 P173 mut	Palmer, J. A. B.	The Mutiny, Outbreak at Meerut in 1857	Cambridge : 1966
58. 954.05 P277des Vol. 3-4	Prasad, S. N.	Descriptive List of Mutiny Papers in the National Archives of India, Bhopal, Vol. 3-4	1973

59. 954.0296 R888i	Ray, P. C.	India Before and After the Mutiny	Edinburgh: 1886 Calcutta: Indian ed. 1995
60. R. K. M. 954.05 R328s	Rees, L. E. Rnutz	Personal Narrative of the Siege of Lucknow	London: 1858
61. 954.0317 R643L	Robert, Fred	Letters Written During the Indian Mutiny	London: 1924
62. 954.0317 R645e	Roberts, Field Marshal	An Eye Witness Account of the Indian Mutiny	Delhi: 1983
63. 923.5540351 R968m	Russal, W. H.	My diary in India in the year 1858-59	London
64. 954.03 S532n	Sahani, Savitri (tr.)	Nana Sahib	Pune: 1980
65. 954.0317 S474e	Sen, Surendranath	Eighteen Fifty-Seven	Calcutta: 1957
66. 954.0317 S476r	Sengupta, Kalyan Kr.	Recent Writings on the Revolt of 1857 : A Survey	ICHR: 1975
67. 954.0317 E34S.	Sharma, Suresh K. (ed.)	1857 : A Turning Point in Indian History, Vol. 1-4	Jaipur: 2005
68. Banga 891.449 R165s	Shastri, Sibnath	Ramtanu Lahiri & Tatkalin Banga Samaj	Calcutta: 2nd ed. 1957
69. 954.0317 S547 per	Shepherd, W. J.	Personal Narrative of the Outbreak and Massacre at Cownpore During the Sepoy Revolt of 1857	New Delhi: 1st Indian ed. 1980
70. 954.06 S561rev	Srivastava, Khushhalilal	The Revolt of 1857 in Central India : Malwa.	Bombay: 1966

No.	Call No.	Author	Title	Place / Year
71.	922.945 T128a	Tagore, Devendra Nath	The Autobiography of Maharsi Devendra Nath Tagore.	Kolkata : Rep. ed. 1994
72.	923.554 T245w	Tayler, P. J. O.	What Really Happened During the Mutiny.	Oxford : 1997
73.	954.05 T237p	Tayler, W.	The Patna Crisis.	London : 1858
74.	RR 954.0317 C737t	Taylor, P. G. O.	A Companion to the Indian Mutiny of 1857.	Delhi : 1966
75.	954.0317 T363r	Thackery, Edward	Reminiscences of the Indian Mutiny (1857-58) and Afghanistan (1879).	London : 1916
76.	923.1542 H192f	Thamankar, D. V.	The Rani of Jhansi.	London : 1958
77.	954.0317 T452s	Thomson, Mowbray	The Story of Cawnpore.	London : 1859
78.	954.03 T812c	Trevelyan, G.O.	Completion Wallah	London : 1864
79.	954.05 M588CT	Tuker, Francis	The Chronicle of private Henry Metcalfe	London : 1953
80.	954.0317 V532d	Verney, G. L.	The Devils Wind : The Story of the Naval Brigade at Lucknow	London : 1956
81.	954.0317 V624s	Vibart, Edward, Col.	The Sepoy Mutiny as Seen by a Subaltern from Delhi to Lucknow	London : 1898
82.	954.05 D352h	---	History of the Siege of Delhi by an Officer Who Served There.	Edinburgh : 1861
83.	954.0317 S887	---	The Story of the Indian Mutiny (1857-58)	Edinburgh

Index

T

V

W

Z